COMPUTER BOOK SERIES FROM IDG

Word For Windows For Du...

D1418895

Word for Windows Screen

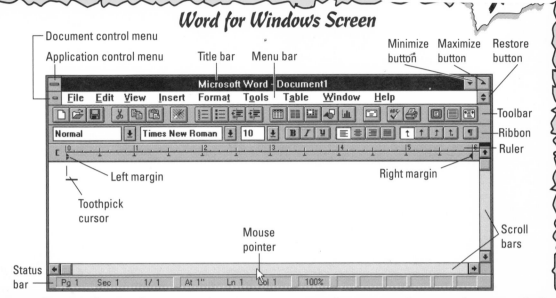

- Document control menu
- Application control menu
- Title bar
- Menu bar
- Minimize button
- Maximize button
- Restore button
- Toolbar
- Ribbon
- Ruler
- Left margin
- Right margin
- Toothpick cursor
- Mouse pointer
- Scroll bars
- Status bar

General Information

To start WinWord, first start Windows at the DOS prompt:

```
C> WIN
```

Then, locate the WinWord icon in the Program Manager. Double-click the mouse on that icon.

- ✔ Use the Insert key to switch between Insert and Overtype modes.
- ✔ Use the Backspace key to backup and erase.
- ✔ Use the Delete key to delete a character.
- ✔ Press the Enter key to start a new paragraph.
- ✔ Press the Tab key to indent or line up text.
- ✔ F1 is the Help key.
- ✔ Press the Escape key to cancel things and make dialog boxes go away.

Alt,I,S means to press and release the Alt key, press and release the I key, and press and release S.

Shift+Ctrl+F12 means to hold down the Shift and Ctrl keys and then press F12. Then release all keys.

Choose the Exit command from the File menu when you're ready to quit WinWord. Follow the instructions on-screen; save your document to disk.

Always quit WinWord and then quit Windows itself before you turn off your computer.

Common WinWord Character Formatting Key Commands

Command	Keys
Center text	Ctrl+E
Left align	Ctrl+L
Right align	Ctrl+R
Bold	Ctrl+B
Italic	Ctrl+I
Underline	Ctrl+U

The Kindergarten Keys

Command	Keys
Copy	Ctrl+C
Cut	Ctrl+X
Paste	Ctrl+V
Undo	Ctrl+Z

Common WinWord Key Commands

Command	Key(s)
Cancel	Esc
Go back	Shift+F5
Help	F1
Mark block	F8
Print	Ctrl+Shift+F12
Save	Shift+F12
Repeat	F4
Repeat Find	Shift+F4

. . . For Dummies: #1 Computer Book Series for Beginners

Word For Windows For Dummies

Cheat Sheet

The Toolbar

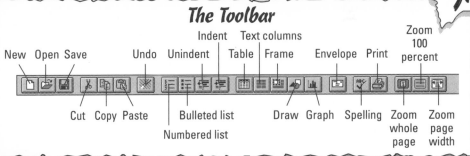

New Open Save   Undo Unindent   Indent   Text columns   Envelope Print   Zoom 100 percent

Cut Copy Paste   Bulleted list   Table Frame   Draw Graph Spelling   Zoom whole page   Zoom page width

Numbered list

The Ribbon

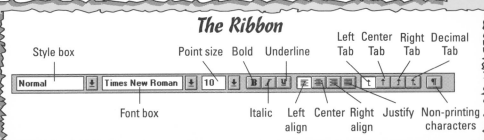

Style box   Point size Bold Underline   Left Tab Center Tab Right Tab Decimal Tab

Normal   Times New Roman   10   B I U

Font box   Italic   Left align Center Right align Justify Non-printing characters

Helpful Tips

- Let the computer do the work! Let WinWord format your pages, insert page numbers, headers, and footers. Don't ever do that stuff "manually" on-screen.
- Always save your documents to disk!
- If a document has already been saved to disk, press Shift+F12 to update the document on disk.

Useful Tools

- To check your spelling, press Alt,O,S.
- Check your grammar by pressing Alt,O,G.
- Look up synonyms by using the thesaurus, Shift+F7.

Document Filenames

A document must be saved to disk using a DOS filename. Here are the rules:

- The filename can be from 1 to 8 characters long.
- The filename can contains letters and numbers in any combination.
- The filename cannot contain a space or a period or any other symbol.
- Be brief and descriptive with your filenames.

Getting Around in a Document

Key	Action
↑	Moves toothpick cursor up one line of text
↓	Moves toothpick cursor down one line of text
→	Moves toothpick cursor right to next character
←	Moves toothpick cursor left to next character
Ctrl+↑	Moves toothpick cursor up one paragraph
Ctrl+↓	Moves toothpick cursor down one paragraph
Ctrl+→	Moves toothpick cursor right one word
Ctrl+←	Moves toothpick cursor left one word
Ctrl+PgUp	Moves the toothpick cursor to top of screen
Ctrl+PgDn	Moves the toothpick cursor to bottom of screen
PgUp	Moves toothpick cursor up one screen
PgDn	Moves toothpick cursor down one screen
End	Moves toothpick cursor to end of current line
Home	Moves toothpick cursor to start of current line
Ctrl+Home	Moves the toothpick cursor to top of document
Ctrl+End	Moves toothpick cursor to bottom of document

WORD FOR WINDOWS FOR DUMMIES™

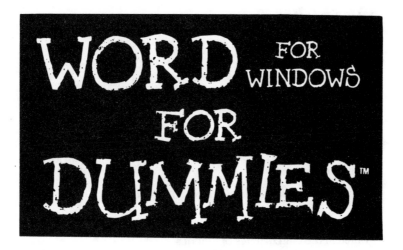

WORD FOR WINDOWS FOR DUMMIES™

by Dan Gookin
author of best-selling *DOS For Dummies, 2nd Edition*
and *WordPerfect 6 For Dummies*
and Ray Werner

IDG Books Worldwide, Inc.
An International Data Group Company

San Mateo, California ✦ Indianapolis, Indiana ✦ Boston, Massachusetts

Word For Windows For Dummies

Published by
IDG Books Worldwide, Inc.
An International Data Group Company
155 Bovet Road, Suite 310
San Mateo, CA 94402

Library of Congress Catalog Card No.: 93-78746

ISBN : 1-878058-86-X

Printed in the United States of America

10 9 8 7 6 5 4 3

Distributed in the United States by IDG Books Worldwide, Inc.

Distributed in Canada by Macmillan of Canada, a Division of Canada Publishing Corporation; by Computer and Technical Books in Miami, Florida, for South America and the Caribbean; by Longman Singapore in Singapore, Malaysia, Thailand, and Korea; by Toppan Co. Ltd. in Japan; by Asia Computerworld in Hong Kong; by Woodslane Pty. Ltd. in Australia and New Zealand; and by Transworld Publishers Ltd. in the U.K. and Europe.

For information on where to purchase IDG Books outside the U.S., call Christina Turner at 415-312-0633.

For information on translations, contact Marc Jeffrey Mikulich, Foreign Rights Manager, at IDG Books Worldwide; Fax number 415-358-1260.

For sales inquiries and special prices for bulk quantities, write to the address above or call IDG Books Worldwide at 415-312-0650.

Acknowledgments

We would like to thank a bunch of folks for helping make this book possible. Unfortunately, we're only limited to a single paragraph, so we'll be brief: At IDG Books, we'd like to thank John Kilcullen, David Solomon, Mary Bednarek, and Leigh Davis. Thanks also go to Waterside Productions and Matt Wagner for many reasons we can't even describe right now because it's so late at night and these acknowledgments are kind of a last-minute thing.

— *Dan Gookin*
— *Ray Werner*

The publisher would like to give special thanks to Patrick J. McGovern, without whom this book would not have been possible.

About the Authors

Dan Gookin

Dan Gookin got started with computers back in the post slide rule age of computing: 1982. His first intention was to buy a computer to replace his aged and constantly breaking typewriter. Working as slave labor in a restaurant, however, Gookin was unable to afford the full "word processor" setup and settled on a computer that had a monitor, keyboard, and little else. Soon his writing career was underway with several submissions to (and lots of rejections from) fiction magazines.

The big break came in 1984 when he began writing about computers. Applying his flair for fiction with a self-taught knowledge of computers, Gookin was able to demystify the subject and explain technology in a relaxed and understandable voice. He even dared to add humor, which eventually won him a column in a local computer magazine.

Eventually Gookin's talents came to roost as he became a ghost writer at a computer book publishing house. That was followed by an editing position at a San Diego computer magazine, at which time he also regularly participated on a radio talk show about computers. In addition, Gookin kept writing books about computers, some of which became minor bestsellers.

In 1990, Gookin came to IDG Books with a book proposal. From that initial meeting unfolded an idea for an outrageous book: a long overdue and original idea for the computer book for the rest of us. What became *DOS For Dummies* blossomed into an international bestseller with hundreds and thousands of copies in print and many foreign translations.

Today, Gookin still considers himself a writer and computer "guru" whose job it is to remind everyone that computers are not to be taken too seriously. His approach to computers is light and humorous yet very informative. He knows that the complex beasts are important and can help people become productive and successful. Yet Gookin mixes his knowledge of computers with a unique, dry sense of humor that keeps everyone informed — and awake. His favorite quote is, "Computers are a notoriously dull subject, but that doesn't mean I have to write about them that way."

Gookin's most recent titles include *WordPerfect 6 For Dummies* and the *Illustrated Computer Dictionary For Dummies*. He is the series editor for the . . . *For Dummies Quick Reference* books. He also is the author of the bestselling *DOS For Dummies*, 2nd Edition, *WordPerfect For Dummies*, and the coauthor of *PCs For Dummies*. All told, he's written more than 30 books on computers and contributes regularly to *DOS Resource Guide, InfoWorld* and *PC Computing Magazine*. Gookin holds a degree in communications from the University of California, San Diego, and recently moved with his wife and boys to Idaho.

About the Authors

Ray Werner

Ray Werner started computing when 48K of RAM was considered to be an awesome, if wasteful, display of power, and any self-respecting computer had several wires emanating from its insides with alligator clamps connecting all sorts of sundry stuff. Over the years, he has learned a lot about these semi-intelligent bundles of silicon and has gradually accumulated enough equipment so that his computer room is often compared to the cockpit of a 747.

Ray is a freelance editor and writer with several computer books under his belt. He authored *The First Book of CorelDRAW! 3* and *50 Ways To Get Your Money's Worth from Prodigy*, among others, and has co-authored books, including *At Ease with FoxPro 2.5 for Windows*. He is known for a laid-back attitude and a playful writing style that is . . . well . . . friendly.

Ray teaches computer literacy courses at Indiana Vocational Technical college and has trained introductory through advanced subjects for several Fortune 500 firms. He lives in Indianapolis with his computers, Amazing, Awesome, and Little Bit Who Possesses Many Bites, and his cats, Bruce and Mandy. He does promise, however, to move back to Cincinnati if he ever gets as famous as Dan Gookin.

Credits

Publisher
David Solomon

Managing Editor
Mary Bednarek

Acquisitions Editor
Janna Custer

Project Editor
H. Leigh Davis

Editorial Assistant
Pamela Mourozis

Technical Reviewer
Michael J. Partington, *Partington Design*

Production Manager
Beth J. Baker

Production Coordinator
Cindy L. Phipps

Production Staff
Tony Augsburger
Mary Breidenbach
Drew Moore

Proofreader
Vickie West

Indexer
Anne Leach

University Graphics Production Staff
Peppy White
Francette M. Ytsma
Tracy Strub
Dana Sadoff

university graphics

palo alto, california

About IDG Books Worldwide

Welcome to the world of IDG Books Worldwide.

IDG Books Worldwide, Inc., is a division of International Data Group, the world's largest publisher of computer-related information and the leading global provider of information services on information technology. IDG publishes over 194 computer publications in 62 countries. Forty million people read one or more IDG publications each month.

If you use personal computers, IDG Books is committed to publishing quality books that meet your needs. We rely on our extensive network of publications, including such leading periodicals as *Macworld*, *InfoWorld*, *PC World*, *Computerworld*, *Publish*, *Network World*, and *SunWorld*, to help us make informed and timely decisions in creating useful computer books that meet your needs.

Every IDG book strives to bring extra value and skill-building instruction to the reader. Our books are written by experts, with the backing of IDG periodicals, and with careful thought devoted to issues such as audience, interior design, use of icons, and illustrations. Our editorial staff is a careful mix of high-tech journalists and experienced book people. Our close contact with the makers of computer products helps ensure accuracy and thorough coverage. Our heavy use of personal computers at every step in production means we can deliver books in the most timely manner.

We are delivering books of high quality at competitive prices on topics customers want. At IDG, we believe in quality, and we have been delivering quality for over 25 years. You'll find no better book on a subject than an IDG book.

John Kilcullen
President and C.E.O.
IDG Books Worldwide, Inc.

IDG Books Worldwide, Inc. is a division of International Data Group. The officers are Patrick J. McGovern, Founder and Board Chairman; Walter Boyd, President. International Data Group's publications include: **ARGENTINA's** Computerworld Argentina, InfoWorld Argentina; **ASIA's** Computerworld Hong Kong, PC World Hong Kong, Computerworld Southeast Asia, PC World Singapore, Computerworld Malaysia, PC World Malaysia; **AUSTRALIA's** Computerworld Australia, Australian PC World, Australian Macworld, Network World, Reseller, IDG Sources; **AUSTRIA's** Computerwelt Oesterreich, PC Test; **BRAZIL's** Computerworld, Mundo IBM, Mundo Unix, PC World, Publish; **BULGARIA's** Computerworld Bulgaria, Ediworld, PC & Mac World Bulgaria; **CANADA's** Direct Access, Graduate Computerworld, InfoCanada, Network World Canada; **CHILE's** Computerworld, Informatica; **COLOMBIA's** Computerworld Columbia; **CZECH REPUBLIC's** Computerworld, Elektronika, PC World; **DENMARK's** CAD/CAM WORLD, Communications World, Computerworld Danmark, LOTUS World, Macintosh Produktkatalog, Macworld Danmark, PC World Danmark, PC World Produktguide, Windows World; **EQUADOR's** PC World; **EGYPT's** Computerworld (CW) Middle East, PC World Middle East; **FINLAND's** MikroPC, Tietoviikko, Tietoverkko; **FRANCE's** Distributique, GOLDEN MAC, InfoPC, Languages & Systems, Le Guide du Monde Informatique, Le Monde Informatique, Telecoms & Reseaux; **GERMANY's** Computerwoche, Computerwoche Focus, Computerwoche Extra, Computerwoche Karriere, Information Management, Macwelt, Netzwelt, PC Welt, PC Woche, Publish, Unit; **HUNGARY's** Alaplap, Computerworld SZT, PC World; **INDIA's** Computers & Communications; **ISRAEL's** Computerworld Israel, PC World Israel; **ITALY's** Computerworld Italia, Lotus Magazine, Macworld Italia, Networking Italia, PC World Italia; **JAPAN's** Computerworld Japan, Macworld Japan, SunWorld Japan, Windows World; **KENYA's** East African Computer News; **KOREA's** Computerworld Korea, Macworld Korea, PC World Korea; **MEXICO's** Compu Edicion, Compu Manufactura, Computacion/Punto de Venta, Computerworld Mexico, MacWorld, Mundo Unix, PC World, Windows; **THE NETHERLAND'S** Computer! Totaal, LAN Magazine, MacWorld; **NEW ZEALAND's** Computer Listings, Computerworld New Zealand, New Zealand PC World; **NIGERIA's** PC World Africa; **NORWAY's** Computerworld Norge, C/World, Lotusworld Norge, Macworld Norge, Networld, PC World Ekspress, PC World Norge, PC World's Product Guide, Publish World, Student Data, Unix World, Windowsworld, IDG Direct Response; **PANAMA's** PC World; **PERU's** Computerworld Peru, PC World; **PEOPLES REPUBLIC OF CHINA's** China Computerworld, PC World China, Electronics International, China Network World; **IDG HIGH TECH BEIJING's** New Product World; **IDG SHENZHEN's** Computer News Digest; **PHILLIPPINES'** Computerworld, PC World; **POLAND's** Computerworld Poland, PC World/Komputer; **PORTUGAL's** Cerebro/PC World, Correio Informatico/Computerworld, MacIn; **ROMANIA's** PC World; **RUSSIA's** Computerworld-Moscow, Mir-PC, Sety; **SLOVENIA's** Monitor Magazine; **SOUTH AFRICA's** Computing S.A.; **SPAIN's** Amiga World, Computerworld Espana, Communicaciones World, Macworld Espana, NeXTWORLD, PC World Espana, Publish, Sunworld; **SWEDEN's** Attack, ComputerSweden, Corporate Computing, Lokala Natverk/LAN, Lotus World, MAC&PC, Macworld, Mikrodatorn, PC World, Publishing & Design (CAP), Datalngenjoren, Maxi Data, Windows World; **SWITZERLAND's** Computerworld Schweiz, Macworld Schweiz, PC & Workstation; **TAIWAN's** Computerworld Taiwan, Global Computer Express, PC World Taiwan; **THAILAND's** Thai Computerworld; **TURKEY's** Computerworld Monitor, Macworld Turkiye, PC World Turkiye; **UNITED KINGDOM's** Lotus Magazine, Macworld, Sunworld; **UNITED STATES'** AmigaWorld, Cable in the Classroom, CD Review, CIO, Computerworld, Desktop Video World, DOS Resource Guide, Electronic News, Federal Computer Week, Federal Integrator, GamePro, IDG Books, InfoWorld, InfoWorld Direct, Laser Event, Macworld, Multimedia World, Network World, NeXTWORLD, PC Games, PC Letter, PC World Publish, Sumeria, SunWorld, SWATPro, Video Event; **VENEZUELA's** Computerworld Venezuela, MicroComputerworld Venezuela; **VIETNAM's** PC World Vietnam

 The text of this book is printed on recycled paper.

Say What You Think!

Listen up, all you readers of IDG's international bestsellers: the one — the only — absolutely world-famous ...*For Dummies* books! It's time for you to take advantage of a new, direct pipeline to theauthors and editors of IDG Books Worldwide.

In between putting the finishing touches on the next round of ...*For Dummies* books, the authors and editors of IDG Books Worldwide like to sit around and mull over what their readers have to say. And we know that you readers always say what you think.

So here's your chance. We'd really like your input for future printings and editions of this book — and ideas for future ...*For Dummies* titles as well. Tell us what you liked (and didn't like) about this book. How about the chapters you found most useful — or most funny? And since we know you're not a bit shy, what about the chapters you think can be improved?

Just to show you how much we appreciate your input, we'll add you to our Dummies Database/Fan Club and keep you up to date on the latest ...*For Dummies* books, news, cartoons, calendars, and more!

Please send your name, address, and phone number, as well as your comments, questions, and suggestions, to our very own ...*For Dummies* coordinator at the following address:

...For Dummies Coordinator
IDG Books Worldwide
3250 North Post Road, Suite 140
Indianapolis, IN 46226

(Yes, Virginia, there really is a ...*For Dummies* coordinator. We are not making this up.)

Please mention the name of this book in your comments.

Thanks for your input!

**IDG
BOOKS**

Contents at a Glance

xiv

Cartoons at a Glance

By Rich Tennant

page 304

page 244

page 68

page 1

page 235

page 7

page 269

page 155

page 199

page 89

Table of Contents

• •

Introduction

● ●

*W*elcome to *Word For Windows For Dummies*, a book that's not afraid to say, "You don't need to know everything about Word for Windows to use it." Heck, you probably don't *want* to know everything about Word for Windows. You don't want to know all the command options, all the typographical mumbo-jumbo, or even all those special features that you know are in there but terrify you. No, all you want to know is the single answer to a tiny question. Then, you can happily close the book and be on your way. If that's you, then you've found your book.

This book informs and entertains. And it has a serious attitude problem. After all, we don't want to teach you to love Word for Windows. That's sick. Instead, be prepared to encounter some informative, down-to-earth explanations — in English — of how to get the job done by using Word for Windows. After all, you take your work seriously, but you definitely don't need to take Word for Windows seriously.

The 5th Wave　　　　　　　　　　　　**By Rich Tennant**

"Well, McNab, I hear the good news is that you've found us an excellent word processor for the editorial staff."

About This Book

This book is not meant to be read from cover to cover. If that were true, the covers would definitely need to be put closer together. Instead, this book is a reference. Each chapter covers a specific topic in Word for Windows. Within a chapter, you find self-contained sections, each of which describes how to do a Word for Windows task relating to the chapter's topic. Sample sections you encounter in this book include:

  ✔ Saving your stuff

  ✔ Cutting and pasting a block

  ✔ Making italicized text

  ✔ Creating a hanging indent

  ✔ Printing envelopes

  ✔ Cobbling tables together

  ✔ "Where did my document go?"

There are no keys to memorize, no secret codes, no tricks, no pop-up dioramas, and no wall charts. Instead, each section explains a topic as if it's the first thing you read in this book. Nothing is assumed, and everything is cross-referenced. Technical terms and topics, when they come up, are neatly shoved to the side where you can easily avoid reading them. The idea here isn't for you to learn anything. This book's philosophy is to look it up, figure it out, and get back to work.

How To Use This Book

This book helps you when you're at a loss over what to do in Word for Windows. I think that this situation happens to everyone way too often. For example, if you press Ctrl+F9, Word for Windows displays a {} thing in your text. I have no idea what that means, nor do I want to know. What I do know, however, is that I can press Shift+← and press the Delete key to make the annoying thing go away. That's the kind of knowledge you find in this book.

Word for Windows uses the mouse and menus to get things done, which is what you would expect from Windows. Yet, there are times when various *key combinations,* several keys you may press together or in sequence, are required. This book shows you two different kinds of key combinations.

This is a menu shortcut:

    Alt,I,L

This means you should press and release the Alt key, press and release the I key, and then press and release the L key. Don't type the commas or any period that ends a sentence.

This is a keyboard shortcut:

Ctrl+Shift+F12

This means you should press and hold Ctrl and Shift together, and then press F12, and release all three keys.

Any details about what you type are explained in the text. And, if you look down at your keyboard and find ten thumbs — or scissors and cutlery — instead of hands, consider reading Chapter 3, "Using Your Keyboard Correctly," right now.

This book tells you the easiest and best way to perform tasks and offers you alternatives when appropriate. Sometimes it's best to use the mouse — others the keyboard. This book also presents the best keyboard shortcuts and inserts toolbar icons in the margin for those who like to use the toolbar.

Menu commands are listed like this:

File➔Open

This means you open the File menu (with the mouse or the keyboard — it's your choice) and then choose the Open command.

If we describe a message or something you see on-screen, it looks like this:

    This is an on-screen message!

This book never refers you to the Word For Windows manual or — yech! — to the DOS manual. It does refer you to some companion books in this series, *DOS For Dummies, 2nd Edition,* and *Windows For Dummies,* both published by IDG Books Worldwide.

What You're Not To Read

Special technical sections dot this book like mosquito bites. They offer annoyingly endless and technical explanations, descriptions of advanced topics, or alternative commands that you really don't need to know about. Each one of them is flagged with a special icon or enclosed in an electrified, barbed wire and poison ivy box (an idea I stole from the Terwilliker Piano Method books). Reading this stuff is optional.

Foolish Assumptions

Here are my assumptions about you: You use a computer. You use Windows. Word for Windows is your word processor. Anything else involving the computer or DOS is handled by someone whom I call your *personal guru*. Rely on this person to help you through the rough patches; wave your guru over or call your guru on the phone. But always be sure to thank your guru. Remember that computer gurus enjoy junk food as nourishment and often accept it as payment. Keep a bowl of M&Ms or a sack of Doritos at the ready for when you need your guru's assistance.

Beyond you, your PC and the guru, you also should have a computer worthy of running Windows, Version 3.0 or 3.1 preferably. That means you need color graphics, preferably of the VGA or SuperVGA variety. You also need a computer mouse. We make no bones about it: Without a mouse, Word for Windows cannot be done. (By the way, when this book says to click on the mouse button, we mean the left button — unless your mouse is setup differently in some way.)

How This Book Is Organized

This book contains six major parts, each of which is divided into three or more chapters. The chapters themselves have been Ginsu-knifed into smaller, modular sections. You can pick up the book and read any section without necessarily knowing what has already been covered in the rest of the book. Start anywhere.

Here is a breakdown of the six parts and what you find in them:

Part I: Basic Word for Windows Stuff

This is baby Word for Windows stuff — the bare essentials. Here you learn to giggle, teethe, crawl, walk, burp, and spit up. Then you can move up to the advanced topics of moving the cursor, editing text, searching and replacing, marking blocks, spell-checking, and printing. (A pacifier is optional for this section.)

Part II: Formatting — or Making Your Prose Look Less Ugly

Formatting is the art of beating your text into typographical submission. It's not the heady work of creating a document and getting the right words. No, it's "you will be italic," "indent, you moron!" and "gimme a new page *here*." Often, formatting involves a lot yelling. This part of the book contains chapters that show you how to format characters, lines, paragraphs, pages, and entire documents without raising your voice (too much).

Part III: Working with Documents

Document is a nice, professional-sounding word — much better than *that thing I did with Word for Windows. Document* is quicker to type. And you sound important if you say that you work on documents instead of admitting the truth that you sit and stare at the screen and play with the mouse. This part of the book tells you how to save and shuffle documents.

Part IV: Working with Graphics

Graphics play a major role in Windows, and Word for Windows is geared toward having many interesting graphical bits and pieces. This part of the book discusses how graphics can work in your documents, how you can use Word for Windows' own *applets* to create your own graphics, and how to do some things that previously required a knowledge of desktop publishing (or at least knowing what a Merganthaller was). The idea here is to make your document look o' so purty.

Part V: Help Me, Mr. Wizard!

One school of thought is that every copy of Word for Windows should be sold with a baseball bat. I'm a firm believer in baseball-bat therapy for computers. But, before you go to such an extreme, consider the soothing words of advice provided in this part of the book.

Part VI: The Part of Tens

How about "The Ten Commandments of Word for Windows" — complete with Bill Gates (the President of Microsoft) bringing them down from Mt. Redmond. Or, consider "Ten Features You Don't Use But Paid for Anyway." Or the handy "Ten Things Worth Remembering." This section is a gold mine of tens.

Bonus Appendix

This book assumes that you have WinWord installed and ready to go. In case you haven't, turn to the Appendix, "Installing Word for Windows."

Icons Used in This Book

This icon alerts you to overly nerdy information and technical discussions of the topic at hand. The information is optional reading, but it may enhance your reputation at cocktail parties if you repeat it.

This icon flags useful, helpful tips or shortcuts.

This icon marks a friendly reminder to do something.

This icon marks a friendly reminder not to do something.

This icon flags information about using Word for Windows with a mouse (the computer kind — although if you like to work with the mammal variety, that's OK too).

This icon identifies the quick, no-commentary way to accomplish a WinWord task.

Where To Go from Here

You work with Word for Windows. You know what you hate about it. Why not start by looking up that subject in the table of contents and seeing what this book says about it? Alternatively, you can continue to use Word for Windows in the Sisyphean manner you're used to: Push that boulder to the top of the hill, and when it starts to roll back on you, whip out this book like a bazooka and blow the rock to smithereens. You'll be back at work and enjoying yourself in no time.

Part I
Basic Word for Windows Stuff

In this part . . .

Primitive peoples first made their marks by slamming rocks into stone tablets. Then came the Egyptian papyrus, the clay tablets of the Babylonians, and then Greek and Roman scrolls. In the 1400s, Gutenberg's press ushered in a new era of printed communication. Then came the typewriter, the patented IBM Selectric, the PC running Microsoft Windows, and then Microsoft Word for Windows word processing software, belovedly called "WinWord." So if we've made this much progress, why do we still feel like slamming a rock into the computer screen? The answer is that no one has bothered to explain it all to you in simple, clay tablet terms. That's what in this part of the book — your basic WinWord stuff.

Chapter 1

Word Processing 101

● ●

In This Chapter

▶ Starting Word for Windows

▶ Reading the WinWord screen

▶ Entering text

▶ Editing a document on-disk

▶ Getting Help

▶ WinWord's less-than-cuddly way of talking to you

▶ Printing

▶ Save your stuff!

▶ Closing a document

▶ Moving on

▶ Exiting WinWord

● ●

*T*his chapter offers an overview of how WinWord works — how you can use the program every day to get various word processing stuff done. *The Basics*. More specific stuff happens in later chapters and is cross-referenced here for your page-flipping enjoyment.

Starting Word for Windows

To begin using WinWord, you must do the following:

1. **Prepare yourself mentally.**

   Do I really want to do this? You know, those rocks were quite good enough for my ancestors, and there really isn't anything wrong with that old typewriter. A computer? Do I have to go out and buy pocket protectors? Tape up my glasses? OK. Deep breath. I will be brave.

2. Turn on the computer, the monitor, and anything else of importance.

The important stuff can usually be identified by the number of lights it has — it's kind of a status symbol in the computer community, you know.

3. Contend with DOS.

This should be brief. Windows is the creature you're fighting for when you use Word *for Windows*. A few lucky users may not have to deal with DOS if the warm, fuzzy Windows interface starts immediately and the beloved Program Manager opens on-screen. Skip on up to Step 5.

4. Start Windows.

If Windows doesn't start already, you'll see the ugly DOS prompt, C> or sometimes C:\>, which is a kind of warning sign on the road to computer purgatory. You need to type **WIN** and press Enter to start up Microsoft Windows, which is a little bit this side of paradise and has plastic palm trees.

```
C:\> WIN
```

That is, type **WIN** at the DOS prompt and press the Enter key. This step starts Microsoft Windows, which will appear in brazen, god-like splendor on your screen. Don't be fooled.

5. Contend with Windows.

6. Locate the Word for Windows icon.

Somewhere entombed on your screen — on the Windows *desktop* — is an *icon* that represents WinWord's heart and soul. You use this picture to start Word for Windows. A copy of the icon is shown in Figure 1-1. Look for the icon on your screen in the Program Manager. If you're lucky, there may be a Word for Windows (or WinWord) group window, which is a subwindow inside the Program Manager; there, you'll find the icon.

7. Start the WinWord program.

Double-click on the WinWord icon with your mouse. Click-click.

Microsoft
Word

Figure 1-1: The WinWord icon as seen in the Program Manager.

Watch in amazement as your computer whizzes and whirs. Before too long, you'll see a screen that looks like Figure 1-2. It's WinWord stumbling into town! The whatzits of the screen are discussed in the following section, "Reading the WinWord Screen."

✔ Your computer can be set up to automatically run WinWord. Think of the time that would save! If you want your computer setup in this manner, grab someone more knowledgeable than yourself — an individual we call a *computer guru*. Tell your guru to "make my computer always start in WinWord." If your guru is unable, frantically grab other people at random until you find someone bold enough to obey you.

✔ It's best to run WinWord *full screen*. After the program starts, click on the upward-pointing arrow button in the very upper-right corner of the window. This button *maximizes* WinWord to fill the entire screen. If WinWord is already maximized, there will be two arrows (up and down) displayed on the button; no need to click anything in that case.

✔ Additional information on starting your PC and contending with the DOS prompt can be found in the book *DOS For Dummies, 2nd Edition*, which does for DOS what this book does for WinWord: Make it understandable!

✔ Additional information on starting your PC and contending with Windows can be found in the book *Windows For Dummies*, which does for Windows what this book does for WinWord, and what *DOS For Dummies* does for DOS!

Reading the WinWord Screen

After WinWord starts, you'll be faced with the electronic version of "The Blank Page." This is the same idea-crippling concept that induced writer's block in several generations of typewriter users. With WinWord it's worse; not only is the screen mostly blank, it is surrounded by bells, whistles, switches, and doodads that would be interesting if only they were edible.

Figure 1-2 shows the typical, blank WinWord screen. There are three things worth noting:

1. Five, count 'em, separate strips of stuff: bars, ribbons, rulers, and other horizontal holding bins for horrendous heaps of hogwash. Each strip performs some function or gives you some information. I warn you not to memorize this list: the *title bar*, the *menu bar*, the *toolbar*, the *ribbon*

(which was once a bar, but closed because they let minors drink), and the *ruler* (who thinks he's the king or something). Refer to the following, easily avoidable technical information box if you want to load your brain with the details of these strips and bars: "Forbidden information on strip bars."

2. A large empty space. This is where text you type and edit appears. Somewhere in this empty space is the flashing *insertion pointer* — looks like a blinking toothpick — that tells you where the text you type appears.

3. The bottom of the screen contains the *status bar*. It contains a lot of information that would impress a bureaucrat but, frankly, makes my eyes glaze over. The gibberish that is usually there explains "where you are" in your document. There are always seven word fragments followed by numbers (like a 10th grade algebra problem). Table 1-1 explains what this stuff means.

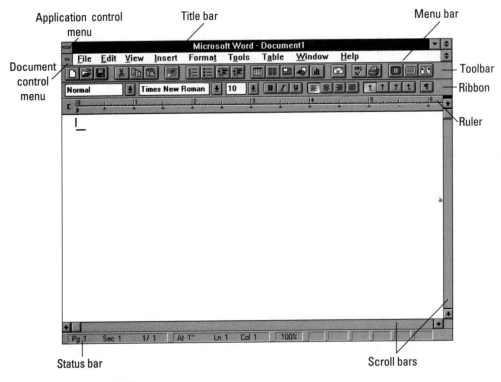

Figure 1-2: WinWord on-screen.

Table 1-1	Stuff in the Status Bar
Word Fragment	**What It Means**
Pg xx	The page number you're editing: 1 = the first page, 8 = the eighth page, and so on.
Sec xx	The section of the document you're editing: 1 = the first section, 8 = the eighth, and so on. (For most of us, this is always section 1.)
x/x	The page of the document that you're editing *over* the total number of pages in the document. So, 1/8 would mean you're on page one of an eight page document. (This is not a math problem; 1/8 does not mean .125.)
At x.xx"	How far from the top of the document your text is in inches. At 4.89" means that the line you're editing is 4.89 inches from the top of the page.
Ln xx	What line you're editing. Ln 5 means that you're working on line 5.
Col xx	What column you are in, columns being these vertical support structures for Greek-style architecture. In WinWord, the first column starts on the left side of the page and the Col (column) numbers get bigger as you type toward the right side of the page.
xx %	The Zoom percentage. Have you had your Zoom this morning? Actually, this refers to how big the document looks on-screen as compared to how big it will print. A value of 100% means that the document is as big on-screen as it will be when printed, a 100% zoom. 150% means that the document is 1 1/2 times as big on the screen, shown larger than real size to make it readable; 50% means it's half size (which is kinda teensy on-screen).
Empty boxes	These boxes are filled with various status indicators. Press the Caps Lock key and CAPS appears in one of the blank boxes. Press the Num Lock key and NUM appears.

✔ My advice? Ignore the weird numbers on the status bar; concentrate instead on your writing. After all, only the truly disturbed would whip out a ruler and measure a piece of paper in a typewriter as they go along. (The numbers will come in handy later to tell you how much stuff you've written or to find your way to a particular spot in a long document. Pretend they don't exist for now.)

✔ Any weird stuff you see on the screen, a ¶ for example, is a WinWord secret symbol. Refer to Chapter 22, the section "All My Words Have Spots Between Them!" for additional information.

✔ The exact spot where the text appears is called the *cursor*. Normally it's also called an *insertion pointer*, because traditional computer cursors are underlines that slide under what you type. I prefer the term *toothpick cursor*, because insertion pointer is just too medically geometric for my tastes. Characters you type will appear immediately to the left of where the toothpick cursor is flashing, and then the cursor will move forward and wait for the next character.

✔ The *mouse pointer* is different from the toothpick cursor. Normally it's an arrow pointer-like thing. But if you move the mouse around the writing part of the screen, the pointer changes. Over your text, the pointer becomes what's commonly called an *I-beam*. The I-beam means "I will beam the insertion pointer to this spot when I click the mouse."

✔ The status bar on the bottom of the screen will tell what some WinWord menu commands do. To see how this works, click on a menu command with the left mouse button. As long as you press and hold the mouse button, the status bar will try to explain what the command does.

Forbidden information on strip bars

This section has nothing to do with strip bars. Instead, the topic here is the information you get from those five strips of information on the WinWord screen. Some of them may be visible — others may not show up at all. You can turn some of them on or off by selecting their names from the View menu.

Title bar: The first strip shows the name of your document. Every window in Windows has a title bar, as well as the various buttons and gizmos Windows is famous for: the Control menu, maximize and minimize buttons, and the scroll bars you may see in the middle part of the screen. (Please refer to *Windows For Dummies* for an explanation of how all this stuff works and what relevance it has.)

Menu bar: The second strip contains a list of menus, each of which disguises a pull-down menu that you use to select the many WinWord commands at your beck and call.

Toolbar: The third strip has lots of tools you can click to quickly use some of the more common WinWord commands. This strip may or may not be visible on your screen, depending on how WinWord is setup. The setup is discussed in Chapter 22.

Ribbon: The fourth strip probably has the word Normal in it, on the left side. As with the toolbar, this is an optional strip. In the ribbon you will find the commands that apply styles, type sizes, fonts, attributes (bold, italic, and underline) justification choices (left, center, right, and full), tabs, and other fun formatting frivolity. Again, refer to Chapter 22 for more information on the ribbon.

Ruler: The fifth strip looks like a ruler. It is. And as with the toolbar and ribbon, your screen may not show the ruler — especially if the country you're in despises monarchy.

To make the Toolbar, Ribbon, or Ruler visible, select that option from the View menu. If the item already has a check mark (✔) by it, then — it's already visible.

Entering Text

To compose text in WinWord, use your *keyboard* — that typewriter-like thing sitting in front of your computer and below the monitor. Go ahead, type away; let your fingers dance upon the keycaps! What you type appears on-screen, letter for letter — even derogatory stuff about the computer. (Your PC doesn't care, but that doesn't mean *WinWord* lacks feelings.)

New text is inserted right in front of where the cursor is blinking. For example, you can type:

```
Mother emphasized, "Don't say a thing about Grandma's mustache."
```

If you want to change emphasized to *reemphasized*, you move the toothpick cursor to the start of `emphasized` and type **re**. Those two letters are inserted into the text. There's nothing to delete, and all the text afterwards falls neatly into place.

- ✔ You compose text on-screen by typing. Every character key you press produces a character on-screen. This holds true for all letter, number, and symbol keys. The other keys, mostly gray on your keyboard, do strange and wonderful things, which the rest of this book tries hard to explain.

- ✔ If you make a mistake, press the Backspace key to backup and erase. This key is named Backspace on your keyboard, or it may have a long, left-pointing arrow on it: ←.

- ✔ There is no cause for alarm if you see spots — or dots — on-screen when you press the spacebar. These special doohickeys let you "see" spaces on-screen. Refer to Chapter 22 for the low-down.

- ✔ Moving the toothpick cursor around the screen is covered in Chapter 2, "Navigating Your Document."

- ✔ The Shift key produces capital letters.

- ✔ The Caps Lock key works like the Shift-Lock key on a typewriter. After you press that key, everything you type will be in ALL CAPS.

- ✔ The Caps Lock light on your keyboard comes on when you're in All Caps mode. Also, note that the word `CAPS` appears in the status bar when Caps Lock is on.

- ✔ The number keys on the right side of the keyboard are called the *numeric keypad*. To use those keys, you must press the Num Lock key on your keyboard. If you don't, the keys will take on their "arrow key" function. Refer to Chapter 2, "Navigating Your Document."

- The Num Lock light on the keyboard comes on when you press the Num Lock key to turn the numeric keypad on. Most PCs start with this feature activated. Also, note that the word NUM appears in the status bar when the Num Lock is on.

- Refer to Chapter 3, "Using Your Keyboard Correctly," for some handy tips on typing and using your keyboard.

- No one needs to learn to type to become a writer. But the best writers are typists. My advice is to get a computer program that will teach you to type. It will make a painful experience like WinWord a wee bit more enjoyable.

Typing away, la la la

Eons ago, a word processor was judged superior if it had the famous *word-wrap* feature. This feature eliminated the need to press the Enter key at the end of each line of text, which is a requirement when using a typewriter. WinWord, and all other modern word processors, has this feature. If you're unfamiliar with it, you should get used to putting it to work for you.

With WinWord, when the text gets precariously close to the right margin, the last word will be picked up and placed at the start of the next line. There's no need to press Enter, except when you want to end a paragraph.

- Press Enter to create a new paragraph. If you want to split one paragraph into two, move the toothpick cursor to the middle of the paragraph, where you want the second paragraph to start, and press Enter.

- You need to press the Enter key only at the end of a paragraph, not at the end of every line.

- Don't be afraid to use your keyboard! WinWord will always offer ample warning before anything serious happens. There also is a handy undo feature that will recover anything you accidentally delete. Refer to Chapter 3, "Using Your Keyboard Correctly."

"That Annoying Line of Dots"

Occasionally, you'll see a row of dots stretching from one side of the screen to another — like a line of ants marching in an uncharacteristically straight line across your screen. Don't swat at it! That thing marks the end of one page and the beginning of another, a *page break*. The text you see above the ants, er, dots, is on the previous page; text below the dots is on the next page.

✔ You cannot delete the line of dots. It's like stepping on a roach. Instead, just ignore it. After all, it is a useful way of telling you where text stops on one page and starts on the next.

✔ You can see how the line of dots works by looking at the scrambled statistics in the status bar. For example, when the toothpick cursor is above the dots, it will say Pg 5 for page 5. When the cursor is below the dots, you'll see Pg 6 for page 6.

✔ A row of dots close together — very friendly ants — marks a *hard page break*. This is a definite "I want a new page now" command given by the person who created the document. Refer to Chapter 11, "Formatting Pages and Documents."

Editing a Document on-Disk

You use WinWord to create *documents*. The documents can be printed or saved to disk for later editing or printing. When a document has been saved to disk, it's considered a *file* "on" the disk. (You can still refer to it as a document.)

There are several ways to load and edit a document already on disk. Because this is Windows, why not use the mouse-menu method?:

1. Choose the File→Open command.

Using the mouse, click on the word File in the menu bar and a drop-down menu, well, drops down. Click on the Open menu command, and the Open dialog box appears, shown in Figure 1-3. (You also can click on the Open tool.)

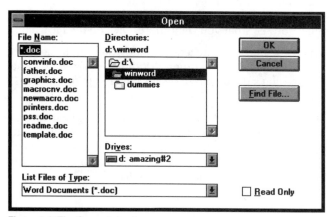

Figure 1-3: The Open dialog box.

2. Select the name of the document (or file) you want to open and edit.

Find the document name in the list and double-click on it with the left mouse button. You can use the controls in the Open dialog box to whisk yourself around your disk drive scouting out files. Using the Open dialog box is standard Windows stuff. When you find your file, highlight it, and click on the OK button in the Open dialog box; or just double-click on the filename with the left mouse button.

✔ If the cat is playing with your mouse, you can open the Open dialog box by pressing Alt,F,O (or the shortcut Ctrl+F12). Then you can use the keyboard to type in a filename — although this method is so primitive you'd better lock the door first. No one wants to be seen using a *keyboard* in Windows!

✔ If you do end up typing the name of the document you want to load, make sure that everything is spelled right; WinWord is finicky about filename spelling. You can type it in upper- or lower-case; it's all the same. Or, you can simply select the name with the mouse by clicking on it. You don't have to worry about spelling that way.

✔ The term *editing* means to read, correct, or add to the text you have composed and saved to disk. This involves using the cursor keys, which are covered in Chapter 2, "Navigating Your Document." Also refer to Chapter 4, "Deleting and Destroying Text"; Chapter 5, "The Wonders of Find and Replace"; and Chapter 6, "Text Blocks, Stumbling Blocks, and Mental Blocks."

✔ To edit a document you must "open" its file on-disk. This is done by using the Open command in the File menu, which is a constant thing you do over and over again in any Windows application. If you know how to open a spreadsheet in Excel, then you know how to open a document in Windows. It works the same way.

✔ If you want to edit a file that you recently had open, pull down the File menu and look at the list on the bottom of the menu to see whether it is listed. WinWord "remembers" the last few documents you worked on. If you see what you want there, click on the file's name to open it.

✔ When you finish editing a document, you print it, save it back to disk, or do one and then the other. Printing is covered in the section "Printing"; saving a document to disk is covered in the section "Save Your Stuff!"

✔ Documents must be saved to disk with a DOS filename. If you think stuffing something clever into a 7-character "vanity" license plate is tough, wait until you try to save that letter to Aunt Velma! DOS is very limiting with how files are named; refer to Chapter 17, "Managing Files" for file naming rules and regulations.

> ✔ If the document you typed doesn't exist on disk, or WinWord was unable to find it, you'll see this error message in a dialog box: `This document does not exist!` Click the OK button when this happens and try again, but check your spelling this time. Also, refer to Chapter 17, "Managing Files," which shows you how to locate a file and open it without typing its name.

Getting Help

That group of pocket-protected, bespectacled, Birkenstock-wearing programmers up at Microsoft can make some delightful blunders every once in a while. However, no matter what else they do, they are forgiven. They put a wonderful Help system into WinWord.

WinWord's Help system is actually the same help system you find in just about every Windows program. It's activated by the F1 key, and you can search for helpful topics or, if you're in the middle of something, get help on only that one topic.

The WinWord Help menu

If you click on Help on the menu bar, you open the Word Help menu. The only menu item worth bothering with is the Help Index, shown in Figure 1-4, which displays a list of all the topics relevant to WinWord — including some stuff that borders on being useful. The rest of the menu items in the Help menu can be cheerfully ignored.

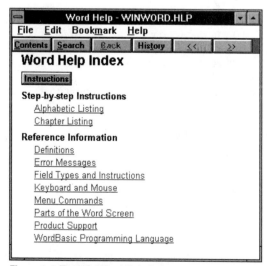

Figure 1-4: The WinWord Help Index.

When you're in the Help Index, you can move the mouse to any of the shown topics. When you hover over a "green" topic, the mouse pointer changes into a flying pointing finger. Click once to select help for that topic.

- ✔ You also can access the Help Index by pressing the F1 key while you're editing.

- ✔ When you press F1 while you're doing something else, such as being mired in a dialog box, you'll see helpful information on that topic only. Click on the Contents button in the Help system to see the Index again.

- ✔ WinWord's Help, like help for all Windows programs, is actually a separate program. Choose Exit from the Help system's File menu, or press Alt+F4, when you're done with help and need to return to your document for more editing fun.

Context-sensitive help

The spiffiest thing about WinWord's help capability is that it can give you help with what you're doing when you're doing it. If you hold down the Shift key while you press the F1 key, the mouse pointer changes into a question mark/arrow.

Point this thing at what you want help with and click on it. For example, point the arrow at the scissors on the toolbar and click the mouse. You'll find out that the scissors are used to cut text, not to give you a haircut. This works with just about anything you see on the WinWord screen — even the really weird stuff.

WinWord's Less-than-Cuddly Way of Talking to You

There are times when you try to do some well-meaning thing in WinWord and the program, for reasons psychologists are still struggling over, just doesn't get it. Or maybe WinWord thinks you're about to do something foolish, and it needs to offer some consoling or hateful words of advice. In those cases, you'll be confronted with one of WinWord's famous question dialog boxes, such as the one simulated in Figure 1-5.

The question in Figure 1-5, which differs depending on what WinWord is trying to tell you, has four options: Yes, No, Cancel, and Help, one of which is highlighted.

Figure 1-5: A question posed to the humble user.

Yes means, "Yes, I agree with you, WinWord. Couldn't have said it better my-self. Please go ahead and do whatever it was I asked you to."

No means, "No."

Cancel means, "I've changed my mind!"

Help begs WinWord, "Try to help me. I dare you. Double-dog dare."

✔ Pressing the Enter key in such a dialog box usually selects the "safe" op-tion. That could be Yes, OK, or even No depending on how the dialog box's warning is worded.

✔ Sometimes only a few of the Yes, No, Cancel, or Help buttons appear — sometimes more!

✔ The dreaded "error" dialog boxes usually have only one button in them, OK. So, regardless of whether it's okay, you must press the OK button. Okay?

Printing

After entering what you feel is the best piece of written work since Tolstoy, you decide you want to print it. After all, dragging the computer around and show-ing everyone what your prose looks like on-screen just isn't practical.

To print your document in WinWord — the document you see on-screen, all of it — do the following:

1. Make sure that your printer is on and ready to print.

Refer to Chapter 8 for additional information on preparing the printer should you need it.

Open the File menu, and then choose the Print command. (You also can choose the Print tool.)

The Print dialog box opens. This is the place where printing and related activities happen.

3. Click the OK button with the mouse.

Zip, zip, zip. The document comes out of your printer. Or, whir, crunch, flap-blap-blap, the document comes out of your laser printer all nice and toasty.

✔ You also can summon the Print dialog box by pressing Alt,F,P or Ctrl+Shift+F12. This is more desirable if you have long fingers, do needle-point, or if the mouse is off eating the cheese again.

✔ Detailed information on printing is provided in Chapter 8. This includes information on making sure your printer is ready to print.

✔ To print only part of your document — a paragraph, page, or a "block" — refer to Chapter 6, "Text Blocks, Stumbling Blocks, and Mental Blocks."

Save Your Stuff!

WinWord doesn't remember what you did last time you used the computer. You must forcefully tell it to *save* your stuff! The document on-screen must be saved in a file on disk. To do this, you need to use WinWord's Save command.

 To save a document to disk, choose the File→Save command Alt,F,S. (You also can click the Save tool.) This saves your document to disk. Or, if the file hasn't yet been saved, a Save As dialog box appears. In that case, type in a name for the file. Click the OK button when you're done.

✔ If the document you created hasn't yet been saved to disk, you need to give WinWord a filename under which the document will be stored. The name is how you'll recognize the file later, when you need to edit or print it again. Think of a clever name, since you have only eight characters (letters and numbers). Type the document's name in the dialog box. Watch what you type! If you make a mistake, use the Backspace key to backup and erase. Click OK to save the file.

 ✔ The fastest way to save a file is to use the function keys. The Save file combination is Shift+F12. Press and hold the Shift key and press the F12 key. If you can't pick up a basketball with one hand this maneuver may take two hands.

✔ When you save a document, look at the lower-left corner of the screen — on the status bar thing. Numbers fly by faster than the government accumulates debt. This movement indicates that the document is being saved.

TECHNICAL STUFF

Complicated — but important — information on DOS filenames

You must name your file according to DOS's file naming rules. This isn't as tough as memorizing stuff for a DMV test, but it's darn close:

1. A filename can be no more than 8 characters long.

2. It can include letters and numbers and can start with a letter or a number.

3. Filenames do not end with a period.

4. WinWord automatically gives your filename a three-letter last name, or file *extension*, of DOC. There is no need to type this in yourself, nor should you mess with giving your documents their own unique last names.

Here are some sample filenames that are okay. I've specified the DOC extension below, although you don't need to type it in when you save a file:

LETTER.DOC	A prim and proper filename, replete with optional period and three-character DOC extension. Mrs. Heinemann, my 3rd grade teacher, would be proud.
CHAP01.DOC	Another okay filename. Note how numbers and letters can be mixed — no oil and vinegar here!
01.DOC	Fine, upstanding DOS filename; numbers are okey-dokey, the extension, DOC, will be added automatically by WinWord.
LTR2MOM4.DOC	No problems here.

Here are some filenames you should avoid (with reasons why you should avoid them):

TO MOM.DOC	The filename contains a space. Heavens! Filenames cannot contain spaces.
BELLYBUTTON.DOC	Too long, and offensive to certain groups of people.
1+1.DOC	Numbers are okay, but the + symbol is not; only use letters and numbers to name files.
I.LOVE.YOU	Weird filename that contains two periods. The period is reserved only to mark the filename extension and not used otherwise.
CHOPSTIK.FOOD	The extension here is too long. They can only be three characters maximum in the extension.
LETTER.1	The number as an extension is okay, but WinWord will not display this file in its Open file dialog box. It only looks for files ending in .DOC, so while the filename is okay, I don't recommend specifying any extension when you save a file.

✔ If you entered a forbidden filename, WinWord will screech at you `ERROR: Invalid filename`. Try again (and read the preceding Technical Stuff box).

✔ Save your documents to disk so that you can work on them later! The documents can be re-loaded into WinWord next time you start. Refer to the section "Editing a Document on-Disk" earlier in this chapter.

✔ After the document has been saved to disk, you'll see its name — actually its complicated DOS pathname with almond clusters — displayed in the title bar. This is your clue that a file has been saved to disk.

✔ If you're not in a clever mood, you may decide to name your file with the name of a file already on disk. This is a boo-boo, because the newer file will "overwrite" the other file with the same name already on disk. For example, if you decide to save your new letter using the LETTER filename, and LETTER already exists on disk, the new file will overwrite the old one. There is no way to get the original back, so use another more clever name instead. WinWord will warn you with the message: `Do you want to replace the existing file?` Click on the No button.

✔ Refer to Chapter 17, "Managing Files," for more information on filenames and such.

Here is how you can quickly save a document you're working on — something you should do all the time. You have three ways to accomplish this task:

1. Choose the File→Save command (Alt,F,S) or;

2. Press Shift+F12, or;

3. Click on the Save tool.

Use the Save command — any version above — often as you work on your document.

Closing a Document

If you're finished with a document, you can make it vanish from your screen by "closing" it, which is similar to ripping a sheet of paper out of your typewriter — without the satisfying sound it makes.

To close a document, choose the File→Close command (Alt,F,C). This closes the document window and makes it vanish from the screen. Zzzipp! (Although you'll have to say "Zzipp!" when you do this; WinWord is mute on the point.)

✔ Why close a document? Because you're done working on it! Maybe you want to work on something else or quit WinWord after closing. The choices are yours, and they're explained in the next section, "Moving On."

✔ If you try to close a document before it has been saved, WinWord will display a warning dialog box. Click on the Yes button to save your document. If you want to continue editing, click on the Cancel button.

✔ If you were working on one document and close it, WinWord will look like it's vacated the premises: ribbons and rulers will disappear as will scroll bars and other screen debris. Don't panic; you've just closed a document and WinWord has little else to do. WinWord will sit patiently and wait for your next command.

✔ If you're working on other documents, another one will appear on-screen in place of the document you just closed. Refer to Chapter 15 for information on working with multiple documents.

Moving On

When the document is closed, you have several options for what to do next. I won't mention the "take a break" or "play with the mouse pointer" options. And if you know how to switch over and play Solitaire for a few eyeball-glazing hours, that's up to you as well. But within WinWord, you have several options.

First, you can start work on another document on disk. Refer to the section "Editing a Document on-Disk" earlier in this chapter.

 Second, you can start work on a new document. Choose the File menu and choose the New command. This starts you off again with a clean, blank sheet of "electric" paper. Now it's up to the word processing muse to get you going again. (You also can choose the New tool.)

Third, you can quit WinWord and do something else in Windows. Refer to the next section, "Exiting WinWord."

 You don't have to quit WinWord when you just want to start working on a new document.

Exiting WinWord

It is the height of proper etiquette to know when to leave. This was personally related to me by the Queen of England in her response to my letter about crashing her Christmas party. Oh, well. Leaving WinWord is accomplished by using the Exit command. This is a common Windows command used to quit all Windows applications and programs.

To politely excuse yourself, get up and leave WinWord, choose the File menu by clicking on it once with the mouse. Then, near the bottom of the list, look for the word Exit. Click on that with the mouse. Poof! WinWord is gone.

✔ If you haven't yet saved your document, WinWord will ask whether you want to before it quits. Again, this is just being polite. A dialog box appears, asking whether you want to save any changes to your file. Click Yes to save them. This is important. Then WinWord will peaceably step aside and let you do something else in Windows, possibly something involving fun. (If the document doesn't yet have a name, WinWord will ask you to think up a name to save your document; refer to the section "Save Your Stuff!" earlier in this chapter.)

✔ The File→Exit command (Alt,F,X or Alt+F4) is the proper way to exit WinWord. Do not, under any circumstances, reset or turn off your PC to "quit" WinWord. This is utterly irresponsible and you'll go to Computer Etiquette Jail for life if you're ever caught — and that's in Redmond, Washington! You also run the very real risk of scrambling stuff on your disk so well that you won't ever get it back.

✔ Suppose that you don't want to quit, but instead you just want to get rid of a document and start on a new one. Refer to the section "Closing a Document." Then refer to "Moving On" for information on starting over with a new document for editing.

✔ Exiting WinWord will return you to the Windows Program Manager or to another running Windows application. If you want to turn your machine off, continue selecting the File→Exit command from the various program menus (or press Alt+F4 till your fingers turn blue) until all applications are closed and you are at the DOS prompt.

✔ When you're at the DOS prompt again, and see that friendly C>, you can start another program, safely shut off your computer, or give up, sell the computer, and start a new hobby like kayaking.

Chapter 2

Navigating Your Document

- -

In This Chapter

▶ Using the basic arrow keys

▶ Using Ctrl with the arrow keys

▶ Moving up and down one screenful of text

▶ Moving to the top or bottom of the current screen

▶ Moving to the end of a line

▶ Moving to the start of a line

▶ Moving to the end of a document

▶ Moving to the start of a document

▶ Using the Go To command

▶ Navigating with the scroll bars

▶ Going back

▶ Using the highly useful Bookmark command

- -

*Y*ou may have noticed by now that unless you believe in minimalist correspondence — documents of one word or less — an entire letter or document seldom fits on a single computer screen. Therefore, there must be an easy way to hop from place to place within your document. How do you get there? Cruise control, of course. Helping you navigate are various keys on the keyboard plus a few WinWord commands geared up to get you moving. Fortunately, this nautical navigation stuff does not go any further than just the name: A document does not have a bow, stern, port, or starboard, and you will not have to learn to tie the cursor into knots. But, you *will* need to learn to move easily within your literary creation.

Using the Basic Arrow Keys

The most common way to move about your document is to use the arrow keys, which are called the *cursor-control keys* because they control the toothpick cursor on-screen.

You can find the cursor control keys on the numeric keypad, and they are duplicated between the keypad and the typewriter keys. The location of these cursor-control keys is shown in Figure 2-1. This duplication allows you to activate the numeric keypad by pressing the Num Lock key and still have access to a set of cursor-control keys.

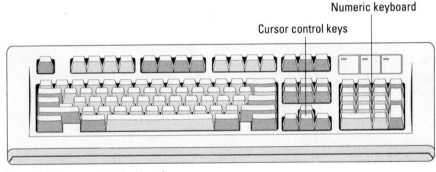

Numeric keyboard

Cursor control keys

Figure 2-1: Cursor control key locations.

The four basic cursor-control keys are the up-, down-, left-, and right-arrow keys. On the numeric keypad, they are found on the 8, 4, 6, and 2 keys:

↑	Moves the cursor up to the preceding line of text
↓	Moves the cursor down to the next line of text
→	Moves the cursor right to the next character
←	Moves the cursor left to the preceding character

Not-so-moving information about moving the cursor

As you move the cursor around, look at the status bar on the bottom of your screen. This gives you some valuable information about your location within a document:

Pg 2 Sec 1 2/6 At 2.5" Ln 6 Col 42

The status bar shows what page you are on, which section you are in, your position with re-

gards to the total number of pages in your document, how far down the document you are in inches, your height, and finally your IQ. Seriously, the Ln and Col values tell you which line (from line one at the top of the page) and column (from the left margin) the cursor is on — useless stuff, but informative.

✔ The cursor-control keys on the numeric keypad and the separate cursor-control keys work in the same way; you can use either set. But, keep your eye on that Num Lock light! It must be off for the keypad cursor-control keys to work.

✔ The mouse provides a quick and easy way to move the toothpick cursor: First, spy a new location for the cursor on-screen. Then, move the mouse pointer to where you want the cursor to be, and click the left mouse button. The cursor is instantly relocated.

✔ If the cursor is on the top line of the screen, and you press the up-arrow key, the document scrolls to reveal the preceding line of text, if there is one. If there isn't, the cursor will stay in place and blink at you with that special look it reserves for the mentally impaired.

✔ When the cursor is on the last line of the screen, and you press the down-arrow key, the document scrolls up to reveal the next line of text, if there is one. If there isn't, the cursor will stay in place and blink at you with that special look it reserves for the soon to be institutionalized.

✔ Moving the cursor does not erase characters.

Using Ctrl with the Arrow Keys

If you press and hold the Ctrl (Control) key and then press an arrow key, the toothpick cursor jumps more than one character. This is the *cursor afterburner* mode:

Ctrl+↑	Moves the cursor up one paragraph
Ctrl+↓	Moves the cursor down to the next paragraph
Ctrl+→	Moves the cursor right one word
Ctrl+←	Moves the cursor left one word

Press and hold the Ctrl key and then press an arrow key. Release both keys. You don't need to press hard; use the Ctrl key as you use the Shift key.

✔ Ctrl+→ and Ctrl+← always move the cursor to the first letter of a word.

✔ Ctrl+↑ and Ctrl+↓ always move the cursor to the start of a paragraph.

✔ If you press Ctrl and click the mouse, you highlight or *select* a sentence in your document. Click again (without the Ctrl key) to move the cursor (refer to Chapter 6 for information on selecting blocks).

Moving up and down one screenful of text

No need to adjust your chair here. The screen does not show you the entire document — usually not even a whole page. To see the next or preceding screen, use the PgUp and PgDn keys. These keys move you or your document (we don't know which) around by the screenful.

PgUp   Moves the cursor up one screen. Or if you're at the tippy top of your document, it moves you to the top of the screen.

PgDn   Moves the cursor down one screen, or to the end of the document if you happen to be there.

It's funny how PgUp and PgDn, where the Pg is rumored to be short for *page,* moves you up and down a *screen* at a time. You'll get used to this illogic, if you're not already.

Moving to the top or bottom of the current screen

There are times when you want to zip to the top or bottom of the current screen. This is easy to do:

Ctrl+PgUp   Moves the cursor to the top of the current screen.

Ctrl+PgDn   Moves the cursor to the bottom of the current screen.

Moving to the end of a line

To get to the end of a line of text, press the End key.

- ✔ To move to the end of a paragraph, press Ctrl+↓, then ←. The Ctrl+↓ actually moves to the start of the *next* paragraph. The ← key moves you back to the end of the current paragraph.

- ✔ Moving to the start of a line is accomplished with the Home key, which is covered . . . well, here it is:

Moving to the start of a line

To get to the start of a line of text, press the Home key.

- ✔ There's no key like home.

- ✔ To move to the start of a paragraph, press Ctrl+↑.

Moving to the end of a document

If you use the Ctrl key with the End key, you will be whisked to the end of the document.

✔ You can use this command to get a feel for how big your document is. Press Ctrl+End and then look at the numbers on the status bar. You can see what page you are on, how far down the page you are, what line you are on, and what column you are in.

✔ Ctrl+End is an easy key combination to mistakenly type in. It will throw you — literally — to the end of your document. If you do this and feel you've boo-booed, then press Shift+F5, the Go Back command, to return whence you came. (Also refer to the section "Going Back" later in this chapter.)

Moving to the start of a document

To go to the beginning — nay, the tippy top — of a document, press the Ctrl and the Home keys: Ctrl+Home.

Using the Go To Command

The Ctrl+Home and Ctrl+End key combinations will let you fly to the beginning and the end of a document, but what if you want to get off somewhere in the middle? The Go To command in WinWord is what you need.

Go To, as in the Shakespearean "Getteth thee outta hereth," allows you to go directly to just about wherever in the document you want to be. To do so, choose the Edit→Go To (Alt,E,G) command and the Go To dialog box appeareth before thine eyes (see Figure 2-2).

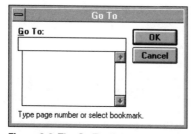

Figure 2-2: The Go To dialog box.

You can type a number of things in the Go To dialog box. The most effective use is typing a page number; WinWord instantly beams you to the top of that page. For example, type **14** into the box and press Enter, and you'll to go to page 14.

✔ You also can press the F5 key twice to open the Go To dialog box.

✔ Feeling kinda loose and fancy free with the Go To command? Then you should know you only really need to press the F5 key once. When you do, a Go To: message appears on the status bar, on the left side. Then, you can discretely tell WinWord to go to any page you want. Press Enter and you're there.

Navigating with the Scroll Bars

If you love your mouse, you can use the power of Windows to help you traverse your documents. You use the vertical scroll bar to the right of your document. It looks like a one-lane highway, but is really used like an elevator shaft (see Figure 2-3).

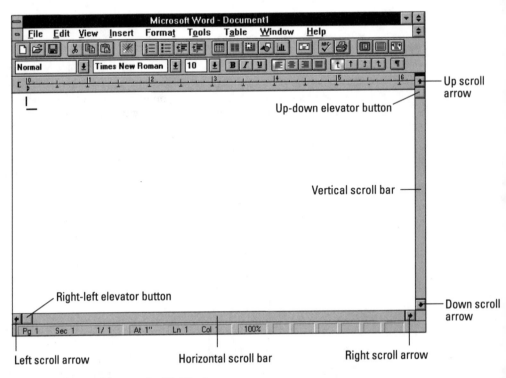

Figure 2-3: The scroll bars on the WinWord screen.

- To scroll your document up one line of text, click the mouse on the up scroll arrow at the top of the scroll bar.

- To scroll down one line of text, click the mouse on the down scroll arrow at the bottom of the scroll bar.

- In the middle of the scroll bar is a scroll box or elevator button. It gives you an idea of which part of your document you're looking at; if the box is at the top of the scroll bar, you're near the top of your document, and vice-versa.

- To see the previous screen of text, click on the scroll bar just above the elevator button.

- To see the next screen of text, click on the scroll bar just below the elevator button.

- To move to a specific position in the document, use the mouse to *drag* the elevator button up or down. The elevator button's position indicates which portion of the document you want to see.

- The scroll bar is not where Greek philosophers went to get drunk.

Going Back

They say that once you commit, there's no going back. Boy, are they wrong. If you go anywhere you don't want to be, press Shift+F5 and WinWord carries you back to where you started.

The Shift+F5 key command only works in WinWord; you can't try this in real life.

Using the Highly Useful Bookmark Command

Have you ever done this: You're working away on great stuff, but occasionally you need to zip off elsewhere in your document? So you try to fold down the edge of the screen — *dog ear* it, if you will — to remember where you were? I do it all the time. Fortunately, WinWord has a command that helps save wear and tear on your monitor. It's the highly useful Bookmark command.

To set a bookmark in your document, follow these steps:

1. **Put the toothpick cursor where you want to place a bookmark.**

2. **Select the Insert→Bookmark command.**

    The Bookmark dialog box opens, as shown in Figure 2-4.

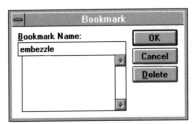

Figure 2-4: The Bookmark dialog box.

3. Type in a name for the bookmark.

Be clever! The name reminds of where you are in your document. So if you're writing about your plans to embezzle millions from your company, the bookmark name *embezzle* would be appropriate.

4. Press Enter or click the OK button with the mouse.

To return to your bookmark, you use the Go To command, as covered in the section "Using the Go To Command" earlier in this chapter. Here are the steps just to keep you from turning the page and losing your train of thought:

1. Press the F5 key twice.

In the Go To dialog box, you see a list of the bookmarks in your document.

2. Highlight the bookmark you want to go to, and press Enter.

Or, you can double-click on the bookmark name by using the mouse.

Chapter 3
Using Your Keyboard Correctly

Some people treat their computer keyboards as if land mines lie under half the keys. But with WinWord's design, one of the best ways to get anything done is to overuse your keyboard. The keys, a lot of them used in combinations with each other, are often much quicker than grabbing for that mouse or perusing the menu.

If there were a theme to this chapter, it would be "Be Bold!" WinWord won't do anything perilous unless you tell it to. Even then, you'll be asked a yes/no question before the dangerous-something happens. You can press the handy Esc key to cancel just about anything before you do it, and the Edit→Undo command will Undo your last action. (You also can click the Undo tool or press the Ctrl+Z shortcut.) Consider these options to be like wearing little high-density uranium thimbles to protect yourself against those keyboard land mines.

Keys on Your Keyboard

Welcome to "Know Your Keyboard 101." Take a look at your keyboard, and then take a look at Figure 3-1.

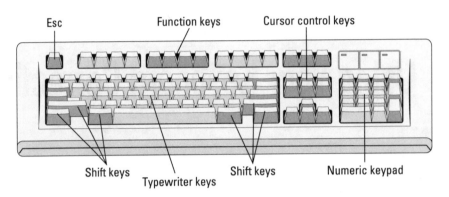

Figure 3-1: Key locations.

Notice how the keyboard is divided into separate areas, each of which has a special function. These are keys you'll be using in WinWord, either alone or in combination with other keys:

Function keys	Along the top row of the keyboard, labeled F1 through F12. These keys are used alone or in cahoots with the Ctrl, Alt, and Shift keys.
Typewriter keys	Standard *alphanumeric* keys you find on any typewriter: A through Z, 1 through 0, plus symbols and other exotic characters.
Cursor keys	Arrow keys that move the toothpick cursor around the screen. Also lumped in are the Home, End, PgUp or Page Up, PgDn or Page Down, and the Insert and Delete keys. Oh, and the big plus and minus keys on the keypad are counted as well.
Car keys	Don't leave these in the car, nor should you have any exposed valuables lying about. Buy The Club.
Numeric keypad	These keys toggle between cursor keys and numbers. The split personality is evident on each key cap, which displays two symbols. The Num Lock key and its corresponding light are on if the numeric keypad (1, 2, 3) is active. If the cursor keys (arrows, Home) are active, Num Lock is off.
Shift keys	These keys don't do anything by themselves. Instead, the Shift, Ctrl, and Alt keys work in combination with other keys.

Two individual keys worth noting are the Enter and Escape key:

Enter   Marked with the word Enter and sometimes a cryptic curved arrow-thing: ↵. You use the Enter key to end a paragraph of text.

Escape   The Escape key may be labeled Esc on your keyboard. It's a handy key to use in WinWord, but it's location may vary. Sometimes Escape is next to the Backspace key. Find its location on your keyboard.

✔ Be thankful: A piano has 88 keys, black and white with no labels. It takes years to master. A computer, by comparison, is easy.

✔ Older PC keyboards have a different layout than the currently popular, 101 key "enhanced" PC keyboard. Some older models have the function keys to the side of the keyboard; some are lacking the separate cursor keys. They all work the same under WinWord, but this book assumes you have the 101 key keyboard. (Go ahead and count 'em; there are 101 keys.)

✔ Laptop keyboards are all goofed-up. Primarily, they lack the numeric keypad. This is okay, but you'll be missing the gray plus and minus keys, which can be used for some special formatting commands, divulged in Chapter 9.

Press and Release!

Sorry to disappoint all you budding third-world dictators. The title of this section is "Press and Release!" and it refers to entering various WinWord key combinations. It's not "oppress and release," which sounds a bit liberal anyway.

WinWord uses key combinations to represent some commands. For example:

    Ctrl+Shift+F12

This command opens the Print dialog box — which isn't really important right now. Instead, what that key combination tells you is to press and hold the Ctrl and the Shift key, and then press the F12. Release all three keys.

These key combinations appear all the time. Always press and hold the first key(s), then press the last key. Press and release.

✔ This works just like pressing Shift+F to get a capital F. It's the same thing, but with the odd Ctrl (control) and Alt (alternate) keys.

✔ Yeah, you have to really reach to get some of those Function key combinations.

✔ There's no need to press hard. If you're having trouble working a command, pressing harder doesn't make the computer think, "Oh, lordy, she's pressing really hard now. I think she means it. Wake up, wake up!" A light touch is all that's required.

✔ Remember to release the keys: Press and hold the Ctrl and the Shift keys, press F12, and then release both keys. If you don't know which to release first, release the second key then the shift key (Shift, Ctrl, Alt) last.

✔ There also are menu key shortcuts, which aren't the same as function key combinations. For example, Alt,F,P chooses the File→Print command, the same as Ctrl+Shift+F12. However, Alt,F,P is a menu shortcut, not a function key combination.

When to Press the Enter Key

On an electric typewriter, you press the Return key when you reach the end of a line. With a word processor, you only need to press Enter when you reach the end a paragraph.

You don't need to press Enter at the end of each line because WinWord will *word-wrap* any words hanging over the right margin and move them down to the next line on the page. Therefore, you only need to press Enter at the end of a paragraph, even a short paragraph that is just a line of text by itself.

✔ Some people end a paragraph with two presses of the Enter key, others use only one press.

✔ If you want to indent the next paragraph, press the Tab key after pressing Enter. This works just like it does on a typewriter.

✔ If you want to double-space a paragraph, you need to use a special line formatting command. This is covered in Chapter 10, "Formatting Sentences and Paragraphs." You do not use the Enter key to double-space lines.

✔ If you press the Enter key in the middle of an existing paragraph, WinWord inserts a new paragraph and moves the rest of the text to the start of the next line. This works like any other key inserted into your text. The difference is that you insert an Enter character, which creates a new paragraph.

✔ You can delete the Enter character by using the Backspace or Delete keys. Removing Enter joins two paragraphs together or, if you press Enter more than once, cleans up any extra blank lines.

Trivial information on the Enter and Return keys

Enter or Return? Some keyboards label the Enter key "Return." Most PCs use the word "Enter"; even so, some yahoos call it the Return key. Why? (And you really have to be hard-up for trivia if you're continuing to read this.)

The reason has to do with the computer's background. On a typewriter, the key is named Return. It comes from the pre-electric days of typewriters when you had to whack the carriage return bar to move the paper over to the other margin and continue typing. From the computer's calculator background, the Enter key was pressed to enter a formula into the calculator. This is why some computers can't make up their mind whether it's the Enter or Return key. My keyboard says Enter on it — and in two places. So that's what I use in this book.

When to Use the Spacebar

A major vice committed by many WinWord users is mistakenly using the spacebar instead of the Tab key. Allow me to clear the air on this one.

Use the spacebar to insert space characters, such as you'd find between words or between two sentences. You only need to press the spacebar once between each word or sentence, although some former touch typists (myself included) put two spaces between two sentences. That's fine.

To indent, align columns of information, or organize what you see on-screen, you need to use the Tab key. The Tab key indents text to an exact position. When you print, everything will be lined up nice and neat. This doesn't happen with the space characters.

✔ Use the Tab key to indent; only use the spacebar when putting spaces between words and paragraphs. I'm serious: Do not use the spacebar to indent or line up your text. You're stuff will look tacky, tacky, tacky if you do.

✔ To set the Tab stops in WinWord, refer to Chapter 10, "Formatting Sentences and Paragraphs."

The Undo Keys

Be Bold! Why not? WinWord has a handy Undo command. It remembers the last thing you did or deleted.

To undelete any text you just accidentally zapped, do any of the following:

1. Press Ctrl+Z.

2. Choose Edit→Undo with the mouse.

3. Press Alt,E,U.

4. Click the Undo tool on the toolbar.

When you choose Edit→Undo, the last action you did is undone, and if you choose Edit→Undo again, you will toggle back to the way things were before you chose Edit→Undo the first time.

The quickest way to undo something is to press Ctrl+Z. This is the handy undo key combination used in almost all Windows applications.

The Kindergarten Keys: Cut, Copy, and Paste

Cutting, copying, and pasting text are covered in Chapter 6. However, three of the keys you use to perform those feats are covered here because by the time you get to Chapter 6, this stuff won't make any sense. The three keys are:

Cut	Ctrl+X
Copy	Ctrl+C
Paste	Ctrl+V

Now, Copy as Ctrl+C I can understand. *C* is Copy. But Cut is Ctrl+X? And Paste is Ctrl+V? Yeah. Looks like they put all the *English as your second language* new hires in the Keyboard Department at Microsoft Corporation.

Actually, these keys are common in many programs to represent the Cut, Copy, and Paste command. The logic is that all three keys (plus Z for Ctrl+Z, the Undo shortcut) are together on the keyboard. Go ahead an look at your keyboard now. Or refer to Figure 3-2.

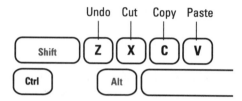

Figure 3-2: How the kindergarten keys line up.

Because these keys are so commonly used and are located together on the keyboard, these are four handy shortcuts to learn. When you get the hang of them, you'll use them often to save time.

The Help Key

The handiest key on the keyboard is F1, the help key. Here are some tips for using it in your fleeting moments of panic:

✔ Press F1 when you're doing something to display help and options available for that something. If you're just editing text, F1 displays the Help Index, from which you can select a topic you're interested, or just waste time using the Help system.

✔ Press Shift+F1 to get context-sensitive help. This will tell you almost everything you need to know about what you are trying to do.

✔ Getting help in WinWord actually means you're running another program — the Windows Help engine. You must quit this program when you're finished using Help. Do this by double-clicking on the Control menu in the upper-left corner of the Help window or by choosing File→Exit from the Help window to close the Help screen.

The Repeat Key

Here's a good one: The F4 key in WinWord is known as the repeat key, and it can be a real time saver. If you press a WinWord command, cursor key or character, and then press the F4 key, that command, cursor key, or character will be repeated. (You also can choose the Edit→Repeat command.)

For example, type the following into WinWord:

```
Did I hear an echo?
```

Now press the F4 key. WinWord repeats the last few things you typed, which includes the above sentence plus anything else you typed before it.

> ✔ A practical use of this command is creating forms. Type a bunch of under-lines on-screen — your form's blank lines — and then press Enter. Press the F4 key a few times and the page will soon be filled with blank lines.
>
> ✔ Not only does F4 echo text, it's especially useful when issuing the same command over and over, like when you are doing a find and replace, in-serting the date, inserting special characters, or extensively formatting a document.
>
> ✔ If you use the F4 key along with the Shift key, WinWord will repeat your last Find or Go To command. Refer to Chapter 5, "The Wonders of Find and Replace."
>
> ✔ The F4 key isn't your only access to the Repeat command. It's also found under the Edit menu, although it may be listed as Repeat Typing, Repeat Formatting, or any of a number of Repeat-*blank* options.

Chapter 4
Deleting and Destroying Text

· ·

In This Chapter

▶ Insert and Overtype modes

▶ Your basic delete keys: Backspace and Delete

▶ The "Backspace-blip" phenomenon

▶ Deleting a word

▶ Deleting a line of text

▶ Deleting odd shapes with blocks

▶ Undeleting

· ·

*N*othing gives you that satisfying feeling like blowing away text — especially if it's someone else's document you're "editing." Of course, most of the destroying and deleting that goes on in WinWord is minor stuff: You delete that extra "E" in *potato*, slay a word here, yank out a sentence there. It's much easier than using White Out on paper; because you delete text on-screen, it happens quickly and painlessly in the electronic ether. No mess, no white goop, and if you change your mind, you can press Ctrl+Z, the Undo shortcut key, (or click the Undo tool) to bring your text back to glowing phosphorescent perfection.

Insert and Overtype Modes

The Insert key on your keyboard controls WinWord's two methods of putting text on-screen. Normally, new text is inserted just before the blinking toothpick cursor. New text pushes any existing text to the right and down as you type. This is the *Insert mode.*

If you press the Insert key, you enter *Overtype mode.* The letters OVR appear in the lower-right section of the status bar, indicating *over* as in *Overtype mode* or "all of this is over your head." Any next text you type will overwrite existing text on-screen.

If you press the Insert key again, the OVR disappears from the screen and you're back in Insert mode.

- ✔ The Insert key appears two places on the enhanced 101-key keyboard. The word Ins appears on the zero key on the keypad, and Insert appears just to the right of the Backspace key. Both keys perform the same function.

- ✔ The new characters you type in Insert mode appear right in front of the flashing cursor. Then the cursor moves to the right, awaiting the next character you type.

- ✔ The OVR in the status bar indicates that you are in Overtype mode. Any new text you type will overwrite existing text. I point this out because a stray finger or elbow can press the Insert key and put you in that mode when you don't want it. If you're typing along and suddenly notice that part of your text seems to be missing, check your status bar to see whether you're in Overtype mode.

- ✔ Leaving WinWord in Insert mode all the time is a safe bet. If you need to overwrite something, just type in the new text and then delete the old.

Your Basic Delete Keys: Backspace and Delete

You can use two keys on the keyboard to delete single characters of text:

Backspace key   Deletes the character to the left of the toothpick cursor

Delete key   Deletes the character to the right of the toothpick cursor

```
No one will notice thos|e white socks, Dan.
```

In the text above, the toothpick cursor is "flashing" between the S and the E in "those." Pressing the Backspace key would delete the S in "those"; pressing the Delete key deletes the E.

- ✔ After deleting a character, any text to the right or below the character moves up to fill in the void.

- ✔ If you're in the Overtype mode, the Backspace key still pulls the rest of the text to the right.

- ✔ Backspace works like the Backspace key on a typewriter. The difference is that when you press Backspace in WinWord, the cursor backs up and erases. (The WinWord equivalent of the typewriter's Backspace key is the left-arrow key.)

- ✔ You can press and hold Backspace or Delete to continuously, "machine gun" delete characters. Release the key to stop your wanton destruction.

The "Backspace-Blip" Phenomenon

WinWord's child-like reaction to something it doesn't like is the *blip*, a nice and brief beep of your PC's speaker. Sometimes you may hear the blip when you press Backspace to delete. Nothing is deleted; you only hear the blip, blip, blip once for each desperate stab at the Backspace key.

The blipping is WinWord's way of warning you. What you're trying to do is delete one of the secret, hidden codes littered about the document — codes that change paragraph formatting and other covert stuff. You can indiscriminately delete this stuff with the Backspace key.

- ✔ If you really want to delete the codes, press the ← key and then press the Delete key. No blip.

- ✔ Any time you want to hear the blip, press the End key more than once. Keep holding down the End key to hear WinWord's equivalent of a raspberry.

- ✔ Don't be surprised by the mystery codes in your document. You put them there as you create and format your text.

 ✔ If you want your old formatting back, choose Edit→Undo or press Ctrl+Z, before you do anything else (or click the Undo tool.)

Deleting a Word

WinWord lets you gobble up entire words at a time by using one of two delete word commands:

Ctrl+Backspace   Deletes the word that is in front (to the left) of the cursor

Ctrl+Delete   Deletes the word that is behind (to the right) of the cursor

To delete a word with Ctrl+Backspace, position the cursor at the last letter of the word. Press Ctrl+Backspace and the word is gone! The cursor then sits at the end of the previous word or the end of the line (if you deleted the last word in a paragraph).

To delete a word with Ctrl+Delete, position the cursor at the first letter of the word. Press Ctrl+Delete and the word is gone. The cursor then sits at the start of the next word or the end of the line (if you deleted the last word in a paragraph).

> ✔ If the cursor is positioned anywhere in the middle of a word, Ctrl+Backspace deletes everything from where the cursor is to the last letter of the preceding word.
>
> ✔ If the cursor is positioned anywhere in the middle of a word, the Ctrl+Delete command deletes everything from where the cursor is to the first letter of the next word.
>
>
>
> ✔ To delete a word, position the mouse pointer on the offending critter and double-click the mouse button. The word is highlighted and the Delete key erases it.

Deleting a Line of Text

There is no command in WinWord for deleting a line of text from the keyboard (at least, not a single command). But, with the mouse it is only a matter of a click and a keypress. Follow these steps:

1. Move the mouse into the left margin of your document.

The cursor changes into an arrow pointing northeast instead of northwest. The winds of change are a-blowin' . . . .

2. Point the mouse pointer arrow at the line of text that you want to obliterate.

3. Click the left mouse button.

The line of text will be highlighted or *selected.*

4. Press the Delete key to send that line into the void.

> ✔ When the mouse cursor is pointing northeast, you can drag it down the left margin and select as many lines of text as you care to. They can all then be deleted with one stroke of the Delete key.
>
> ✔ Northeast = ➹

Deleting Odd Shapes with Blocks

WinWord can delete characters, words, and lines all by itself. To delete anything else, you need to mark it as a block of text, and then delete the block.

To delete a block of text, follow these steps:

1. **Mark the block.**

   The block can be highlighted by using the mouse; click the mouse at the start of the block and then drag it to the block's end. Using the keyboard, you move the toothpick cursor to the start of the block; then press F8 and use the cursor keys to highlight the block.

2. **Press the Delete key to remove all of the highlighted text.**

Chapter 6 contains more information on selecting, highlighting, and otherwise playing with blocks.

Undeleting

Deleting text can be traumatic, especially for the timid WinWord user. But editing is editing, and mistakes happen. If you want some of your freshly deleted text back, you can use the Undo command, Ctrl+Z, to undelete text. It usually works like this:

1. **Panic! Oh, lordy! I just deleted cousin Jimmy from the will!**

2. **Press Ctrl+Z.**

This should put cousin Jimmy back in line.

✔ Don't forget the Undo command in the Edit menu — first item, by the way. If you can't remember Ctrl+Z, or find yourself pressing other keys by mistake, just select Edit→Undo *whatever.* (Or click the Undo tool.)

✔ You must be quick with the Undo shortcut. It only remembers the last thing you deleted — everything from single characters to full pages and more.

Chapter 5

The Wonders of Find and Replace

*L*ittle Bo Peep has lost her sheep. Too bad she doesn't know about WinWord's Find and Replace commands. She could locate the misplaced ruminants in a matter of microseconds. Not only that, she could find and re-place — replace all the sheep with Miatas. It's all really cinchy once you force the various purposes of the Find and Replace commands into your head. Sadly, only words are replaced. If WinWord could find and replace real things, there'd be at least one more wonderful house with swimming pool and sauna in this world, I bet you.

Finding Text

WinWord can locate any bit of text anywhere in your document. Well, not re-ally. It can only locate text below the toothpick cursor's position — from where you are to the end of your document — or above the cursor to the start of the document. It can't do both at once.

The command used to find text is called, surprisingly enough, the Find com-mand. It lurks in the Edit menu. Follow these steps to use the Find command and locate text in your document:

1. **Think of some text you want to find.**

   For example, "sheep."

2. **Choose the Edit→Find command.**

   You see the Find dialog box shown in Figure 5-1.

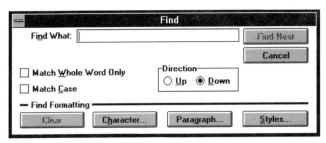

Figure 5-1: The Find dialog box.

3. **Type in the text you want to find.**

   Enter the text into the box titled Find What. For example, **sheep**. Type in lower-case letters.

4. **Click the <u>F</u>ind Next button to start the search.**

   Or you can press Enter.

If any text is found, it will be highlighted on-screen. The Find dialog box will not go away until you click the Cancel button or press the Escape key. (This allows you to keep searching for more text if you're so inclined.)

✔ Type in the text you want to find exactly. Do not end the text with a period unless you want to find the period too.

✔ If the text isn't found, you'll see the message The search text is not found. Oh, well. Try again and check your typing.

✔ You may see a message displayed that says Word reached the end of the document. Do you want to continue searching at the beginning? Word is being uncharacteristically nice here and will search for your text back at the start of the document. Click the <u>Y</u>es button to keep looking for your text.

✔ To find any additional occurrences of the text, click on the <u>F</u>ind Next button.

✔ After you close the Find dialog box, you can use the handy Shift+F4 key to repeat finding the next matching bit of text in your document. This saves time over using the full-on Find command again.

✔ You can search for a variety of things using the Find command — text, spaces, the Enter character, and formatting codes. This is covered in the following section, "Finding Secret Codes."

✔ Typing in lower-case helps you find just about any text in the document. But when you want to find text that matches upper-case and lower-case the way you type it in, be sure to select the Match <u>C</u>ase check box. This will make the Find command know the difference between Mr. Sheep and a sheep.

Finding or not finding bits and pieces of words

WinWord finds any matching text in your document. It can find things so well that it can drive you crazy. If you ask WinWord to find *ant*, for example, it will find ants in places that you never thought existed — like rumin*ant*, w*ant*, triumph*ant*, eleph*ant*, or w*ant*on.

To make WinWord more precise — for example, to locate only instances of the word *ant* — select the Match Whole Word Only check box in the Find dialog box. When that box is checked, the Find command logically locates only words and not things nestled in other words.

Finding Secret Codes

Laced throughout a document are secret codes and printing instructions. You don't see these codes on-screen, but they affect how your document looks and prints. Basically, the secret commands — bold, underline, center, and special paragraph formatting — can be searched for just like text.

To search for a secret code, choose Edit→Find, and then click on the Character button to open the Find Character dialog box shown in Figure 5-2. You can find a bunch of character-related stuff with this dialog box. If, for example, you want to search a document for words in italic, you select the Italic check box and then select OK. The dialog box closes, and you can then select Find Next to look for any italic stuff.

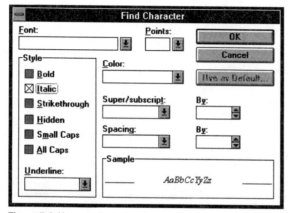

Figure 5-2: You can find a bunch of character-related stuff by using this dialog box.

- The Character formatting boxes — Italic, Bold, Underline, etc. — are three-way switches. When the box is filled (solid gray), it is ignored in the search. When it is checked, the Find command looks for occurrences of that format. When the box is empty (white), the Find command looks for cases where text is not formatted that way — such as everything that is not italic. To change a block, click on it using the mouse.

- You can use this box to look for specific occurrences of a font, like Courier or Times New Roman by selecting the font from the selection list. Click on the down-pointing arrow button below the word Font to see what you can choose.

- You can look for a particular size of type, say 24 point, by selecting that from the Points selection list. See Chapter 9, "Formatting Characters," for information on character formatting.

- You can look for occurrences of anything shown in this box (or any combination of things) by putting in what you want to look for.

- You also can search for paragraph formatting by selecting Paragraph instead of Character from the Find dialog box. See Chapter 10, "Formatting Sentences and Paragraphs," for information on paragraph formatting.

Finding special characters: don't read this — just keep it handy

Hey little space character, you can't run, because WinWord has ways of finding you. And that goes for your buddies Enter, Tab, and the rest of the gang, too.

There are times when you want to search for special things, like two spaces together, a hyphen, or a paragraph mark (the Enter key). For your enjoyment, and future reference, the following is a table of what you would type in the Find (or Replace) dialog box to locate each special character.

To Find:	Type:
Tab	^t
Paragraph (Enter)	^p
Hard Page Break	^d
Hyphen	^-
Question Mark	^?
Caret Character	^^

- The ^t means type the caret or "hat" character (^) and then a lower-case T. It must be a little T.

- Additional characters, mostly specific advanced stuff can also be looked for. The WinWord Help system lists them under the title *special characters*.

> ✔ You also can search for styles by selecting Styles instead of Character
> from the Find dialog box. Refer to Chapter 13, "Formatting with Style," for a
> discussion of styles.
>
> ✔ To clear all your searching options and doodads, click on the Clear button.

Find and Replace

Find and replace is the art of finding a bit of text and replacing it with something
else. This happens all the time. For example, you can replace the word "goat"
with "caprine." WinWord will do it in a snap, by using the Replace command.

1. **Position the toothpick cursor to where you want to start searching for
   text.**

   The search always happens from the cursor's position *down*, to the end of
   the document.

2. **Choose Edit→Replace.**

   The Replace dialog box, shown in Figure 5-3, appears on your screen.

3. **Type the text you want to find in the Find What box.**

   This is the text that will be found and replaced with something else. For
   example, you could type **goat**. Press the Tab key when you're done typing.

4. **Into the Replace With box, type the text you want to replace the original
   text.**

   For example, type **caprine**, which is the fancy-schmancy biologically
   dooded-up term for the goat family — neighbors you definitely want to
   have downwind.

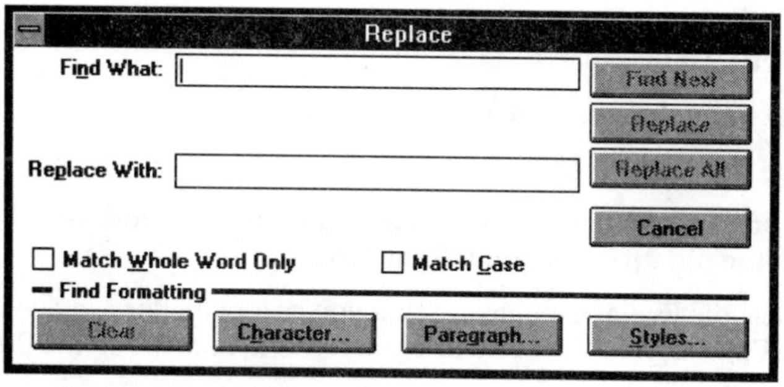

Figure 5-3: The Replace dialog box.

5. **Ask yourself, "Do I want WinWord to ask permission before replacing each bit of found text?"**

If so, select the Find Next button. This is a good idea. If not, you can select the Replace All button; text will be found and replaced automatically, giving you no chance to change your mind.

6. **If you selected Find Next, WinWord pauses at each occurrence of the text and asks whether you want to replace it.**

Select Replace to replace it; Find Next to skip and find the next bit of text. Click on the Cancel button or press the Escape key when you tire of this.

Always type something in the Replace With box. If not, you'll systematically delete all the text found in a wanton round of wholesale slaughter. This is called "Find and Delete," and it's covered in a later in this chapter in a section by the same name.

✔ My advice is to select Find Next most of the time. Only if you're replacing something and you're certain (a rare occurrence, at least in my book) should you select Replace All. Because . . . .

✔ There is no way to undelete any text you've searched and replaced. Sorry.

✔ A good way to restore your document after an adverse search and replace is to save your document *before* you do a search and replace. If you make a mistake, then you can close your document then re-load the older, unsearched and replaced document from disk.

Find and Replace Spaces

Here's a practical use for the Replace command. Too many WinWord users litter their documents with excessive spaces. The most harmless of all these spaces come at the end of a line of text, after the period yet before you press Enter. I do this too. Yet the extra spaces serve no purpose. Here is how to get rid of them:

1. **Press Ctrl+Home.**

This moves you to the top of your document.

2. **Choose the Edit→Replace.**

3. **Enter one space by pressing the spacebar one time followed by the special command ^p in the Find What box.**

This tells the Replace command that you're looking for a space followed by the Enter key. Press Tab when you're done to move to the Replace With box.

4. Type ^p all by itself in the Replace With box.

That's a caret (or hat) and a little P, the symbol for the Enter key. (See "Finding Secret Codes" earlier in this chapter for an explanation of the special codes.)

5. Click Replace All.

It's okay to click Replace All here. Or, if you're not the daring type, select Find Next. You're telling WinWord to replace the space-Enter with just Enter. The end result is to remove the spaces before the Enter key in your document.

✔ To confirm whether any spaces exist before trying this exercise, use the Find command to search for space-Enter.

✔ A quick way to transform extra spaces into a Tab character is to search for five spaces in a row and translate them into Tabs. In the Find What box, enter your five spaces. In the Replace With box, type ^t (a caret and a little T). Those spaces will be replaced with Tabs, which are much easier to align. Refer to Chapter 9 for more information on using and setting Tabs.

Find and Delete

If you don't type anything in the Replace With box, WinWord's Replace command systematically deletes all of the Find Whats. This can be a scary thing, so be sure to select Find Next. Otherwise, you could zap parts of your document irrevocably and, boy, would you be bummed.

Suppose, however, that Bo Peep wants to get rid of her sheep. Instead, she wants to be a truck driver. Here's how to delete the *sheep* from a WinWord document:

1. Position the cursor at the beginning of the document — or to the spot where text needs to be found and deleted.

Press Ctrl+Home to move to the tippy top of your document. Or use the cursor control keys or the Go To command (see Chapter 2) to move to just the right spot. This is necessary because the Replace command always works from the toothpick cursor's position *down*.

2. Choose Edit→Replace.

3. Type the text you want to find in the Find What box.

For example **sheep**. Enter in the text exactly. Any previously searched-for text will appear at the prompt. Edit it, or type in new text, secret codes, or whatever to search for.

4. Type nothing in the Replace With box, leaving it blank.

You're deleting text here, replacing it with nothing — a bold concept that I hope they someday address in a *Star Trek TNG* episode.

5. Click the Replace All button.

In moments, your text will be gone. Bo Peep's sheep will go pop, pop, popping away! If you were timid and selected the Find Next button instead of Replace All, then it takes a bit longer because you have to squint at the screen, and then press the Replace button at each occurrence.

As with any massive replacement operation, you might want to save your document to disk before you proceed:

1. Choose the File→Save command, or stab at Shift+F12 with your fingers.

2. If your document hasn't yet been saved, type in a name. Now you're mentally free to go ahead with the "search and destroy" operation.

3. If the search and destroy operation goofs up, re-load your document. First close the document without saving (avoid the temptation here), then re-open it by selecting the File→Open command. Everything will be as it once was, the universe is safe for you to try again — more carefully this time.

Let's all wish Miss Bo Peep good luck in her new profession.

Chapter 6
Text Blocks, Stumbling Blocks, and Mental Blocks

A major advantage of a word processor over, say, a stone tablet is that you can work with blocks of text. Stone tablets, no way: You can break them up into blocks, but gluing them back together again is *trés gauche*. Hand such a thing with a report on it to your boss and he'll shake his head and mutter, "Tsk, tsk, tsk. This is tacky, Jenson."

A block in a word processor is a marvelous thing. You can rope off a section of text — any old odd section, a letter, word, line, paragraph, page, or a rambling polygon — and then treat the text as a unit, a *block*. You can copy the block, move it, delete it, format it, spell-check it, use it to keep the defensive line from getting to your quarterback, and on and on. Think of the joy: Years after childhood, WinWord has made it okay for us to play with blocks again.

Marking a Block

You can't do anything with a block of text until you *mark* it. Marking a block is telling WinWord, "Okay, my block starts here. No, *here*! Not over there. Here, where I'm looking, where the cursor is." You can mark a block two ways in WinWord: using the mouse or using the keyboard.

Marking a block with your mouse

To mark a block with the mouse, follow these rodent-like steps:

1. **Position the mouse pointer to where you want the block to start.**

2. **Hold down the left mouse button and drag the mouse over your text.**

   As you drag, the text becomes highlighted or *selected*, as shown in Figure 6-1. Drag the mouse from the start to the end of the text you want to mark as a block.

3. **Release the mouse button — stop the dragging — to mark your block's end.**

   ✔ If you drag above or below the blank white space where your document appears, the screen will scroll up or down.

   ✔ To quickly mark a word, position the mouse pointer over that word and double-click.

   ✔ To mark a line of text, move the mouse pointer to the left margin. The pointer becomes an arrow pointing northeasterly. Click on the mouse to highlight one line of text, or drag the mouse to select several lines at once.

Marking a block with your keyboard

Dragging over the screen with the mouse is great for selecting small portions of text. Marking anything larger than a screenful, however, can get a bit out of hand with the mouse — which tends to think there's a cat around or something whenever you scroll-drag and moves too fast to control. In those instances, it's much better to mark text by using the keyboard. Follow these steps:

1. **Press the F8 key.**

   This is the Start Block command. The F8 key "drops anchor" by marking one end of the block.

2. **Use the cursor navigation keys to move to the other end of the block.**

   The navigation keys are discussed in Chapter 2.

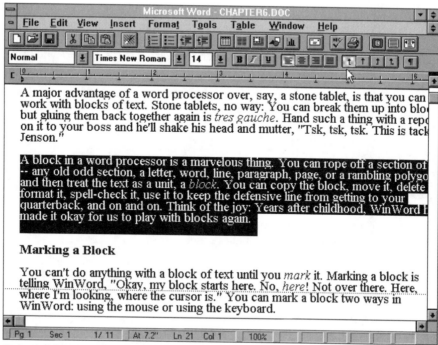

Figure 6-1: A block of text marked on-screen.

WinWord highlights text from the point where you dropped anchor with F8 to wherever you move the toothpick cursor (see Figure 6-1). Text appears in white-on-black. After the block is marked, you're ready to do something with it.

- ✔ After you press the F8 key, you'll see EXT (for Extend Selection) on the status bar. The block-marking mode is active until you type a block or formatting command or press Escape to cancel.

- ✔ To quickly mark a word, position the toothpick cursor on the word and press the F8 key twice.

- ✔ To quickly mark a sentence, position the toothpick cursor somewhere in the sentence and press the F8 key three times.

- ✔ To quickly mark a paragraph, position the toothpick cursor in the paragraph and press the F8 key four times.

- ✔ To mark your whole do-dang document, press the F8 key five times, or press Ctrl+5 (the 5 key on the numeric keypad).

- ✔ Press the Escape key to cancel the block-drop-and-chop F8 method of marking text.

✔ You can use the mouse *and* the F8 key to get real fancy. Position the cursor at either end of the block that you want to mark and press the F8 key. Then, position the mouse cursor at the other end of the block and press the left mouse button. Everything from there to there will be marked.

✔ After a block has been marked, you're ready to type a block command. You can copy the block, cut it, paste it elsewhere, format the block, print it, spell-check it, or a dozen more interesting things all covered in this chapter. Refer to the appropriate section later in this chapter for the next step.

✔ Instead of using the cursor keys to mark a block with the keyboard, you can type a character. WinWord locates the next occurrence of that character and includes all the text between it and the start of the block inside the block. You can do this several times to make the block as large as you like.

✔ Get used to using the keyboard commands to block your text, and you will be much happier, believe me.

Marking a block with the Find command

Marking a block can get sloppy with the mouse or the cursor navigation keys — especially if you're using the PgUp or PgDn keys to mark large acres of text. A better way is to use the Find command to locate the end of the block. Do this:

1. **Position the toothpick cursor at the start of the block.**

   The cursor must be blinking right before the first character to be included in the block. Be precise.

2. **Press the F8 key.**

   This turns on the EXT word-fragment message in the status bar. You're in block-marking mode.

3. **Choose Edit→Find.**

   You see the Find dialog box open on-screen. Yes, you're still in block-marking mode, but now you can use the Find command to locate the end of your block.

4. **Type in the text that you want to locate, which marks the end of the block.**

   After typing the text, press Enter. WinWord stretches the block highlight down to that point in the text and includes the found text in the block.

When the cursor is at the end of the block, you're ready to use a block command. Refer to the proper section later in this chapter for additional details.

✔ Until you type a block command, the block remains highlighted and EXT continues to stare at you from the status bar. Remember to press the Escape key to cancel the block-marking mode.

✔ If text isn't found by using the Find command, you'll see an appropriate not found error message box displayed — but you'll still be in block-marking mode. Click on the OK button to tell WinWord what a good little program it is and that you are sorry that it was unsuccessful.

✔ To find the next occurrence of the matching text, you can press click on the Find Next button in the dialog box. Or . . .

✔ If you don't see the dialog box on-screen, pressing the Shift+F4 key combination will do a "find next" for you.

✔ Although you're using the Find command to help mark your block, you still can use the cursor navigation keys. Heck, you can even use the mouse if you press and hold the Shift key first. Blocking is a liberal thing here; you're not limited to using only the cursor or Find command methods to mark a block.

✔ More details about the Find command can be found in Chapter 5, in the section titled "Finding Text."

Copying and Pasting a Block

After a block is marked, you can copy it and paste that block into another part of your document. The original block remains untouched by this operation. Follow these steps to copy a block of text from one place to another:

1. **Mark the block.**

   Locate the start of the block and select text until you've highlighted to the block's end. Detailed instructions on doing this are offered in the first part of this chapter.

2. **Conjure up <u>E</u>dit→<u>C</u>opy.**

   Choose <u>C</u>opy from the <u>E</u>dit menu. Or, if you're adept at such things, press Ctrl+C for the Copy shortcut. (Or click the Copy tool.)

   WinWord places a copy of the marked block on the Windows Clipboard — a storage area for text or graphics you've cut or copied and are about to paste back into your document.

3. **Move the cursor to the position where you want the block copied.**

   Don't worry if there isn't any room there; WinWord inserts the block into your text just as if you typed it there manually.

4. Do Edit→Paste.

Pressing Ctrl+V is the Paste shortcut. (Or click the Paste tool.)

After doing so — thwoop! (sound effects added) — you now have two copies of the block in your document.

✔ You also can copy blocked text with the mouse. Position the mouse cursor anywhere in the blocked text, hold down the Ctrl key and the left mouse button while you drag the block to the location where the copy is to be placed. The mouse pointer changes to an arrow-with-square-lasso design while you're dragging. Release the mouse button to paste in the block copy.

✔ After a block has been copied, you can paste it into your document a second time. This is covered in the section "Pasting a Previously Cut or Copied Block" later in this chapter.

Here is the quickest way to copy a block in WinWord:

1. Mark the block.

2. Press Ctrl+C.

3. Move the cursor to the block's destination.

4. Press Ctrl+V.

Cutting and Pasting a Block

Cutting a block is like deleting it — but nothing is really gone. Instead, like you snip out an article in the newspaper, the cut block can be pasted into your document at another location. This is technically called a *move*; you move a block of text from one spot to another in your document. (Talk about writing moving text!)

Cutting a block of text works very similarly to copying a block. Follow these steps:

1. Mark the block of text you want to move (cut).

Locate the block's start by using the cursor; press the F8 key and use the cursor keys or use the mouse to highlight the block.

2. Choose the Edit→Cut command.

You also can press Ctrl+X, the Cut shortcut. (Or click the Cut tool.) Either way, the block disappears. That's okay — it's been stuffed into the Windows Clipboard, an electronic storage place, nestled deep in your computer's memory.

3. Move the toothpick cursor to the position where you want the block pasted.

Don't worry if there isn't any room for the block; WinWord makes room as it inserts the block.

4. Summon the Edit→Paste command.

You also can press Ctrl+V to paste in your block. (Or click the Paste tool).

- Additional information on marking a block is found in the first two sections of this chapter.

- Copying a block works just like moving a block, although the original isn't deleted. Refer to the previous section, "Copying and Pasting a Block."

- Moving a block is not the same as deleting a block; the block can be recovered only by positioning the cursor and pasting it in with the Ctrl+V key. The Undo command will not recover a block you moved.

- The Ctrl+Z Undo shortcut will undo a block move.

- After a block has been cut and moved, you can re-paste it into your document a second time. This is covered in the section "Pasting a Previously Cut or Copied Block."

- You also can move blocked text by dragging the mouse — although I recommend using this tip only when the move is just a short distance away. (Scrolling the screen while dragging with the mouse can be unwieldy.) Position the mouse cursor anywhere in the blocked text, and hold down the left mouse button while you drag the bar-looking cursor to the location where the block is to be moved. This dance step is particularly useful when you are rearranging stuff on a page.

Here is the quickest way to move a block in WinWord:

1. Mark the block.

2. Press Ctrl+X.

3. Move the cursor to the block's destination.

4. Press Ctrl+V.

Pasting a Previously Cut or Copied Block

Whenever a block of text is cut or copied, WinWord remembers it. You can re-yank that block into your document at any time — sort of like re-pasting text after it's already been pasted in. This is done by using Ctrl+V, the Paste shortcut.

To paste a previously cut block of text, follow these exciting steps:

1. **Position the toothpick cursor in the spot where you want the block of text to be pasted.**

   This should always be done first. The block will appear right at the cursor's position as if you typed it in yourself.

 2. **Choose the Edit→Paste command.**

   You also can press Ctrl+V, the Paste shortcut. Ctrl+V equals paste? Uh-huh. (Or press the Paste tool.)

3. **Zap. There it is on your screen.**

   - ✔ If nothing has been copied or cut by using the other block commands, nothing will be pasted by this command. Duh.

   - ✔ WinWord has a small brain. It only remembers the last cut or copied block. Anything cut or copied before that is gone, gone, gone.

 Here is the quickest way to retrieve a previously copied or cut block in WinWord:

1. Position the cursor to where you want the block pasted.

2. Press Ctrl+V.

Deleting a Block

There are two ways to delete a block: the complex way and the easy way. What say we do the easy way, eh?

1. **Mark the block.**

   Refer to the first section of this chapter for the best block-marking instructions in any computer book.

2. **Press the Delete key.**

   Thwoop!

   - ✔ You also can press the Backspace key to delete the block.

   - ✔ Additional and detailed information on marking a block is covered in this first section of this chapter.

   - ✔ This time, the block can be recovered by using the Edit→Undo command. This is what makes deleting a block different from cutting and pasting a block. However, when you Undo, the block appears in the same position from where it was deleted.

   - ✔ Chapter 4 covers the vast subject of deleting and destroying text. Turn there to quench your destructive thirsts.

Formatting a Block

When you've roped off a section of text as a block, you can format the text and characters as a single unit. Formatting is covered in detail in Part II of this book, "Formatting — or Making Your Prose Less Ugly." So instead of going over the details, here are the various things you can do to a block for formatting:

- ✔ You can make the text bold, underline (two different flavors), italic, super-script, or subscript by using various Ctrl key combinations, all of which are detailed in Chapter 9.

- ✔ You can change the font for the block's text, which also is covered in Chapter 9.

- ✔ Any formatting changes affect only the text roped off in the block.

- ✔ Information on changing the text style, bold, underline, italic, and all that is offered in Chapter 9, "Formatting Characters." Information on shifting between upper- and lower-case is presented in the same chapter.

- ✔ Information on changing the position of a block — its *justification* — is covered in Chapter 10, "Formatting Sentences and Paragraphs."

Spell-Checking a Block

If you want to spell-check a small or irregularly-sized part of your document, you can block it off and then use WinWord's Spelling command. This is a lot quicker than going through the pains of using the full spell-check.

To see whether your spelling is up-to-snuff, follow these steps:

1. **Mark the block.**

   Refer to the first section in this chapter.

   The highlighted area marked by the block will be the only part of your document spell-checked.

2. **Select the T<u>o</u>ols→<u>S</u>pelling command.**

   No muss, no waiting, the block is spell-checked. (You also can click the Spelling tool.)

3. **WinWord compares all words in the block with its internal dictionary.**

   If a misspelled or unrecognized word is found, it is highlighted and you are given a chance to correct or edit it. If you tire of this, click on the Cancel button.

4. **After the block has been spell-checked, WinWord asks whether, by the way, you want to continue checking the rest of your document. Press N.**

Or press Y if you really want to see how poor your spelling has gotten outside the block.

Chapter 7 covers using WinWord's spell-checker in glorious detail. Refer there for additional information on changing or correcting your typos.

Using Find and Replace in a Block

You cannot find text in a marked block, but you can use WinWord's Replace command. When a block is on, Replace will find and replace only text in the marked block. The rest of your document will be unaffected.

- ✔ A full description of this operation is offered in Chapter 5's section "Find and Replace." I'm too lazy to re-write all that stuff here.

- ✔ The Find command cannot be used in a block because the Find command is used to mark the block; see "Marking a Block with the Find Command" earlier in this chapter.

Printing a Block

WinWord's Print command allows you to print one page, several pages, or an entire document. If you want to print only a small section of text, you need to mark it as a block and then print it. Here's the secret:

1. **Make sure your printer is on and ready to print.**

Refer to Chapter 8 for additional printer setup information.

2. **Mark the block of text you want to print.**

Move the cursor to the start of the block, press F8 to turn on block-marking mode; move the cursor to the end of the block, or use the mouse for wrist-action block marking.

3. **Choose the File→Print command.**

You also can press Ctrl+Shift+F12 (and qualify for the Finger Gymnastics event at the next Olympics). The Print dialog box appears.

4. **Tickle the button by the word Selection.**

Press the E key or click on the word Selection with your mouse. This tells WinWord that you want to print only your highlighted block.

5. Click the OK button or press the Enter key.

In a few moments, you'll see the hard copy sputtering out of your printer.

✔ Additional information on marking a block of text is found in the first section of this chapter.

✔ The full subject of printing is covered in Chapter 8, "Send *This* to the Printer!" Refer there for information on printing options and setting up your printer.

✔ The Selection item appears in the Print dialog only if you have a block selected on-screen.

The 5th Wave By Rich Tennant

"I SAID I WANTED A NEW MONITOR FOR MY BIRTHDAY! MONITOR! MONITOR!"

Chapter 7

The Electronic
Mrs. Heinemann

*E*veryone should have a third grade teacher like Mrs. Heinemann. The woman was a goddess in the annals of proper English, pronunciation, and, of course, spelling. Nothing pleases an eight-year-old more than a smile from Mrs. Heinemann: "Very good, Danny. There is no E at the end of potato." The woman could probably correct the Queen.

What ever happened to Mrs. Heinemann? The folks at Microsoft somehow scooped the essence out of her brain, sliced it thin, and distributed it on the WinWord diskettes. Every copy of WinWord comes with a spelling checker that's as efficient and knowledgeable as Mrs. Heinemann (but without the little red check marks). Somehow, her vast knowledge of English vocabulary has been included as well: WinWord's thesaurus offers alternative word suggestions quicker than Mrs. Heinemann could frown disapprovingly over the misuse of the word "boner." But to top it all off, WinWord can correct your grammar quicker than Mrs. Heinemann could say, "Me, Danny. Woe is me."

Checking Your Spelling

One of the miracles of modern word processing is that the computer knows English spelling better than you do. Thank goodness. I really don't know how to spell. Not at all. The rules are obtuse and meaningless. There are too many exceptions. And with WinWord, you don't need to worry about being accurate. Just be close, and the Spell command does the rest.

To check the spelling of the words in your document, use the Spelling command in the Tools menu. Follow these steps:

1. Press Ctrl+Home.

The toothpick cursor moves to the top of your document. Spelling always starts at the cursor's position and goes toward the end of your document. To spell-check an entire document, you must start at the top.

2. Get the Tools→Spelling command.

You also can choose the Spelling tool.

3. Word scans your document for offensive words that would de-bun Mrs. Heinemann's hair.

4. A misspelled word is found!

The Spelling dialog box appears, and the misspelled or unknown word appears highlighted in your text on-screen. The dialog box displays the misspelled word and suggests alternative spellings — most of them correct. Figure 7-1 shows an example.

5. Pluck the correctly spelled word from the list.

Highlight the correct word and click on the Change button. If the word isn't in the list, you can type it into the Change To box. Or if the word is okay, you can click on the Ignore button to skip over the word without making any changes.

6. WinWord continues to check every word in your document.

When it's done, you'll see a dialog box proclaim: `Spell check complete`. Okay, it's complete.

✔ If the cursor isn't at the top of the document when you start the spell-check, WinWord checks all the words from the toothpick's cursor to the end of your document. At that point, a dialog box asks whether you want to check the first part of your document. Click OK to do so.

✔ Click on the Ignore All button if your word is really a word and you don't want to be stopped every time WinWord encounters it in this document.

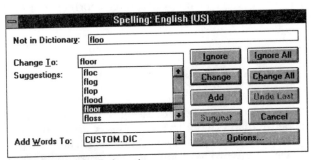

Figure 7-1: A misspelled word.

✔ Select Change All if you want to change every instance of a misspelled word to whatever is in the Change To box. For example, if you have the annoying habit of typing in *teh* instead of *the*, you can click on Change All so that WinWord automatically makes the substitution without bothering you.

✔ You can click on the Add button to place words WinWord doesn't know into its dictionary. For example, your last name, street name, city, and other frequently used words probably won't be in WinWord's dictionary. When the word is flagged as "misspelled," click on the Add button and it will become a part of WinWord's dictionary for life.

✔ Undo Last will undo your last spelling change, most of the time. This is great for those sleepy night spell-checks when you quickly select the wrong replacement word and aren't sure. Just click on Undo Last and check out the last word again. (Undo Last may not work all the time; don't count on it.)

✔ To check the spelling of only one word — which does come in handy — refer to the next section in this chapter, "Checking Only One Word."

✔ To check the spelling of a paragraph or irregularly shaped block of text, refer to Chapter 6, the section "Spell-Checking a Block."

✔ The WinWord dictionary is not a substitute for a real dictionary. Only in a real dictionary can you look up the meaning of a word, which tells you whether you're using the proper word in the proper context. No computer writer works with an electronic dictionary alone; there's usually a good, thick Webster's sitting right within arm's length.

✔ If two identical words are found in a row, WinWord highlights them as a Repeated Word. Error, Error! Click the Ignore button to tell WinWord to forget about the double word, or click on the Delete button to blow the second word away.

✔ My, but this is a long list of check marks.

✔ The Spelling command also locates words with weird capitalization. For example, bONer. You're given an opportunity to correct the word to proper capitalization just as if it were misspelled.

✔ The WinWord dictionary is good but definitely not as good as Mrs. Heinemann. For one thing, it doesn't check your words in context. For example "your" and "you're" can be spelled correctly in WinWord's eye, but you may be using them improperly. The same thing goes for "its" and "it's." For that kind of in-context checking you need something called a *grammar checker*, and you've got one. Its use is discussed later in this chapter.

✔ *Spell* here refers to creating words by using the accepted pattern of letters. It has nothing to do with magic. Many people assume that a spell-check will instantly make their document better. Wrong! You need to read what you write, edit, look, and read again. Spell-checking doesn't fix things up other than finding rotten words and offering suggested replacements.

Checking Only One Word

There's no need to spell-check an entire document when all you want to check is one word. Actually, this is a great way to mentally deal with English spelling: Go ahead and spell the word how you think it *should* be spelled. Then check only that word. WinWord looks up the accurate, wretched English spelling and you're on your way. And the cool part is, you don't need to learn a thing!

To check the spelling on a single, suspect word, do the following:

1. **Put the cursor somewhere on the word or just before it.**

2. **Highlight the word.**

   Press F8 twice or double-click on the word with the mouse and you can skip Steps 1 and 2.

 3. **Spell-check it!**

   Choose the T<u>o</u>ols→<u>S</u>pelling command.

4. **WinWord checks that word.**

   If it's okay (and the way I spell, the odds are 50-50), WinWord reports that it has finished checking the selection. If it's not okay, you'll see the Spelling dialog box that lists possible alternative spellings and suggestions.

5. **Click on a word from the suggested spellings.**

6. **Press the <u>C</u>hange button.**

WinWord replaces the word you thought was spelled correctly with its proper and non intuitive English spelling.

  ✔ Refer to the first section of this chapter for additional information on working WinWord's Spell feature.

  ✔ Single-word checking is often a good way to immediately tackle a word you know is hopelessly wrong. Of course, my philosophy (or "filosofy") is to spell any old which way, and then use a document spell-check to catch everything at once.

Adding Words to the Dictionary

There are common words that don't appear in the dictionary. My last name, for example. Perhaps your last name is as unique as mine, or maybe your first name, city, business name, and so on are all spelled correctly, yet unknown to

WinWord. This means that each time you spell-check your document, it's going to come up with alternative suggestions for those words. There are two options for avoiding this tautological conundrum:

The first, and most stupid option, is to press the Ignore button when the spell-checker finds the word. This means that WinWord will ignore that word during the spell-check. But next time you spell-check, you'll have to do the same thing. Dumb, dumb, dumb.

The second, and wise option, is to Add said word to your supplemental dictionary. This is a list of words kept by WinWord that it will skip every time you spell-check, because you've told it they're all okay. Here's how:

1. **Start your spell-check as you normally would.**

   Refer to the first section of this chapter for the persnickety details.

2. **Lo, you stumble upon a word unbeknownst to WinWord yet beknownst to you.**

   It's spelled just fine.

3. **Select the Add button.**

That stuffs the word into the supplemental dictionary and you'll never have to mess with it again.

✔ When a word is in the supplemental dictionary, WinWord knows and recognizes it as it does the words that come in the real dictionary — the one they made from Mrs. Heinemann's brain.

✔ Be careful when you decide to add a word to the dictionary, because it isn't easy to un-add a word from the dictionary. This is something you may want to do when you commit a flub and inadvertently put a seriously misspelled word into the dictionary. (I once added "fo" to the dictionary and spent three weeks in the WinWord penalty box — and that's in Seattle of all places!) You can get the word out again, which is covered in the nearby technical information box (optional reading).

✔ You actually can maintain several supplemental dictionaries on disk. To select or create a new dictionary, select the Add Words To text box in the spelling dialog box and give the new dictionary a name. WinWord adds the word and uses the supplemental dictionary (along with the real one) for the spell-check.

No need to bother with this trivial drivel on the supplemental dictionary

The supplemental dictionary is actually a text document on disk. It contains all the words you added in alphabetical order. And, as a special bonus, you can edit the list and remove any deleterious words you may have added.

The filename for the standard WinWord supplemental dictionary is:

CUSTOM.DIC

It's actually a text document that you can edit by using the Windows Notepad or WinWord if you like.

The file can be found in the WINWORD directory, or sometimes in the \WINDOWS\MSAPPS\PROOF subdirectory. (Refer to Chapter 17, "Managing Files," for information on locating the WinWord directory.)

You can edit this file to remove extra words from the supplemental dictionary. For example, suppose that you accidentally stuck "fo" in the dictionary. Only by editing the CUSTOM.DIC file can you get "fo" out of there.

My advice is to make a copy of the file before you edit it. That way, if the edited copy gets fouled, you can restore the duplicate. Needless to say, this isn't something for the timid, which is why I wisely stuck it in this box, out of the way, where only the true WinWord goof-offs bother to read.

Checking Your Grammar (Woe is I)

WinWord's grammar checker is a wonderful tool, and I hate it. It keeps telling me how far I have strayed from the boring writing style that the folks who gave the checker life think is the "one true path." Don't get me wrong, it does a great job distinguishing between *I* and *me*, *neither/nor*, and other similar stuff. I just think it's snooty.

For example, running the grammar check on the above paragraph results in the dialog box shown in Figure 7-2. Regardless of the results, if you didn't have enough trauma in English class, and want some more browbeating, select Grammar from the Tools menu. The checker checks, and the dialog box opens, unless you are simply perfect.

- ✔ If you are going to run the grammar checker, don't bother running the spell-checker first. The grammar checker checks your spelling as well as your grammar.

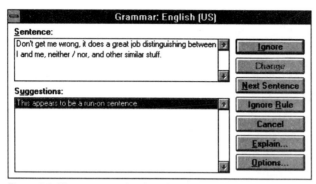

Figure 7-2: The grammar checker chewing the author out.

✓ The grammar checker works a lot like the spell-checker; it tells you what's wrong and then suggests, in a patronizing tone, how to fix it.

✓ You can select buttons to ignore the suggestion, make the changes, move on to the next sentence, ignore the offending rule (my favorite), demand an explanation about why it didn't like what you did, or get out.

✓ You can select the Options button to set the way the grammar checker works. This sets some rather rough parameters, allowing you to select between three sets of writing rules: Strict, Business, and Casual.

✓ You also can check the box that presents the grammar statistics after the checker is done. You should probably check this box, because this is about the only way to get a word count.

✓ If you really want to get into the grammar thing, open the Grammar dialog box, click on the Options button, and then click on the Customize Settings dialog box. Yea verily, although you're several dialog boxes in the thick of things, the one you see on your screen contains a lot of switchable-offable things you can set or reset to control the Grammar Checker's level of fastidiousness.

Using the Thesaurus

If you think I'm smart enough to use all the big words in this chapter, you're grievously mistaken. Witness: *tautological conundrum*. That ain't me talkin'; that's WinWord's thesaurus in action. An amazing tool, astounding utensil, or marvelous implement. You get the idea. The thesaurus helps look up synonyms or other words that have the same meaning but more weight or more precision.

Here's how to instantly become a master of big, clunky words in English:

1. **Hover the cursor on a simple word, such as "big."**

   Adjectives are best for the thesaurus, although the WinWord Statistical Department tells me that the thesaurus contains more than 120,000 words.

2. **Do the Thesaurus command.**

   Choose Tools→Thesaurus, or press the Thesaurus shortcut, Shift+F7. Instantly, the Thesaurus dialog box opens. (See Figure 7-3.) You can still see your original word, highlighted in context, at the top of the screen.

   WinWord displays several alternatives for the word. They're grouped into categories by meanings on the left and synonyms on the right.

3. **To replace the word in your document, highlight your choice and select Replace.**

   After selecting a word, you return to your document. If you don't find a word, select Cancel to return to your document.

✔ A thesaurus is not a colossal, prehistoric beast.

✔ If one of the words in the left column is close, but not exactly what you want, select it and its synonyms will appear in the right column. Repeat Step 3 if you find a word you like.

✔ If there is no synonym for the word you select, the thesaurus will display an alphabetical list of words. Type in a new, similar word, or select Cancel to get back to your document.

✔ After inserting a new word, you may need to do a bit of editing: add "ed" or "ing" to the word, replace "a" with "an" in front of it. There is usually a bit of editing required whenever you replace one word with another.

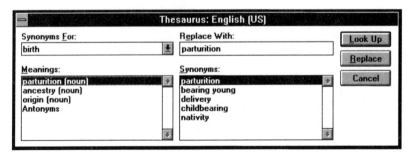

Figure 7-3: Looking up a word in the thesaurus.

Chapter 8

Send *This* to the Printer!

● ●

● ●

Two guys are riding a bus. One of them, a WinWord dummy, says to the other, a typical nondescript dummy, "I'm having trouble sending my document to the printer." And the nondescript dummy says, "Try Quicky-Printy, it's where Marge and I had our Christmas letter done last year." Ba-dum, bum.

The woes of using a computer are so subtle that, well, they drive to you create inane jokes. "Sending something to the printer," means nothing until you explain that a *printer* is a device connected to a computer that allows you to print things.

Getting the Printer Ready

Before printing, you must make sure that your printer is ready to print. This involves more than flipping on its power switch.

Start by making sure that your printer is plugged in and properly connected to your computer. A cable connects the computer and your printer. It should be firmly plugged in at both ends. (This only needs to be checked if you're having printer problems.)

Your printer should have a decent ribbon installed. Old frayed ribbons produce faint text and are bad for the printing mechanism. It will cost you more later in repair bills if you're trying to save a few bucks now by using a ribbon longer than necessary. Laser printers should have a good toner cartridge installed. If the laser printer's "toner low" light is on, replace the toner at once!

There must be paper in the printer for you to print on. The paper can feed from the back, come out of a paper tray, or be fed manually one sheet at a time. However your printer eats paper, make sure you have it set up properly before you print.

Finally, your printer must be *on-line* or *selected* before you can print anything. Somewhere on your printer is a button labeled *on-line* or *select*, and there should be a corresponding light. You need to press that button to turn the option (and the light) "on." Although your printer may be plugged in, the power switch on, and it's doing its warm-up, stretching exercises, it won't print unless it's on-line or selected.

✔ Before you can print, your printer must be: plugged into the wall; plugged into your computer; turned on; full of paper; and *on-line* or *selected*. (Most printers turn themselves on in the *on-line* or *selected* mode.)

✔ Never plug a printer cable into a printer or computer that is on and running. Always turn your printer and computer off whenever you plug anything into them. If not, you may damage the internal electronic components.

✔ Some special — okay, weird — printers are called *serial printers*. These plug into the computer's serial port instead of the more logical printer port. I don't need to bore you with details about which is which. However, if you have a serial printer (and I pity you), some extra setup is necessary before you can start printing. Refer to your printer manual, or go out and buy *DOS For Dummies, 2nd Edition,* and look in Chapter 9.

✔ If you're printing to a network printer — and it makes me shudder to think of it — then *Someone Else* is in charge of the printer. It should be setup and ready to print all for you. If not, there's usually someone handy you can complain to.

✔ The printer that you use affects how WinWord displays and prints your document, so before you do a lot of formatting, check to be sure that you have the correct printer selected. For help installing your printer and connecting it to your computer, see your Windows documentation and the manual that came with your printer.

✔ Some additional information on setting up, or *installing*, your printer for use with WinWord is covered in Chapter 24, "The Printer Is Your Friend." That chapter also contains troubleshooting information and a detailed anatomical guide to popular printers that tells you where to shoot the printer for a quick death or a lingering, slow, and painful one.

Selecting a Printer

One of the joys of printing with any Windows application is its capability for using many different printers. WinWord will even remember the capabilities of several different printers and automatically format your work to show you, on-screen, what it will look like when it gets to paper. This is called *WYSIWYG*, (wizz-i-wig) or *what you see is what you get* (more-or-less).

After the joy, depression sets in when you realize that you can only select a printer that has been installed in Windows. This is definitely Windows Guru time, although you should rest happy in the knowledge that if your printer works with other Windows programs, it will work swell in WinWord too. This is perhaps Windows only redeeming quality over DOS. That, and it isn't as ugly.

To select a printer — if you *really* need to — follow these steps:

1. **Choose the File→Print Setup command.**

   This opens the Print Setup dialog box, shown in Figure 8-1.

2. **Select the printer that you want to use, then click on OK.**

3. **You're done.**

   That's it.

   ✔ Selecting a printer is necessary only if you have more than one printer connected to your PC.

   ✔ If you're using a network printer, an appropriate section for your needs is hidden in Chapter 24, "The Printer Is Your Friend."

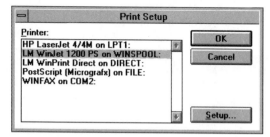

Figure 8-1: The Print Setup dialog box allows you to choose any of the printers already installed in Windows.

Printing a Whole Document

If you think that your work is worthy enough to be enshrined on a sheet of paper, follow these steps. This will print your entire document, top to bottom, head to toe, from *Once upon a time* to *happily every after*:

1. **Make sure the printer is *on-line* and ready to print.**

   What's that noise? Is Bobby at it again with the Playskool Li'l Plumber Kit? No, it's the printer, humming its ready tune.

2. **Summon the Print command.**

    Choose the File→Print command or, if you can pick up a basketball with one hand, press Ctrl+Shift+F12. (You also can click on the Print tool.) You'll see the Print dialog box displayed, looking suspiciously like Figure 8-2.

3. **Click OK or press the Enter key.**

4. **The printer warms up and starts to print.**

Printing may take some time. Really. A long time. And you can't do anything else while the little "I'm printing, don't bother me" dialog box is displayed. Ho-hum.

- ✔ When printing is done, you'll be returned to your document for further editing, saving, or more laborious writing — the beads of sweat dotting your brow like bees of fury as you painstakingly wrestle the selfish muses for their inspiration!

- ✔ If nothing prints, don't hit the Print command again! There's probably nothing awry — the computer is still thinking or sending (downloading) fonts to the printer. If you don't get an error message, everything will probably print, eventually.

- ✔ If you have a manual feed printer, then the printer itself will be begging for paper. Your printer will say, "Beep, feed me!" You must stand by, line up

Figure 8-2: The Print dialog box.

paper, then shove it into the printer's gaping maw until your document is done printing. Refer to the section "Printing Envelopes" later in this chapter to figure this one out.

✔ Before you print, consider saving your document to disk and — if we're talking final draft here — do a spell-check. Refer to Chapter 15, the section "Saving a document to disk (after that)" as well as Chapter 7, the section "Checking Your Spelling."

Here are the shortcut keys for printing an entire document:

Press Ctrl+Shift+F12, Enter.

Printing a Specific Page

Follow these steps to print only one page of your document:

1. **Make sure that your printer is on and anxious to print something.**

2. **Move the toothpick cursor so that it's sitting somewhere in the page you want to print.**

   Check the cryptic Pg counter at the lower-left corner of the screen to make sure that you're at the page you want.

3. **Do the <u>P</u>rint command.**

   Choose <u>F</u>ile→<u>P</u>rint or press Ctrl+Shift+F7. The Print dialog appears. (You also can click on the Print tool.)

4. **Select Cur<u>r</u>ent Page.**

   Click on Cur<u>r</u>ent Page or press Alt+E to select the radio button.

5. **Click OK or press Enter.**

6. **You'll be returned to your document when that sole page is printed on your printer.**

The page will have a header, footer, all formatting — and even a page number — just as if you printed it as part of the complete document.

Printing a Range of Pages

WinWord allows you to print a single page, or even a range of pages. To print a range or group of pages, follow these steps:

1. **Make sure the printer is on-line, happy, and ready to print.**

2. **Conjure up the Print command.**

   Choose File→Print, or press Ctrl+Shift+F12. You see the Printer dialog box.

3. **Choose Pages.**

   Click on Pages with the mouse, or press Alt+G. The toothpick cursor zooms down into the From text box.

4. **Enter the starting page number.**

   For example, enter 5 for page 5.

5. **Press the Tab key or click on the To text box with your mouse.**

   This zooms you over to the To text box.

6. **Enter the ending page number.**

   For example, enter 8. This sets the page range from 5 to 8, meaning pages 5, 6, 7, and 8 will print.

7. **Choose OK.**

   Click the OK button or press the Enter key . The pages you specified — and only those pages — will print.

Printing a Block

When a block of text is marked on-screen, you can beg the Print command to print only that block. Refer to "Printing a Block" in Chapter 6 for the down-and-dirty details.

Printing Several Documents

It may seem that the best way to print several documents at once is to load them one at a time and print them one at a time. There is a better way, however, and it is hidden in the Find File command tucked away in the File menu. You can use this command to mark files on the disk and do a "gang-print." This is rumored to be easier than loading each file into WinWord, printing it, putting the file away, and then loading in another file. You be the judge.

To print several files at once, follow these steps:

1. Make sure the printer is on, selected, and rarin' to print.

2. Choose File→Find File.

The Find File dialog box shown in Figure 8-3 opens.

If you are the one person in a thousand who is familiar with the Find File dialog box, skip ahead to Step 7. If this is the first time you have used it, you will need to tell it where to look for your files. To do this:

3. Click on the Search button.

4. Select All Drives from the Drives list.

This tells WinWord to look at all of the drives that your computer has.

5. Enter *.doc in the File Name box.

That's an asterisk, then a period, then DOC. This tells WinWord to look only for files that end in the DOC extension — WinWord documents.

6. Select Start Search.

Your computer will whiz and whirl, and you will eventually be presented with a list of all of the WinWord document files on your computer — the whole lot of them.

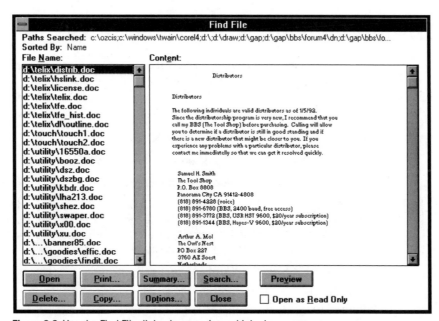

Figure 8-3: Use the Find File dialog box to print multiple documents.

You can see the contents of the file in the Cont̲ent window. This is a real help when you forget what you wrote or when you have several different versions of the same file and you only want to print one of them.

7. Select the files that you want to print.

The files are all listed in the Find File window. You select them by clicking on them with the mouse. To select more than one, hold down the Ctrl key while you click. You can select several files.

8. Click on the P̲rint button.

The Print dialog box opens. Deja vu!

9. Choose OK.

WinWord happily prints all the documents you selected.

- ✔ Yes, as with printing a single document, printing multiple documents takes a while. Be prepared to sit and stare at the tiny "I'm printing so you can't be doing anything" dialog box or go off and get a cup of coffee — *in another state!*

- ✔ If you're adept with DOS, you can direct the Find File dialog box to display only those files in a specific subdirectory on your hard drive. This subject is tackled in Chapter 17, "Managing Files."

Printing Envelopes

Yes, WinWord can print envelopes. Yes, it can even be a snap. There's even a little button on the toolbar specifically designed for this purpose — an envelope, complete with a stamp. (Alas, WinWord does not print the stamp as well. And if it could, it might as well print money.)

To print an envelope, follow these steps:

1. Make sure your printer is oh-so anxious to print something.

2. Choose the T̲ools→Create E̲nvelope command.

(Or click the Envelope tool.) This opens the Create Envelope dialog box shown in Figure 8-4. If an address had been selected in your document, or WinWord has somehow magically located the address near the toothpick cursor, it will appear in the Addressed T̲o box.

If you didn't have WinWord automatically fill in the address, type it in now.

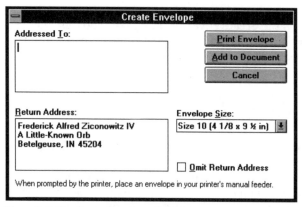

Figure 8-4: The Create Envelope dialog box.

3. Stick an envelope in your printer.

I mention this step because most printers must be spoon-fed envelopes one at a time. (Mine works like this.) In some fancy-schmancy offices, there may be printers with *envelope feeders*. La-di-da.

4. Choose Print Envelope.

Click on that button with the mouse. Your printer may beep or otherwise prompt you to insert the envelope, or it may just print it right then and there.

✔ Check the envelope to make sure you didn't address the backside or put the address on upside down — as I so often do. This is an important last step because you can just repeat the above steps to reprint your envelope should you goof.

✔ Place the envelope in your laser printer's manual-feed slot-thing. The envelope will go in face up with the top side to your left. Draw a picture of this or print the previous two sentences on a piece of paper and tape it to the top of your laser printer for future reference.

✔ On a dot-matrix printer, the envelope goes into the feeder upside-down and faces away from you. It helps to wedge it in there a bit to make sure the printer grabs it. Or you may have a new-fangled printer that has a special envelope slot. And if you do, well, la-di-da.

✔ Printing envelopes on a dot-matrix printer is a study in frustration. They usually look like something that a four-year-old did in preschool, all smeared up and not legible. You may be able to reduce the amount of smear by increasing the distance between the paper and the roller; you will have to experiment.

🖌 If you don't want the return address to print, check the Omit Return Address box in the Create Envelope dialog box. I do this routinely because my printer munges the top part of the envelope and the return address never prints right.

Canceling a Print Job

Sometimes you'll print something, and then change your mind. This happens all the time. (Rumor has it that Gutenberg originally wanted to print a hanging floral wall calendar.) Or maybe your printer is so slow that you repeatedly press Ctrl+Shift+F12, Enter too many times. Then you find yourself accidentally printing several dozen copies of the same document. Ugh.

Because WinWord prints "in the background," there is no obvious way to cancel printing. It can be done if you're crafty, however. Follow this step:

1. **If the "I'm printing now, don't bother me" dialog box hasn't yet disappeared from your screen, select Cancel.**

   This should halt printing, but don't expect it to stop right away. Your printer has RAM memory just like the PC and may take a few seconds (or pages) to "empty its tank."

If the printing dialog box has already disappeared, you are probably too late. Your only hope is to switch to the Windows Print Manager and try to stop printing there. Your chances of success here are low, so muster your courage and take these steps:

1. **Press Ctrl+Esc.**

   This summons the Windows Task Manager. Somewhere in the list displayed, look for Print Manager. If you can't find it (and do try scrolling the list if it's that long), then click on the Cancel button. You're doomed.

2. **Click on the Print Manager to select it.**

3. **Click on the Switch To button.**

   The Print Manager appears. It contains a list of stuff that is currently waiting to be printed. You may see your WinWord document named somewhere toward the bottom of the list. If not, you're sobbing new lakes in your backyard. Skip to Step 6.

4. **Click on the name of your WinWord document "job" in the Print Manager's list.**

   Items in the Print Manager's list are called *print jobs*. Your task is to fire one of them.

5. Click on the big _D_elete button at the top of the Print Manager.

You may be asked whether you really want to terminate the employee, er, print job. Click on the OK button.

6. Press Alt+Tab.

This zaps you back to WinWord, ready for more editing action.

✔ Obviously, canceling a print job is the act of a desperate person. In its efforts to make life easy for computer users, Windows tries hard to help us change our minds. Canceling something that's printing may or may not work as planned. My advice is just to be careful with the Print command in the first place.

✔ More information on using the Print Manager can be found in IDG Books' *Windows For Dummies*.

✔ The Alt+Tab key combination discussed in Step 6 above only works with Windows Versions 3.1 or later. If you have an older version of Windows, press Alt+Esc a few times until you see WinWord back on your screen.

Part II
Formatting — or Making Your Prose Look Less Ugly

The 5th Wave   By Rich Tennant

"NOPE - I'D BETTER WAIT 'TIL ALL MY FONTS ARE WORKING. A HATE LETTER JUST DOESN'T WORK IN *Filigree Flowerbox Extended*."

In this part . . .

Formatting makes your documents shine. It's what makes
you boast when you show your printed labors to a —
dare I say it — WordPerfect user, who snivels, "Gosh, how'd
you get it to look so good?" Few other things in life will make
you swell with such pride.

Yet, formatting isn't without its dark side. It involves a lot of
key pressing and other secret rituals. This section describes
the intricacies of how formatting works in WinWord and how
to make your documents look oh, so purty.

Chapter 9
Formatting Characters

*T*he most basic thing you can format in a document is a character. Characters include letters, words, text in paragraphs, and weird Uncle Lloyd who trims the hair in his ears with a butane lighter. You can format characters to be bold, underlined, italicized, little, big, or in different fonts. WinWord gives you a magnificent amount of control over the appearance of your text and allows you to generate documents that are truly professional in quality — fooling everyone in the process.

If you want to learn to access everything in this chapter through menus, see the last section in this chapter, "Doing it the hard way."

Making Bold Text

 To emphasize a word, you make it bold. Bold text is, well, bold. It's heavy. It carries a lot of weight, stands out on the page, speaks its mind at public meetings, wears a cowboy hat — you know the type.

To make new text stand out, follow these steps:

1. Press the Ctrl+B key combination.

This activates bold mode, and everything you type will be bold. Go ahead — type away. La-la-la. (You also can click the Bold tool in the ribbon to turn it on.)

2. Press Ctrl+B again.

This turns off the bold character format. All your text will be normal. (Turn off the Bold tool.)

If you already have text on-screen and you want to make it bold, you need to mark it as a block and then make it bold. Follow these steps:

1. Mark the block of text you want to make bold.

Move the toothpick cursor to the start of the block; press F8 to turn on the block-marking mode; move the cursor to the end of the block. Or you can use the mouse to drag and select the block. The block appears highlighted on-screen.

2. Press Ctrl+B, the Bold key command.

The block is bold. (You also can click on the Bold tool.)

✔ Everything you type after pressing Ctrl+B will appear in boldface on-screen and in your printed document. However, if you wander with the toothpick cursor, you may turn off the bold command. My advice is to do this: Press Ctrl+B; type bold stuff; press Ctrl+B; and type normal stuff.

 ✔ When the Bold **B** tool is depressed (it's crying or bemoaning something trivial), the text the toothpick cursor is nestled in has the bold attribute. (This feature helps when you can't tell by looking at the screen whether text is already bold.)

✔ You can mix and match character formats; text can be bold and underline or bold and italic. To do so, you need to press the proper keys to turn on those formats before typing the text. Yes, this means you may have to type several WinWord character formatting commands before typing your text. Ctrl+B, Ctrl+I, and Ctrl+U for bold, italic, and underlined text all at once, for example. It's a hassle, but everyone has to do it that way.

✔ You can turn off all character formatting at one stroke by pressing the Ctrl+spacebar key combination. Granted, it helps to have a block of formatted text marked, first.

✔ Refer to Chapter 6, the section "Marking a Block," for more information on marking blocks.

Making Italicized Text

 Italics are replacing underlining as the preferred text emphasis format. I'm not embarrassed to use italics to emphasize or highlight a title just because it looks so much better than shabby underlined text. It's light and wispy, poetic and free. Underline is what the DMV does when it feels creative.

To italicize your text, follow these steps:

1. **Press the Ctrl+I key combination.**

   Italics mode is on! (You also can click the Italic tool.)

2. **Type away to your heart's content!**

   Watch your delightfully right-leaning text march across the screen.

3. **Press Ctrl+I when you're done.**

   Italic formatting is turned off. (Turn off the Italic tool.)

If the text you want to italicize is already on-screen, you must mark it as a block and then change its character format to italics. Follow these steps:

1. **Mark the block of text you want to italicize.**

   Do the block-marking thing here. Detailed instructions are offered in Chapter 6 and earlier in this chapter.

2. **Press the Ctrl+I key combination.**

   This italicizes the block. (You also can click the leaning *I* Underline tool.)

✔ If you want to double up on a character font — say make something italic and bold, you can press both character formatting keys while you hold down the Ctrl key. Holding down the Ctrl key and pressing I and then B seems to be easier than doing the Ctrl+I and Ctrl+B dance.

✔ You also can use Ctrl+spacebar to turn Italics off, but then you turn off all other formatting as well.

Making Underlined Text

 Underlined text just isn't as popular as it used to be. Instead, people now use *italicized* text for subtle emphasis. Still, underlined text still does have its place. I don't know where, or else I'd come up with a cheesy example here.

To underline your text, follow these steps:

1. Press the Ctrl+U key combination.

This turns on the underline character format. (You can also use the Underline tool-button thing on the ribbon.)

2. Type!

You're now free to type the text you want underlined.

3. Press the Ctrl+U key combination again.

This returns you to typing normal text. (Or click off the Underline tool-button.)

If you already have text on-screen that you want to underline, you need to mark the text as a block, and then press the Ctrl+U keys. Here are the steps to take:

1. Mark the block of text you want to underline.

Refer to Chapter 6 or the first section of this chapter for exciting block marking rules and regulations.

2. Press the Ctrl+U keys.

The block is underlined. (Or click the Underline tool.)

✔ After you finish typing underlined text, you can press Alt+spacebar, Alt+U, or click the Underline **u** tool to turn off underlining.

✔ Chapter 6, the king of the block chapters, contains a section called "Marking a Block," which tells you more about marking blocks.

Text Attribute Effects

The most common character formats are bold, italics, and underlining. These are covered in previous sections. WinWord has other text formats, not so common, that work through Ctrl+*key* combinations to format characters or blocks of text. All character formats are presented in Table 9-1 with their corresponding key commands.

Table 9-1	Text Format Samples and Commands
Ctrl+key	*Applies this format*
A	ALL CAPS
B	Bold
D	<u>Double Underline</u>
H	Hidden Text (it won't print — shhh!)
I	*Italic*
K	SMALL CAPS
U	<u>Continuous Underline</u>
W	<u>Word</u> <u>Underline</u>
=	Subscript
+	Superscript
spacebar	Return to Normal

✔ To apply one of these weird text formats to a character you type or text that is blocked, refer to the preceding section, "Making Underlined Text," and substitute the proper shortcut from Table 9-1.

✔ Ctrl+spacebar is the easiest way to recover when your character formatting seems to have gotten rambunctiously encumbered.

✔ Although these formats lack the cool B, I, and U buttons on the ribbon that the Bold, Italics, and Underline attributes have, they can be controlled from the Character dialog box, discussed at the butt end of this chapter.

✔ Hidden text, what good is that? Good for you, the writer, to put down some thoughts and then hide them when the document prints. Of course, you won't see the text on-screen either. To find hidden text, you must use the Find command (covered in Chapter 5) to locate the special hidden text attribute. This information is tucked away in a technical box in that chapter. (It really should have been hidden to begin with.)

Text Size Effects

Attributes — bold, italics, underline, and so on — are only half the character formats. The other half deal with the text size. By using these commands, you can make your text teensy or humungous.

To change the size of text as you type, follow these steps:

1. **Press Ctrl+P, the point size shortcut.**

   The point size box is highlighted in the ribbon.

2. **Type in the new point size and press Enter.**

   The text you type from that moment on will be in the new size.

- ✔ Bigger numbers mean bigger text — smaller numbers mean smaller text.

- ✔ The *points* in point sizes are actually a measurement. There are 72 points to the inch, so if you type the number **72**, your characters will be one inch tall when printed. The average point size is 12 or sometimes 10.

- ✔ TrueType or Adobe Type 1 fonts can be sized from 4 points to 127 points.

- ✔ Refer to Chapter 14, "The Power of Glossaries," to learn about applying complex text attributes with simple key presses.

- ✔ If you want to apply a size format to text already on-screen, you need to mark those characters as a block before modifying the size.

- ✔ To quickly change the point size of a marked block you can use the F2 key. Ctrl+F2 makes text larger; Shift+Ctrl+F2 makes it smaller. Because F2 and text size aren't mnemonically connected, this is one you'll need to remember.

Making Superscript Text

Superscript text is above the line, for example the 10 in 2^{10}. To produce this effect, type Ctrl+Shift+= (the equal key) and then the text you want to superscript. Or, mark a block of text, then press Ctrl+Shift+= (the equal key) to superscript the text in the block.

- ✔ To return your text to normal, press Ctrl+spacebar.

- ✔ Some people prefer superscript text that's a tad bit smaller than regular-sized text. WinWord doesn't automatically shrink its superscript text; you'll have to refer to the previous section for information on changing the text's size.

- ✔ Here's a reason to be glad for alcohol: Ctrl+Shift+= is the art of pressing the Ctrl and Shift keys at the same time — which anyone can do after a light lunch — and then pressing the equal key. Actually, Shift+= is the plus key. So this is really Ctrl++ or Control-plus. Ugh. I'd bet if they made a bigger keyboard, Microsoft would find things to do with all the keys, no sweat.

Making Subscript Text

Subscript text is below the line, for example the 2 in H_2O. To subscript your text, type Ctrl+= (the equal key), and then type away. If you mark a block of text and then press Ctrl+= (equal), all the text in the block will be subscript. To return your text to normal, press Ctrl+spacebar (long boney key under thumb).

> ✔ Refer to the section "Text Size Effects" for information on making your subscript text smaller than other text on the same line.

Making Normal Text

Sometimes, you have so many character attributes going that you don't know what to press to get back to normal text. This can be very frustrating. Fortunately, WinWord has lent a tiny ear to the cries of help. You can use the Reset Character text formatting command to shut off everything — size and attribute formats — and return the text to normal. Here's how:

Press Ctrl+spacebar, the Reset Character shortcut.

Everything you type from that point on will be normal (or at least have the normal attributes).

> ✔ If you mark a block, then press Ctrl+spacebar, all text in the block will be returned to normal. Refer to "Marking a Block" in Chapter 6 for more information on marking blocks of text.
>
> ✔ Ctrl+spacebar will not work on cousin Melvin.

Changing the Font

One of the fun things about WinWord is its capability to use lots of different fonts. Sure, text can be made bold, italics, underline, big, little, and on and on, but adjusting the font to match your mood takes expression to an entirely new level.

To switch to a different font, follow these steps:

1. Press Ctrl+F.

This highlights the font box on the ribbon. You also can click on the font box with the mouse.

2. Press the down-arrow key.

This displays all the fonts that have been installed for Windows. (You also can click on the down-arrow button to the right of the font box.)

3. Scroll down to the font you want.

They're listed by name in alphabetical order.

4. Press Enter to select a font.

Or click on it once with your mouse.

Everything you type after selecting a new font appears on-screen in that font. It should print and look the same as well.

- ✔ You can change a font for text already in your document by first marking the text as a block (refer to Chapter 6) and then selecting the font you want from the ribbon.

- ✔ The last section in this chapter, "Doing it the hard way," contains information on previewing certain fonts, which allows you to see how they will look before you use them.

- ✔ The fonts are listed in the font box by name and appear in the drop-down list with little icons before the name. A printer icon identifies a *printer font*, one that's part of your printer. This type of font may not show up on-screen as it will print; Windows is odd this way. Fonts with a double $^{\mathsf{T}}\mathsf{T}$ by them are *TrueType fonts*, which look on-screen as they will print.

- ✔ In WinWord, fonts are the responsibility of Windows alone. You install new fonts by using the Windows Control Panel. Thousands of fonts are available for Windows, and they work in all Windows applications. (Windows users trade fonts like characters in cheesy sitcoms trade insults; refer to a local computer club or scour the back of a computer magazine to look for some cool Windows fonts.)

Upper- and Lower-Case Conversion

Upper- and lower-case effects aren't considered part of a font, character attribute, or format. Anyway, WinWord lets you switch from ALL CAPS to lower-case exclusively with a fun key, the Switch Case key. This can come in handy.

To switch text to ALL CAPS, follow these steps:

1. Mark the text you want to convert to ALL CAPS as a block.

Refer to the first section of this chapter for the details, or home in on Chapter 6 for the best block-marking advice since the ancient Babylonians.

2. Press Ctrl+A.

Ctrl+A is the ALL CAPS shortcut.

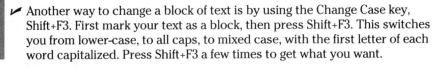

- ✔ To switch your text back, press Ctrl+A again.

- ✔ Another way to change a block of text is by using the Change Case key, Shift+F3. First mark your text as a block, then press Shift+F3. This switches you from lower-case, to all caps, to mixed case, with the first letter of each word capitalized. Press Shift+F3 a few times to get what you want.

Inserting Oddball Characters

Look over your keyboard's keys. Yeah, there are the letters of the alphabet, plus numbers, and some weird symbols. WinWord can display all those characters just fine; you see it on your screen every day.

But there are several dozen to several hundred additional, interesting characters you can display. These are WinWord's oddball characters, and they seem to accumulate like coat hangers.

Oddball characters are inserted by using the Insert→Symbol command. Here is how you work it:

1. **Position the toothpick cursor to where you want the oddball character to appear.**

2. **Select the Insert→Symbol command.**

   You see the Symbol dialog box shown in Figure 9-1.

3. **Select the symbol you want.**

   Point the mouse at the character that interests you, and then double-click on that character. Or you can use the cursor keys to move a highlight box around, and then press Enter.

4. **The oddball character is inserted into your text.**

Well, I'll be ♥☎➤&⊗♠!

✔ To get a good look at a particular symbol, point the mouse cursor at it, and press and hold the mouse button. That one symbol will be magnified as long as you hold down the button.

✔ Just about any font you have installed that has symbols in it appears in the drop-down list at the top of the Symbol dialog box. To look at other symbols, click on the down arrow next to the Symbols From box and select a different symbol set by clicking on its name. The best symbols can be found in the various *Wingdings* fonts.

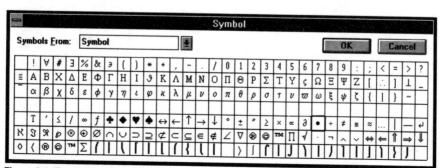

Figure 9-1: The Symbol dialog box.

Doing it the hard way — taking a Yellow Line bus tour of the Character dialog box

Too many choices can overwhelm you. Most people prefer simple, straight forward information — all the options explained right there on the menu, with pictures of what they look like. Or a smell may waft from two tables over and you'll point and say, "I want what the nun is having."

Then again, there are times when — providing you know what you're doing — you want all the options right there at once. You know which levers you want pulled — the salad dressing, potato fixings, and how burnt the meat should be — all at once. For those times, WinWord offers the Character dialog box, a place where almost all your character formatting can take place simultaneously. This is definitely not for the timid.

When you select Format→Character, you open up the rather imposing Character dialog box, as shown in the figure below. All sorts of interesting things happen here, depending on at which bus stop you disembark.

Day #1	**Font**	If you click on the drop-down list under the word Font, you see the name of each and every font on your machine. There can be anywhere from a handful to a kabillion of them. If you highlight the name of one, a sample appears in the window.
Day #2	**Points**	If you click on the drop-down list under Points, you see all available whole number sizes of the font in question. The available sizes run from 4-point to 127-point, or teensy-weensy to really big.
Day #3	**Style**	Look at the list of different styles you can have: **Bold**, *Italic,* ~~Strikethrough~~, Hidden, SMALL CAPS, ALL CAPS, and Three Different Flavors of Formatting for Underline.
Day #4	**Super/subscript**	You can have Superscript and Subscript.
Day #5	**Spacing**	This controls how close the letters in your text appear together. Your options are expanded or condensed or normal.
Day #6	**Color**	Create text in living color by selecting a new color from the Color drop-down list. The color shows on-screen only if you have a color monitor, and it prints only if you have a color printer.

You can make all sorts of text settings in the Character dialog box, and then click OK to apply them to your text. That's any new text you type or text already in a block you highlight on-screen.

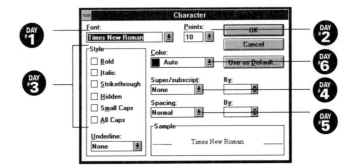

Chapter 10

Formatting Sentences and Paragraphs

*T*he next biggest things you can format in a document, after characters or text, are sentences and paragraphs. This formatting involves the position of text on the page, alignment with tabs or indents, and line spacing. This stuff can be done on the fly, but I recommend doing it just before printing (along with page formatting — see Chapter 11) or by including the formatting in a style sheet (see Chapter 13). That way, you can pull out half your hair while you struggle with spelling and grammar and getting your ideas on paper. Then, when that's perfect, and your blood pressure has dropped, you can pull out the rest of your hair while you struggle anew with line and paragraph formatting. Ugh. Will it never end?

If you want to learn to access everything in this chapter through menus, see the last section in this chapter, "Doing it the hard way."

Centering Text

 WinWord lets you *center* a single line of text or an entire block of text. Your text is miraculously centered down the middle of the page on-screen and when printed. This is yet another miracle of modern computing.

If you just want to center a single line, follow these steps:

1. **Start on a new line, the line you want to be centered.**

   If the line is already on-screen, skip to the second set of instructions following.

2. **Use the Center command, Ctrl+E.**

   I know that E doesn't mean *center* in your brain. But, the word center does have two Es in it. How about E means *equator*. Na, that goes side-to-side. I give up.

   You also can center text by clicking on the Center tool on the ribbon. It looks like the thing you yell into when you order burgers in a drive-thru.

3. **The cursor zips over to the center the of the screen (or thereabouts).**

4. **Type your title or heading.**

5. **Press Enter when you're done.**

 If you want to center more than a line, say a paragraph or more, keep typing away. When you tire of seeing your text centered, press Ctrl+L to return to *left justification*, or press the Left Align tool. (Left justification is the way text normally appears in WinWord; everything is even on the left side of the page on the left margin.)

Follow these steps to center text already in your document:

1. **Mark as a block the text you want to center.**

   Refer to Chapter 6 for the best block-marking directions you'll ever read in a computer book.

2. **Use the Center command, Ctrl+E.**

   You see the blocked text, along with any paragraph it is in, promptly displayed as center-justified. (You also can click on the Center tool.)

✔ The Center command, Ctrl+E, actually centers paragraphs only. If you want to center just one line at a time, you must end each line by pressing the Enter key — which makes that single line a paragraph.

 ✔ The easiest way to accomplish quick paragraph formatting, such as centering, is to use the tools on the ribbon. Just click one of them instead of pressing Ctrl+E, Ctrl+L, or whatever and your text will be formatted accordingly.

 ✔ To *justify* text — the left *and* right margins align — click on the Justify tool or press Ctrl+J.

Flushing Text Right

 Flush right describes the way text aligns on-screen. (You'll soon discover there is a lot of flushing in paragraph formatting.) Text is usually *flush left*, with each line aligning at the left margin. Flush right text aligns at the right margin. In other words, all the text is slammed against the right side of the page — like picking up the paper and jerking it wildly until the text slides over.

You can right align a single paragraph of text or mark any size of text as a block and flush it right. If you just want to flush a single paragraph, follow these steps:

1. Position the toothpick cursor where you want to type a line flush right.

The cursor will be on the left side of the screen; this is okay. Don't use the spacebar or Tab key to move the cursor; the Flush Right command will do so in just a second.

If the text you want to flush right is already on-screen, skip to the second set of instructions following.

2. Press Ctrl+R, the Flush Right command.

Golly, R equals Right. This is amazing. The cursor skips on over to the right margin, on the right side of the screen. (You also can click on the Right Align tool.)

3. Type your line.

The characters push right, always staying flush with the right side of the document. It's like writing in Hebrew!

4. Press Ctrl+L to return to left justified text when you're done.

Again, put the cursor on a new line, otherwise the Ctrl+L command will undo all your right-justified text. (Or press the left Align tool.)

For flushing right more than a single paragraph or text you already have in your document, you need to mark it all as a block. Follow these steps:

1. Mark as a block the text you want to flush right.

Chapter 6 has block-marking details to soothe your furrowed brow.

2. Press Ctrl+R, the Flush Right command.

You see the text zip over to the right margin. Og say block flush right. Block good. (You also can click the Right Align tool.)

- ✔ Be careful not to flush large objects, cardboard, or other foreign objects when adjusting your text.

- ✔ Do not flush while the train is parked at the station.

- ✔ *Flush right* is a design term that means the same thing as *right align* or *right justification.*

- ✔ Typographers use other words besides *justification.* They occasionally use the word *ragged* to describe how the text fits. For example, left justification is *ragged right*; right justification is *ragged left.* A "rag top" is a convertible with a soft top, and a "rag bottom" is any child still in diapers.

Flushing your dates right

A good thing to flush right at the top of the document is the date. This is the way most people start their letters. To flush right the date at the top of a document, follow these handy steps:

1. Move to the top of the document to the line where you want to put the date. It must be a blank line.

2. Press Ctrl+R, the Flush Right command. The cursor zooms over to the right side of the page.

3. Press Alt+Shift+D. This inserts the current date into your document. (No need to memorize this command; just flag this page.)

4. Press Enter.

5. Press Ctrl+L to go back to left justification.

You can continue editing with the current date proudly flushed right at the top of the page.

Changing Line Spacing

On a typewriter, you change the line spacing with a double or triple whack of the carriage return. Sadly, although whacking your computer twice or thrice will help your attitude, it won't do diddly for your document's line spacing. Instead, you'll need to use WinWord's Line Spacing command.

To change the line spacing for new text you have three options:

1. Press Ctrl+1 for single-space lines.

Hold down the Ctrl key and press 1. (That's Ctrl and the one key, not the L key.) Release both keys and WinWord single-spaces your text. Any text you type or a highlighted block on-screen is affected after you press Ctrl+1.

1 ½. Press Ctrl+5 for 1.5-spaced lines.

The 1.5 spacing means your lines are between single and double spacing — which gives editors (and teachers) less room to mark up your stuff but still lets in all that "air" that makes the text readable. You press Ctrl+5 to get 1.5 line spacing in your document or to change the spacing for a highlighted block.

2. Press Ctrl+2 for double-space lines.

Double spacing is often required by fussy editors who, without enough room in their precious 1-inch margins, want to write under, over, and between what you write. Press Ctrl+2 to make your text double spaced.

✔ Refer to Chapter 6 for information on marking a block. The Ctrl+1, Ctrl+2 and Ctrl+5 shortcuts affect any block marked on-screen.

✔ Ctrl+5 means 1 ½ line spacing, not 5 line spacing.

Unnecessary, more-specific spacing stuff

If you want line spacing other than single, double, or 1.5, you can select the Format→Paragraph command. The Paragraph dialog box opens, which is covered at the end of this chapter. Choose Exactly in the Line Spacing box, and the measurement that you want in the At box. For example, to triple-space lines, you select Exactly under Line Spacing and enter the number 3 in the At box. You don't need to put the 1i after the three, unless you really want to; WinWord fills in the default measurement for you.

Indenting a Paragraph

To offset a paragraph of text, you can indent it. This doesn't mean just indenting the first line of a paragraph, which you can do with the Tab key. Instead, you can indent, or *nest*, the entire paragraph by aligning its left edge against a tab stop. Here's how:

1. Move the toothpick cursor anywhere in the paragraph.

The paragraph can already be on-screen, or you can be poised to type in a new paragraph.

2. Press Ctrl+N the Indent shortcut.

N-dent, N-dent. Say it over and over. It kinda works. (You also can click the Indent tool.)

3. Type your paragraph if you haven't already.

If the paragraph is blocked, it will be indented to the next tab stop.

✔ Ctrl+N is the *Nest* key (okay, not *N-dent*). It works like the Tab key but indents the entire paragraph's left margin to the same tab stop.

✔ To return the original margin, Press Ctrl+M or, heck, Ctrl+Z the Undo command (which is why it's there). You also can click the Unindent tool.

✔ To indent the paragraph to the next tab stop, press Ctrl+N again.

✔ Although the Ctrl+N and Ctrl+M shortcuts aren't mnemonic, they are right beside each other on the keyboard. So, when you get used to using them, they're easy to remember.

✔ To indent both the right and left sides of a paragraph, refer to the following section, "Double-Indenting a Paragraph." Also check out "Making a Hanging Indent" later in this chapter.

✔ If you're in a fair mood, refer to the section "The Tab Stops Here" for information on setting tab stops.

Double-Indenting a Paragraph

Sometimes an indent on the left just isn't enough. There are those days when you need to suck a paragraph in twice: once on the left and once on the right. For example, when you lift a quote from another paper but don't want to be accused of plagiarism. I do this to Abe Lincoln all the time. When I quote his stuff, I follow these steps:

1. Move the toothpick cursor to the start of the paragraph.

If the paragraph hasn't been written yet, then move the cursor to where you want to write the new text.

2. Select the Format→Paragraph command.

The Paragraph dialog box appears. In the upper-left region, you see the Indentation area. It contains three items, From Left, From Right, and First Line.

3. Enter the amount of left and right indent.

Click in the From Left box. Type in a value, such as **.5** to indent the paragraph ½-inch. Then click in the From Right box (or press the Tab key once) and type in **.5** again. This indents your paragraph half an inch from the left and right.

4. **Click OK or press Enter.**

5. **Type your paragraph if you haven't already.**

> ✔ The Paragraph dialog box is given a shave and a haircut at the end of this chapter. (See the technical sidebar at the end of this chapter.)

> ✔ When you modify a paragraph in the Paragraph dialog box, notice the Sample in the lower-right corner. Your paragraph's format is shown in dark lines on the sample page.

> ✔ To indent only the left side of a paragraph, refer to the previous section, "Indenting a Paragraph."

Making a Hanging Indent

A hanging indent has committed no felonious crime. Instead, it's a paragraph where the first line sticks out to the left and the rest of the paragraph is indented. To create such a beast, follow these steps:

1. **Move the toothpick cursor into the paragraph you want to hang and indent.**

   Or, you can position the cursor to where you want to type a new, hanging indent paragraph.

2. **Press Ctrl+T, the Hanging Indent shortcut.**

   You can remember Ctrl+T because the English always hang felons just before Tea Time.

   The Ctrl+T in WinWord moves the paragraph over to the first tab stop but keeps the first line in place.

3. **Ta-da! You have a hanging indented paragraph.**

> ✔ If you want to indent the paragraph even more, press the Ctrl+T key more than once.

> ✔ See the section "Indenting a Paragraph" earlier in this chapter for more information on indenting paragraphs.

> ✔ If you want to undo a hanging indent, press the Ctrl+G, Unhang key, and your paragraph's neck will be put back in shape.

> ✔ Hanging indents depend on the placement of tab stops. See "The Tab Stops Here" later in this chapter for help on tabs.

Paragraph formatting survival guide

The table contains all the paragraph formatting commands you can summon by holding down the Ctrl key and pressing a letter or number. By no means should you memorize this.

Ctrl+ key	Does this:	Ctrl+ key	Does this:
E	Center Paragraph	R	Right Align (flush right)
G	Unhang Indent	T	Hanging Indent
J	Full Justify Paragraph	1	Single space Lines
L	Left Align (flush left)	2	Double space Lines
M	Unindent (or unnest)	5	1.5 space Lines
N	Indent (or nest)		

The Tab Stops Here

When you press the Tab key, indent a paragraph, or make a hanging indent, WinWord moves the cursor or text over to the next *tab stop*. Normally, the tab stops are set every half inch. You can change this to any interval or customize the tab stops if you like. Use these steps:

1. **Position the toothpick cursor to a place in the document before where you want to change the tabs.**

   If you want to change the tab stops in more than one paragraph, mark the paragraphs that you want to change. Refer to Chapter 6 for block-marking instructions.

2. **Click the mouse on the ruler where you want a new tab stop.**

   The mouse pointer changes into an arrow shape when it's not hovering over text. Point that pointer at the spot on the ruler where you want your new tab stop to appear.

   After clicking the mouse button, a little arrow with a curved step appears and marks the tab stop location.

3. **Modify or fine-tune the tab position by dragging the tab indicator to the left or right.**

   You also can drag the little upside-down T tabs to move them if you like.

✔ Clicking on the ruler is something that must be done just so. You need to click a little below the ruler's center line, below the numbers and tick marks. If you don't get it just right, you can drag the little arrow to the left or right to a new position. If you decide that you don't want the tab after all, you can drag the tab arrow off of the ruler altogether.

✔ When I'm working with a lot of tabs, I usually press the Tab key only once between each column of information. Then I select all of the paragraphs and drag the tab indicators around so that each of my columns align. Using one tab instead of two or three is a lot easier to edit. And, it lets me do fancy stuff like sorting and math. You will learn about this neat-o stuff in Chapter 12.

Meddlesome nonsense about tab types

WinWord uses four different types of tabs, as seen by the four different buttons on the ribbon. The one selected looks depressed and is the type of tab WinWord sticks on the ruler. You can select a left, right, center, or decimal tab by first selecting the tab type from the ribbon and then following the preceding steps. Here is what each type does:

The most common tab is the left tab. This works like the tab key on a typewriter: Press Tab and the new text appears at the next tab stop. No mental hang-ups here.

The right tab causes text to line up right-justified at that tab stop. This gives you leeway to do some fancy paragraph justification on a single line, which you can read about in Chapter 21 on fancy document titles.

The center tab centers text on the tab stop. Good for one-word columns.

The decimal tab aligns numbers by their decimals. The number is right-justified before you press the period key then left-justified on the decimal.

The Fearless Leader Tab

The leader tab is interesting but not required for most writing. It produces a row of dots when you press Tab. You see this all the time in indexes or a table of contents. WinWord gives you the choice of three different leaders:

Fearless dot leader tabs 109
Zipper line leader tabs – – – – – – – – – – 109
U-Boat underline leader tabs _____ 109

To select among the different types of tabs, follow these steps:

1. Position the toothpick cursor on the line where you want to have your leader tabs.

For example, you're just starting your table of contents for this year's Christmas letter.

2. Set a tab stop.

This is important. Follow the steps outlined in the section "The Tab Stops Here" earlier in this chapter. Stick the tab where you want it. For example, put a tab under the 3 on the ruler, which sticks a tab just about in the middle of the page: Click under the 3 with the mouse. This puts a left tab stop in that position on the ruler.

3. Choose the Format→Tabs command.

You see the Tabs dialog box, as shown in Figure 10-1. Door number 3, `Leader`, is the one you need to focus on.

4. Select the style of fearless leader tab you want.

Click on the appropriate style, as presented at the start of this section, or press Alt+1 through Alt+4 to select that style using the keyboard.

5. Click on the OK button or press Enter.

6. Type the text to appear before the tab stop.

```
Little Jimmy's tree mulcher accident
```

7. Press the Tab key.

Zwoop! The toothpick cursor jumps to your tab stop and leaves a trail of, well, "stuff" in its wake. That's your dot leader (or dash leader or underline leader).

8. Type in the reference, page number, or whatever.

9. Press Enter to end that line.

✔ Setting the dot leader tabs doesn't work unless you manually stick in your own tab stops, as discussed in the section "The Tab Stops Here" earlier in this chapter.

✔ You can adjust the tab stops after setting them if some of the text doesn't line up.

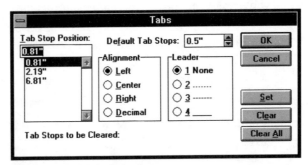

Figure 10-1: The Tabs dialog box.

Doing it the hard way — taking a Yellow Line bus tour of the Paragraph dialog box

It's possible to get all your paragraph formatting done in one place, just as I'm sure the Lord Almighty has this one control panel from which He directs the universe. And like that control panel, the Paragraph dialog box is a complex and dangerous place in which to loiter. The figure below shows you what it looks like.

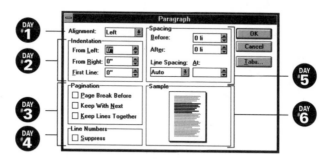

To summon the Paragraph dialog box, choose Format→Paragraph. Most of the stuff that happens here is detailed earlier in this chapter, along with some quick shortcut keys that make avoiding this dialog box a must. Still, I'd be sent to WinWord prison and laughed at during the next WinWord Book Authors' convention if I didn't take you on the whirlwind bus tour of this dialog box. Here is your daily itinerary:

Day #1   Alignment   You can apply any of the following alignments to selected text or to the paragraph where the cursor is currently located: Left; Center; Right; Justified. Each of these alignments is discussed previously in this chapter.

Day #2   Indentation   This is where you can enter the formatting for nested paragraphs and hanging indents. From Left indicates how far from the left margin your paragraph will be in inches. From Right is the same thing but from the right margin. The First Line box tells WinWord how far in (or out) to stick the first line. You can type values into the boxes or use the tiny up or down triangles to "spin the wheels."

Day #3   Pagination   These are pretty sophisticated commands that tell WinWord where it is allowed to start a new page. Page Break Before tells WinWord to start a new page before this paragraph. Keep With Next tells WinWord that it can't start a new page just yet, while Keep Lines Together tells WinWord not to start a new page in the middle of the paragraph.

Day #4   Line Numbers   The bus broke down and we all missed this stop, which is fortunate because another computer group stopped here just yesterday and all the readers got dysentery.

Day #5   Spacing   Hmmm, you hum, "Okay, I press Enter at the end of a *paragraph*. But how can I put extra space between paragraphs?" Here is the place. Before and After allow you to stick extra lines before or after your paragraphs. If you type **.5** into Before, then WinWord puts an extra half line before each paragraph — same thing for After. The Line Spacing box controls the line spacing for a paragraph; type in the proper spacing value into the box or use the up or down triangles to wheel through the values.

Day #6   Sample   The Sample window shows you how your paragraph will look when you click the OK button; your text changes are shown as black lines and current text is shown in gray.

Chapter 11

Formatting Pages and Documents

- -

In This Chapter

▶ Starting a new page — a *hard page break*

▶ Taking a break — a *section break*

▶ Adjusting the margins

▶ Setting the page size

▶ Centering a page, top to bottom

▶ Choosing where to stick the page number

▶ Adding a header or footer

▶ Editing a header or footer

▶ Using footnotes

- -

At last, the formatting three-ring circus has come to this. Formatting pages and documents isn't as common as formatting characters or even formatting paragraphs. This is major league stuff that affects your entire document, and it can really be handy: headers and footers, page numbers — even footnotes. This is the stuff of which professional-looking documents are made. This chapter explains it all so carefully that even we amateurs fool them, too.

Starting a New Page — a Hard Page Break

There are two ways to start a new page in WinWord:

1. **Keep pressing the Enter key until you see the row-o'-dots, denoting the start of a new page.**

   Needless to say, this is tacky and wrong.

2. Press Ctrl+Enter, the hard page break key combination.

Ctrl+Enter inserts a tighter row of dots, also denoting the start of a new page. This is the preferred way to start a new page.

This is a WinWord hard page break:

....

- ✔ The hard page break works just like a regular page break, although you control where it is in your document: Move the toothpick cursor to where you want the hard page and press Ctrl+Enter.

- ✔ Pressing Ctrl+Enter inserts a hard page break *character* in your document. That character stays there, always creating a hard page break no matter how much you edit the text on previous pages. The first approach doesn't take into account any editing you may do on the text.

- ✔ You can delete a hard page break with the Backspace or Delete keys. If you do this accidentally, just press Ctrl+Enter again, or you can use the Ctrl+Z keys to undelete.

Taking a Break — a Section Break

Books have chapters and parts to break up major plot lines. Formatting has something called a *section break* that serves the same function. WinWord uses all kinds of different breaks: page breaks, column breaks, section breaks, but not lunch breaks.

You can use a section break when you want to apply different formatting to several different parts of a document. You might want different margins to appear in different places, put in a banner headline, change numbers of columns, or whatever. You can accomplish this by inserting a section break. It's kinda like building an island — all types of weird formatting can live on it, isolated from the rest of the document.

To insert a section break, do this:

1. Position the toothpick cursor where you want the break to occur.

2. Choose the Insert→Break command.

The Break dialog box opens, as shown in Figure 11-1.

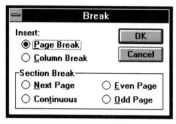

Figure 11-1: The Break dialog box.

3. Select your break.

Click on Next Page if you want the new section to start on a fresh page. Select Continuous if you want the break to happen wherever you happen to be. You use Next Page, for example, to center text on a title page. (See "Centering a page, top to bottom" later in this chapter.) Continuous is used for all other circumstances.

4. Select OK.

A double line of dots appears on-screen. You have your section break and new formatting can begin:

This is a WinWord section break:

....
....

✔ Section breaks also provide a great way to divide a multi-part document. For example, the title page can be a section; the introduction, Chapter 1, Appendix A all can be made into sections. You can then use WinWord's Go To command to zoom to each section. Refer to Chapter 2 for more information on the Go To command.

✔ You can delete a section break with the Backspace or Delete keys. If you do this accidentally, you will lose any special formatting that you applied to the section. Press the Undo command, Ctrl+Z, before you do anything else.

✔ You can use the Break dialog box to insert a Page Break, but Ctrl+Enter is much quicker; refer to the previous section.

Adjusting the Margins

Every page has margins. This is the "air" around your document, that inch of breathing space that sets off the text from the rest of the page. WinWord automatically sets your margins at one inch in from the right, left, top, and bottom of the page. This is how most English teachers and book editors want things, because they love to scribble in margins. But you can adjust the margins to suit any fussy professional.

You have two basic choices when setting margins: from here on and change it all (from the beginning to the end).

To change the margins, follow these steps:

1. **If you want to change "from here on," move the toothpick cursor to the place in your text where you want the new margins to start.**

   It's best to set the new margins at the top of the document, top of a page, or start of a paragraph. If, on the other hand, you want to change it all, it doesn't matter where you place the cursor.

2. **Choose the Format→Page Setup command.**

   The Page Setup dialog box appears, as shown in Figure 11-2.

3. **Enter the new measurements for the margins by typing in new values into the appropriate boxes.**

   For example, a value of 1" in all boxes sets all margins to one inch. A value of 2.5" sets a 2-inch margin. There's no need to type the inch symbol (").

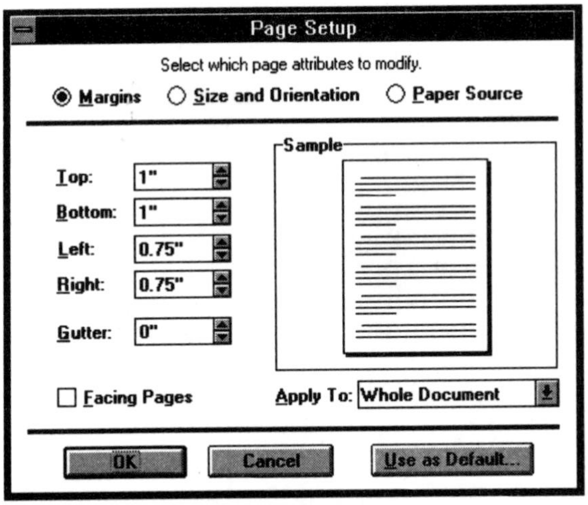

Figure 11-2: The Page Setup dialog box.

4. Select Whole Document or This Point Forward from the Apply To drop-down list.

Whole Document applies the new margins to your document. This Point Forward applies new margins from the toothpick cursor's position to the last jot or tittle you typed.

5. Select OK.

Your new margins appear.

- ✔ Yo! Check it out! You have visual feedback on-screen regarding your new margin settings. The Sample window gives you a view of what the document will look like when the changes are finally made.

- ✔ If you don't want to change one or the other margin, don't change its value or just Tab over it. This tells WinWord to continue using the present margin settings.

- ✔ What's in the Gutter? The Gutter box applies more to documents printed on two pages and intended to be bound in a book-like format. It's a *bonus margin* that appears on the left side of right-facing pages and vice-versa. No need to put your mind in the gutter.

- ✔ If you want to change the margins to a different value later and leave the current settings in place for the first part of your document, move to the place where you want new margins in your document. Start at Step 1 above and select This Point Forward from the Apply To drop-down list. A single document can have several margin changes, just as a single driver on the freeway will have several lane changes.

- ✔ Laser printers cannot print on the outside half inch of a piece of paper — top, bottom, left, and right. This is an absolute margin; although you can tell WinWord to set a margin of 0 inches right and 0 inches left, text will still not print there. Instead, select .5 inches minimum for the left and right margins.

- ✔ If you want to print on three-hole paper, set the left margin to 2 or 2.5 inches. This allows enough room for the little holes, and it offsets the text nicely when you open up something in a three-ring notebook or binder.

- ✔ If your homework comes out to three pages and the teacher wants four, bring in the margins. Set the left and right margins to 1.5 inches each. Then change the line spacing to 1.5. Refer to the section "Changing the Line Spacing" in Chapter 10. (You also can select a larger font; check Chapter 9, the section "Text Size Effects.")

Setting the Page Size

Most printing takes place on a standard, 8½-by-11 inch sheet of paper. But WinWord lets you change the paper size to anything you want — from an envelope to some weird-sized sheet of paper. The following describes how you change the paper size to the legal 8½-by-14 inch sheet of paper:

1. **Position the toothpick cursor at the top of your document or at the top of a page where you want to start using the new paper size.**

2. **Select the Format→Page Setup command.**

   The Page Setup dialog box appears (refer to Figure 11-2).

3. **Select Size and Orientation.**

   It's a radio button at the top of the Page Setup dialog. Click on that radio button or hold down the Alt key and press the S key.

4. **Click on the Paper Size drop-down list.**

   It drops down.

5. **Select Legal.**

   It's legal.

6. **Select Whole Document or This Point Forward from the Apply To drop-down list.**

   Well, which do you want?

7. **Select OK.**

   Okay. Type away on the new size of paper.

   > ✔ Keep an eye on the Sample window in the Page Setup dialog box. It changes to reflect the new paper size.

   > ✔ The following section tells you how to print sideways on a sheet of paper. This really fools the relatives into thinking you're a word processing genius.

   > ✔ If you're printing an odd-sized piece of paper, remember to load it into your printer before you start printing.

   > ✔ Refer to Chapter 8 for information on printing envelopes. (There's a special command for doing that; no sense in finagling a new paper size here.)

Landscape and Portrait

WinWord usually prints up and down on a piece of paper — which is how we're all used to reading a page. However, WinWord also can print sideways. In this case, the page's *orientation* is changed; instead of up-down, the paper is printed sideways. The technical "I'm an important word processing expert" terms for the two orientations are *Portrait mode* for the up-down paper and *Landscape mode* for sideways. A portrait picture is usually taller than it is long to accommodate our faces. Landscape is for those lovely oil paintings of seascapes or lakes and trees that are wider than they are tall.

To make WinWord print the long ways on a sheet of paper — the landscape mode — do the following:

1. **Choose Format→Page Setup.**

   The Page Setup dialog box appears.

2. **Click on the Size and Orientation button at the top-center of the box.**

   The dialog box changes slightly. In the lower-left corner you'll see the Orientation area.

3. **Choose Portrait or Landscape.**

   The Sample document and the tiny icon in the Orientation area change to reflect your perspective.

4. **Click OK.**

Avoid printing standard documents in Landscape mode. Scientists and other people in white lab coats who study such things have determined that human reading speed slows drastically when people must scan a long line of text. Reserve Landscape mode for printing lists and items for which normal paper is too narrow.

Centering a page, top to bottom

Nothing makes a title nice and crisp like having it sit squat in the middle of a page. That's top-to-bottom middle, as opposed to left-right middle. To achieve this feat, follow these steps:

1. **Move the toothpick cursor to the top of the page containing the text that you want centered between the bottom and the top of the page.**

   The text should be on a page by itself — actually a section by itself. If the page you want centered isn't the first page of the document, press Alt,I,B,N,Enter. This inserts the Section/Page Break and you see a double line on-screen (the section separator). That marks a new page, the page you want to center.

2. **Type the text you want centered top to bottom.**

   Refer to Chapter 9 for more information on formatting characters, making text big and fancy, or whatnot for your title or whatever text you want centered. If you also want the lines centered from left to right, refer to Chapter 10 for information on centering a line.

3. Create a new section break.

You need to mark the end of the page you want centered with a section break. Press Alt,I,B,N,Enter. This inserts a *next page* section break — a double line of dots that marks a new page and a new section.

4. Choose the Format→Section Layout command.

The Section Layout dialog box appears. You should focus your laser beams on the lower-left corner, in the area roped in and named Vertical Alignment.

5. Choose Center.

6. Click on OK.

> ✔ In Normal View, there is no visual feedback that you've centered a page on-screen. Choose the View→Page Layout command to get a sneak-peak at the centered page. Choose View→Normal to return to Normal View.

> ✔ All text on the page will be centered top to bottom with the Center Page command. It's a good idea to keep as little text on the page as possible — a title, description, and so forth.

> ✔ Refer to the section titled "Taking a Break — a Section Break" earlier in this chapter for more information on section breaks.

Where to Stick the Page Number

If your document is more than a page long, you should put pages numbers on it. WinWord can do this for you automatically, so stop putting those forced page numbers in your document, and follow these steps:

1. Choose the Insert→Page Numbers command.

The Page Numbers dialog box, shown in Figure 11-3, appears.

2. Where doest thou wantest thine page numbers?

Choose Top or Bottom and Left, Center, or Right Alignment from the dialog box to place your page number in one of those positions. For example, page numbers smartly appearing at the bottom center of every page would have the Bottom and Center buttons filled in with their inky blackness.

3. Choose OK.

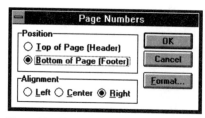

Figure 11-3: The Page Numbers dialog box.

The page numbers are inserted.

✔ You also can create page numbering by sticking the page number command into a header or footer. Refer to the sections "Adding a header or footer" later in this chapter. If you do end up putting the page number in a header or footer, you will not need to use the Page Number command.

✔ If you want to get fancier page numbers, click on the Format button in the Page Numbers dialog box. This opens the Page Number Format dialog box. From there, you can select various ways to display the page numbers from the Number Format drop-down list— even those cute little ii's and xx's.

✔ To start numbering your pages with a new page number, press Alt,I,U,F,Alt+S. Then enter the new page number and press Enter twice. This is something you may want to do for the second, third, or later chapters in a book. By setting a new page number, the page numbers in all chapters will be continuous.

Adding a header or footer

A header is not a quickly poured beer. Instead, it's text running along the top of every page in your document. For example, the top of each page in this book has the section name and chapter name. Those are *headers*. You can stick headers on your work, complete with a title, your name, date, page number, dirty limericks — you name it.

The *footer* is text that appears on the bottom of every page. A great footer is "Turn the page, dummy," although better uses of footers include holding page numbers, listing a chapter or document title, or what have you. The footer is created by using exactly the same steps used to create a header.

To add a header or footer, follow these steps:

1. Choose the View→Header/Footer command.

The Header/Footer dialog box opens, as shown in Figure 11-4.

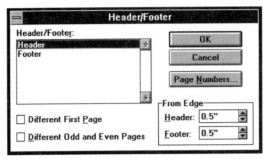

Figure 11-4: The Header/Footer dialog box.

2. **To apply a header or footer to your entire document, select Header or Footer and click OK.**

   The window shown in Figure 11-5 opens so you can enter the header or footer text. You see Header or Footer in the window depending on which you selected from the Header/Footer dialog box.

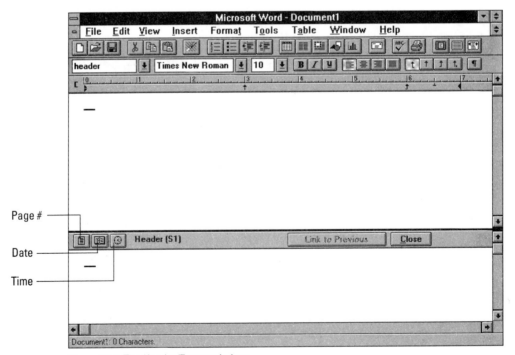

Figure 11-5: The Header/Footer window.

3. Enter your header or footer text.

The text can be formatted just as if it were a separate document.

4. Click on the Close button when you are done.

You're back in your document. The header and footer are there, but you can't see them until you print or choose the File→Print Preview command (refer to Chapter 8).

✔ A header is a section-long thing. You can change parts of a header, such as a chapter name or number, from section to section, without changing other parts of the header, like the page number. Refer to the section "Taking a Break — a Section Break" earlier in this chapter for more information on sections.

✔ You can put anything in a header or footer that you could put in a document, including graphics. This is especially useful if you want a logo to appear on each page. Refer to Chapter 19 for a discussion of inserting graphics.

✔ If you want to insert the page number in the header, put the cursor where you want it to appear and press the button on the header/footer bar that has the # on it. The number **1** appears in the header text, but it will be replaced by the current page number when the document is printed. Other buttons on the header/footer bar allow you to insert the current date and the time.

✔ You probably will want to put some text in front of the page number, because a number sitting all by itself tends to get lonely. You can get real creative and type in the word **Page** and a space before you hit the # button, or you can come up with some interesting text on your own.

✔ To see your header or footer displayed on-screen, choose View→Page Layout. Choose View →Normal to return to the normal way you look at WinWord.

✔ You can have two headers, odd and even, running on different pages — and the same thing with footers. Select the check box Different Odd and Even Pages in the Header/Footer dialog box (Alt,V,H,Alt+D). Then, you can select the odd or the even header or footer. Create an odd and an even header (or footer) in turn, according to the steps above and they will print differently on odd and even pages. Cool.

✔ To prevent the header or footer from appearing on the first page of text, which usually is your title page, select Different First Page from the Header/Footer dialog box, and leave it blank. This places an empty header on the first page; the header will appear on all the other pages as ordered. You also can use this option to place a different header on the first page — a graphic, for example. See Chapter 19 to learn about placing graphics in a document.

Editing a header or footer

To edit a header or footer you already created, follow these steps:

1. **Open the Header/Footer dialog box.**

   Choose View→Header/Footer, or press the Alt,V,H key combination.

2. **Select the header or footer that you want to edit.**

   Click on it to highlight.

3. **Select OK.**

   This opens the header or footer window.

4. **Make any changes or corrections.**

   Do this as you would edit any text on-screen.

5. **Choose Close when you're done.**

   ✔ Editing a header or footer changes the header for footer for your entire document. You don't have to move the cursor to the tippy top of your document before editing.

   ✔ You also can edit a header or footer directly in Page Layout View: Choose View→Page Layout. This command adjusts the way WinWord displays your document and allows you to view the headers and footers just as you would the rest of the text. To edit a header or footer, place the toothpick cursor in the header or footer and make any corrections.

    ✔ You also can get a fast page preview by clicking the Zoom Whole Page tool. To return to regular size, click the Zoom 100 Percent or Zoom Page Width tools right next door.

Using Footnotes

Some folks seem to think that footnotes are pretty advanced stuff. Pooh! A lot of people need them in their documents. I mean, academics use them all the time and look how many people consider them "experts."

Instead of creating footnotes obtusely, follow these handy steps:

1. **Position the toothpick cursor in your document where you want the footnote to be referenced.**

   This is the spot that will display the tiny number and refer to the footnote. For example[1].

---

[1] Made you look!

2. Choose the Insert→Footnote command.

You see the footnote dialog box. It's kind of boring, so I'm not putting a figure of it in this book.

If this will be the first footnote for a document, you need to decide where you want your footnotes placed. Choose Options from the Footnote dialog box, and you see the Footnote Options dialog box (and I'm not showing it either). Select where you want the footnotes to appear: on the bottom of the page where the footnote is referenced; beneath the text that contains the reference; at the end of the current section; or at the end of the document. After this selection is made, you don't need to open this dialog again, unless you change your mind. Click OK.

3. If you want WinWord to number footnotes for you, and who wouldn't, leave Auto-Numbered Footnote selected, and click OK.

This opens, finally, the Footnotes window on the bottom of the page.

4. Type your footnote.

You can place anything in a footnote that you can place in a document — charts, graphs, pictures, even text.

5. Choose Close, and you have done it.

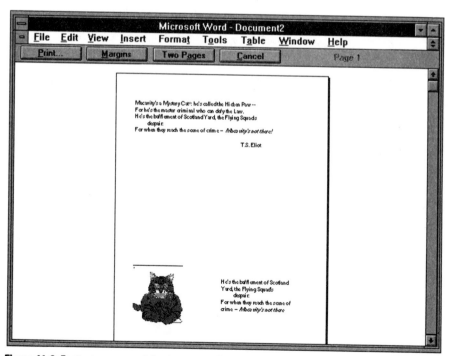

Figure 11-6: Footnotes can contain charts, graphs, pictures, even text.

Figure 11-6 shows what a footnote depicting T.S. Eliot's *Macavity* might look like. It uses very fancy graphics and other cool stuff to show you that footnotes such as "7. Ibid." are very passé and that academics should be weeping bitterly over the fancy stuff we mere mortals can do.

- ✔ To delete a footnote, highlight the footnote's number in your document and press the Delete key. WinWord magically re-numbers any remaining footnotes for you.

- ✔ To view or edit footnotes, choose <u>V</u>iew→<u>F</u>ootnotes.

- ✔ To quick-edit a footnote, double-click on footnote number on page. The footnote text edit area opens.

- ✔ Information on inserting jellical cats into your document can be found in Chapter 19, which tells you almost all you care to know about graphics.

Chapter 12

Using Tables and Columns

*Y*ou can spice up your text with bold and italics and maybe even some large characters when your document doesn't run as long as you like. Paragraph formatting and page formatting add garlic to your document salad — just a touch, not enough to open your mouth, say "Hi," and watch flowers wilt, grown men cry, and women faint. What more can you do? Well, if you're really the daring type, you can pump up your document with fancy tables and formatting that's just one Cicero beneath the official realm of Desktop Publishing. Oh, we've come a long way from the days of word processing with moveable type.

Cobbling Tables Together

A table is this thing with four legs on which you set things — but not your elbows when Grandma is watching. In WinWord, a *table* is a list of items with several rows all lined up in neat little columns. In the primitive days, you'd make this happen by using the Tab key and your handy frustration tool. Face it, making things align can be maddening. Even in a word processor. Even if you think you know what you're doing.

Coming to your rescue, of course, is WinWord. "It's Table Man, Ma, and he's here to rescue us!" WinWord has an able Table command. It lets you create this prison-like grid of rows and columns. Into each cubby hole or *cell* you can type information, or store society's miscreants, and everything will be aligned nice and neat and suitable for framing. The printed result looks very impressive, and if you do things right, your table will even be sturdy enough to eat off.

Creating the table

To create a table in your document, follow these steps:

1. **Place the toothpick cursor on the spot in the text where you want the table.**

   The table will be created and inserted into your text — like pasting in a block — a *cell block*. You fill in the table *after* it's created.

2. **Choose the Table→Insert Table command.**

   Yes, WinWord has it's own Table menu. How handy. Choosing the Insert Table command from that menu opens the Insert Table dialog box, as seen in Figure 12-1.

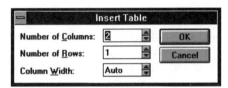

Figure 12-1: The Insert Table dialog box.

3. **Enter the number of columns into the first box.**

   For example, enter **3**. You'll have three columns going across.

4. **Press the Tab key.**

   The cursor moves to the next line.

5. **Enter the number of rows into the second box.**

   For example, enter **5**. There will be five rows, marching down.

   Three columns? Five rows? Who knows? Accuracy isn't a big issue at this stage; you can change your table after it's created if you goof up. (I do this all the time.)

6. **Press Enter to leave the Insert Table mini-dialog boxlette.**

   Welcome to prison! After you tell WinWord how many rows and columns to make, it builds you a table and shows it to you on-screen (see Figure 12-2). It looks like a spreadsheet, smells like a spreadsheet, and if I weren't afraid of electrocuting myself, I'd tell you whether it tastes like a spreadsheet. You're still in WinWord, however.

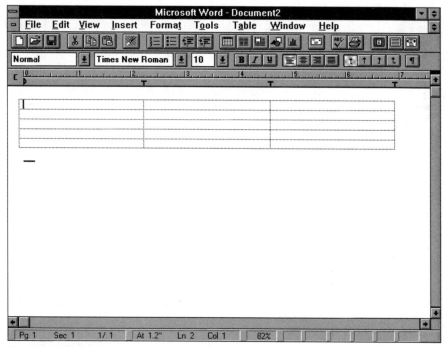

Figure 12-2: A table is born.

7. Fill in the table.

✔ Use crayons on your screen or, better still, refer to the next section.

✔ If you can't see your table, choose Table→Gridlines to display the cell borders.

✔ You also can build a table from the toolbar. If you click on the Table tool, a little tiny baby table drops down. Click and drag the mouse through this table to select the number of rows and columns you want. The table expands as you drag past its borders. When you re-lease the mouse button, the table appears in your document. Clicking the Table tool again lets you insert more cells.

✔ Dogs certainly are the highest form of life on this planet. The other day I was watching my dog and he had the most serious look on his face. He didn't even blink. Then, after observing him for about a minute longer, he opened his mouth and a bee flew out. Dogs must know something we don't.

- ✔ Use a table in your document anytime that you have information that needs to be organized into rows and columns. This works much better than using the Tab key because adjusting the table's rows and columns is easier than fussing with tab stops.

- ✔ Be sure that at least one line of text, or a blank line if the table starts off a new section, is in front of any table. This gives you a place to put the cursor if you ever want to put stuff before the table in your document.

- ✔ You can always add or delete columns and rows to your table after it's created. Refer to the following section.

- ✔ The table may have an ugly lined border around it and between the cells. You can change this, as covered in the later section "Changing the Table."

- ✔ Alas, WinWord does not have a handy Chair command.

Putting stuff in the table

An empty table sits in your document. But before you break out the MinWax and clean it up, why not set the table?

The table is divided into rows and columns. Where they meet is called a *cell* — just like they have in prison, but without the TV and metal toilet. Your job is to fill in the various cells with text, graphics, or whatever. Here are some pointers:

- ✔ Use the Tab key to move from cell to cell. Pressing the Enter key just puts a new paragraph of text into the same cell. (Each cell is like its own little document.)

- ✔ The Shift+Tab combination moves backwards between the cells.

- ✔ If you press the Tab key in the last bottom-right cell, a new row of cells will be added.

- ✔ You can use the cursor keys to move from cell to cell as well (how swell). But if there is text in the cell, the cursor keys will make the toothpick cursor dawdle through the words. After all, you can still use the cursor keys to edit text in the cells. (It's best to use the Tab key to move from cell to cell.)

- ✔ Text formatting commands also work in the cells. You can bold, underline, italicize, center, flush left, and so on. Refer to Chapters 9 and 10 for the details. The formatting affects the text in only one cell at a time — or in the cells you collectively mark as a block.

- ✔ You can apply styles to text in a table. Refer to Chapter 13 for the details.

✔ To format a row or column all at once, you need to select it first.

✔ To utterly remove the table from your document, highlight the whole darn thing as a block, then choose Table→Delete Rows. The table is blown to smithereens.

✔ To erase a cell's contents in a table, mark it as a block and press the Delete key.

Changing the table

Suppose that you create a card table but really need a dining room table — or one of those long dual-time-zone tables rich people eat at — or, because you are participating in a back to nature movement, no table at all. Everything can be changed and adjusted after the table has been created.

Adding and deleting rows and columns

To add rows to your table, follow these steps:

1. Highlight the row below the spot where you want the new row.

Move the cursor into the row and choose Table→Select Row.

2. Choose the Table→Insert Rows command.

Thud! The Government of the People's Democratic Republic of WinWord is proud to add a brand-new story to the existing Worker's Apartment Complex.

3. Repeat Steps 1 and 2 to add as many rows as you want.

If you used the Table tool to create your table, click the Table tool again, and choose Insert Entire Row from the Insert Cells dialog box.

To delete rows from your table, follow these steps:

1. Highlight the row that you want to delete.

Move the cursor into the row and choose Table→Select Row.

2. Choose the Table→Delete Rows command.

3. Repeat Steps 1 and 2 to blast away as many rows as you want.

You also can select rows by moving the mouse cursor into the left margin until it changes its shape to a nor'easterly-arrow. Point the arrow at the row and click the mouse button. You can select multiple rows by dragging the mouse up or down.

To add columns to your table, follow these steps:

1. **Highlight the column to the left of the spot where you want the new one to be added.**

   Move the cursor into the column and choose T<u>a</u>ble→Select <u>C</u>olumn.

2. **Choose the T<u>a</u>ble→<u>I</u>nsert Columns command.**

3. **Repeat Steps 1 and 2 to add as many columns as you want.**

 If you used the Table tool to create your table, click the Table tool again, and choose Insert Entire <u>C</u>olumn from the Insert Cells dialog box.

To delete columns from your table, follow these steps:

1. **Highlight the column that you want to delete.**

   Move the toothpick cursor to that column and pluck out T<u>a</u>ble→Select <u>C</u>olumn.

2. **Choose the T<u>a</u>ble→<u>D</u>elete Columns command.**

3. **Repeat Steps 1 and 2 to blast away as many columns as you want.**

- ✔ You also can select columns by moving the mouse cursor above the column until it changes shape into a down-pointing arrow. Point the arrow at the row and click the left mouse button. You can select multiple columns by dragging the mouse across them.

- ✔ New rows are inserted *above* the current row in a table, which is the highlighted row or the one the toothpick cursor is in.

- ✔ New columns are inserted *to the left* of the current column in a table.

Adjusting the column width

Columns, like my waistline, tend to get fatter, and, unlike my waistline, thinner, too. Fortunately, changing the width of a column in WinWord is a heck of a lot easier than going on a diet.

To adjust the width of a column, follow these steps:

1. **Put the toothpick cursor anywhere in the column that you want to change.**

   Anywhere.

2. **Choose the T<u>a</u>ble→Column <u>W</u>idth command.**

   This opens the cute little box, shown in Figure 12-3, the Column Width dialog box.

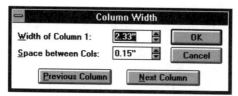

Figure 12-3: The Column Width dialog box.

3. Enter the new width measurement for the column.

The width is measured in inches. So if you want a thinner column, enter a smaller number than the one already in the box. Larger numbers make the columns wider — but keep in mind that a fat table — a gross concept unto itself — will probably not fit all on the page.

4. If you want to change the following or preceding column as well, press the Next Column or Previous Column button.

5. Click OK when you're done.

✔ If you want to make several, or all, of the columns the same width, select them before you open the Column Width dialog box. Any changes you make will apply to all the selected columns.

✔ It's easier to change the width of columns by using the mouse — lots easier because you can see what is going on (like being thin enough to see your feet, I am told). Place the mouse cursor on the border between columns, and it changes its shape into something that looks like a railroad track with arrows pointing east and west. Hold down the left mouse button and drag the column border to a new size.

✔ If you look up at the ruler when the toothpick cursor is in the table, you'll see some heavy black **Ts**. You can adjust the size of your table by dragging those **Ts** around with the mouse.

Doing the One, Two, Three, Four-Column March

Columns — especially those you can see right on your screen — are one of those features all the magazines, gurus, and other pseudo-pundits demanded for word processors. Do we need them? No. Can WinWord do them? Yes. Do you want to mess with this? Sure, why not? It will give you something to do while the electric chair recharges.

Before I divulge my WinWord column secrets, here's a healthy bit of advice: The best way to make columns is in a desktop publishing package, such as PageMaker for Windows. Those programs are designed for playing with text and making columns much easier than WinWord (although figuring out the instructions is like playing an eternal chess match with a guy who wears a size 12 hat). In WinWord, columns remain more of a curiosity than anything you or I want to spend more than 15 minutes of our time on.

To start columns in your document, follow the steps listed below. If your text has already been written, WinWord puts it all into column format. Otherwise, any new text you create will be placed into columns automagically.

1. **Move the toothpick cursor to where you want the columns to start.**

2. **Choose the Format→Columns command.**

   The Columns dialog box opens, as shown in Figure 12-4.

3. **Enter the number of columns you want.**

   Two columns is sufficient enough to impress anyone. More columns make your text skinnier and may be harder to read.

4. **If you want a pretty line between the columns of text, check the Line Between box.**

5. **If you want to start a new column right from where you are, check the Start New Column box.**

   This tells WinWord to put a column break in the document.

6. **Open the Apply To drop-down list and choose to apply the columns to the whole document or just to apply from now on.**

7. **Choose OK!**

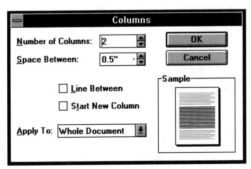

Figure 12-4: The Columns dialog box.

WinWord shows you your columns right there on-screen. That's at least $15 out of the purchase price right there!

- ✔ You also can use the Columns tool. Click the tool, and a baby box of columns appears. Click and drag the mouse to indicate how many text columns you want. When you release the mouse button, the columns appear.

- ✔ The space between columns is called the *gutter*. Unless you have a bunch of columns, or a lot of space to fill, it is best to leave this at .5" — half an inch. This amount of white space is pleasing to the eye without being overly much of a good thing.

- ✔ Editing text in columns is a pain. The cursor seems to hop all over the place and take an eternity to move from one column to another. I'm just complaining here because there's nothing else to do.

- ✔ To get rid of columns, go back and change the number of columns to one. Neat, huh?

- ✔ Using the mouse to poke the cursor to a new spot on a column seems to work nicely.

- ✔ The three-column text format works nicely on landscape paper. This is how most brochures are created. Refer to Chapter 11 for information on selecting landscape paper.

- ✔ All the text and paragraph formatting mentioned in this part of the book also applies to text and paragraphs in columns. The difference is that your column margins — not the page margins — now mark the left and right sides of your text for paragraph formatting.

Chapter 13

Formatting with Style

- -

- -

*W*ant to stand out from the crowd? Then do what I do: Eat massive quantities of garlic. Nothing makes you stand alone like that. When word processing, however, garlic won't help much (unless you buy garlic paper — refer to a funky former-hippie neighborhood in your town for a shop that carries the stuff). Instead, you can stand out by using WinWord's Style command.

No matter how pretty your undies are, style — in WinWord anyway — is not what you wear or even how you wear it. A style is a series of formatting instructions — bold, "about so big," centered, sideways — that are named and stored for future use. Suppose that you have a series of paragraphs that you want indented in bold tiny type with a box drawn around each paragraph — oh, and an extra line placed at the end of each paragraph. You can create a style that slaps on all of these formats with a single keystroke. This may be advanced stuff, but it certainly can come in handy.

Using the Style Command

Styles bring together character and paragraph formatting under one roof — or in one dialog box, which is the case with WinWord. That one roof is found in the Format menu, the Style command. When you choose Format→Style, you see the Style dialog box, shown in Figure 13-1.

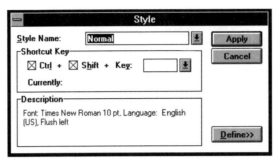

Figure 13-1: The Style dialog box.

Three items are worth noting in the Style dialog box: Style Name, Shortcut Key, and Description.

The Style Name is an easy-to-remember name assigned to a style. WinWord always starts with the Normal style, which is plain boring text on-screen. You can use the Style Name drop-down box to select a new style for your document.

The Shortcut Key area lets you assign a special quick-key option to apply a style. For example, you can click on the Ctrl and Shift boxes and then enter an N into the Key box to make Ctrl+Shift+N a shortcut key for the Normal style.

The Description is the technical mumbo jumbo about the style. For example, it may say bold or list tab stops or mention fonts and such in this area. No need to rest your weary eyes here for long.

✔ You can use WinWord without ever messing with styles. Only if you want to get truly fancy should you ever bother with this stuff.

✔ Styles are combinations of character and paragraph and other formatting, all saved under an easy-to-remember name.

✔ The Normal style is WinWord's standard style, the one that always appears when you open a new document. Yeah, it's pretty plain and ugly, but you can add your own styles to make your text fairly fancy if you like.

✔ To apply the various styles to your document, select the style name from the Style dialog box, or from the first drop-down box on the ribbon.

✔ The new style applies to the paragraph the toothpick cursor is in or any block you select on-screen.

✔ For more information on character formatting, refer to Chapter 9.

✔ Refer to Chapter 10 for the details on paragraph formatting.

✔ The standard styles WinWord provides for your new documents are Normal and heading 1, heading 2, and heading 3. The Normal style is Times New Roman text at 10 points (kinda small), plus no other fancy features. The heading styles are all blocky fonts that share equal unimagination with the Normal style.

Creating a new style

New styles are easy to create. Just follow these loosely outlined steps:

1. **Type a paragraph of text.**

   It doesn't have to be a whole paragraph; a single line will do. Just remember to press Enter at the end of the line, which makes WinWord believe you've typed an entire paragraph.

2. **Mark your paragraph as a block.**

3. **Select the character formatting you want for your style.**

   The character formatting will be applied to the block. Select a font. Select a point size to make the text big or little.

Run wildly through Chapter 9 for more information on character formatting, but here's an important word of advice: Stick to fonts and sizes; avoid bold, italics, or underline unless you want them applied to all of your text. (Styles are broad things; only individual words are given bold, underline, and similar character formats.)

4. **Select the paragraph formatting for your style.**

   With the block still highlighted, use the information presented in Chapter 10 to format the paragraph. Indent it, center it, or apply whatever formatting you want to apply to your style.

5. **Press Ctrl+S.**

   This activates the Style command. Actually, it highlights the Style drop-down box on the ribbon — the one that normally says Normal.

6. **Type in a name for your style.**

   A brief, descriptive one-word title will do nicely. For example, if you create an indented paragraph that you want to use to list things, name the style List. Or if you created a special musical style, name it Liszt.

7. Press Enter.

The style is added to WinWord's repertoire of styles for your document.

✔ To use the style — to *apply* it to other paragraphs in your document — refer to the following section, "Using a style."

✔ You can create a shortcut key for your style by choosing Format→Style. In the Style dialog box, type in a shortcut key into the Shortcut Key box — L for List for example. Click on the Apply button to use the shortcut key and apply the style to text in your document.

✔ Give your style a name that is descriptive of the style's function. Names like Indented List or Table Body Text are great, because it is easy to remember what they do. Names like Orville or Jean are somewhat less desirable.

✔ The styles you create are only available to the document in which they're created.

✔ If you create scads of styles you love and want to use them for several documents, then you need to create what's called a *template*. This is covered later in this chapter, in the section "Creating a Document Template to Store Your Styles."

✔ You also can create a style by using the Style dialog box. Choose Format→Style. Click on the Define button at the bottom of the box and additional buttons appear. You can use the Character button to affect character formatting, Paragraph to control paragraph formatting, or any of the other buttons to change the definition of your style. This is advanced stuff but not difficult to do once you know how to work WinWord's various text formatting dialog boxes.

Using a style

You don't *use* a style as much as you *apply* it. The character and paragraph formatting carefully stored inside the style is applied to text on-screen, text in a block, or text you're about to write. Using a style is easy:

1. Know what you're applying the style to.

If it's a paragraph already on-screen, then just stick the toothpick cursor somewhere in that paragraph. Otherwise, the style will be applied to any text you formatted.

2. Select a style from the ribbon.

Click on the down-arrow button beside the first drop-down list — the Normal list. Select your style from that list. From the keyboard, press Ctrl+S and then the down-arrow key to see the styles. Highlight a style name and click on it with the mouse, or press the Enter key. You also can type the style name directly into the box if you can spell.

- ✔ Applying a style is a paragraph-level thing. You can't put a style on just a single word in a paragraph; the style will take over the whole paragraph instead.

- ✔ To apply a style to your entire document, press Ctrl+5 (the 5 key on the numeric keypad) to select your entire document. (You also can choose Edit→Select All.) Then choose the style you want for *everything*.

- ✔ Refer to the previous section, "Creating a new style," for information on creating your own special styles for a document.

- ✔ Sometimes you can develop a style so sophisticated that it won't show on your monitor. If you exceed the capabilities of your printer or graphics card, you may see some strange stuff. Just don't think it's the '60s all over again.

Changing the style

Styles change. Bell bottoms were once the rage, but now they are only "in" at costume parties or reruns of *The Mod Squad*. Times New Roman — the bane of the *Normal* style — is a wonderful font . . . if you're into bow ties and think merengue is a salted tequila drink or an ex-Nazi who lived in Brazil. Still, Times New Roman is a work horse that is used by everyone for almost everything. Maybe you want to put it out to pasture and use a different font in your Normal style. If so, you can change it.

Here are the instructions for changing a style — any style, not just the Normal style. (In fact, I don't recommend you mess with the Normal style.)

1. **Choose the Format→Style command.**

   The Style dialog box opens.

2. **Select a style to change from the Style Name drop-down list.**

3. **Click on the Define button.**

   The Style box expands a bit to reveal a hoard of buttons on the bottom (see Figure 13-2). Each button allows you to modify a specific aspect of the style: Character to change character attributes, Paragraph to change paragraph formatting, and so on.

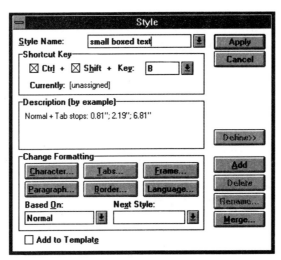

Figure 13-2: The Style box transmogrifies when you click on the Define button.

4. Click on the appropriate button to change part of the style.

For example, select the Character button to open the Character formatting dialog box. There, you can change the font, size, or any of the other things controlled in the Character formatting box (covered near the end of Chapter 9). Other buttons in the Style dialog box control and allow you to change other formatting aspects.

5. Choose OK.

This closes whichever dialog you opened to modify some aspect of a style. For example, if you opened the Character dialog box, clicking on its OK button closes that box and returns you to the Style dialog box.

6. Repeat Steps 4 and 5 as necessary to change the style.

7. When you're finished, click on the Change button in the Style dialog box.

An information box will open and ask you whether this is really what you want to do.

8. Answer Yes.

✔ Changing styles is advanced stuff — not recommended for the timid. It's entirely possible to use WinWord without bothering with styles at all, which is the way most people use the program.

✔ Changing a style means that all paragraphs in your document that have that style will be changed. This is a great way to change a font throughout a document without having to select everything and manually pick out a new font.

✔ If you change a style for the worse, don't worry. Open a new file and leave that messy style behind.

Creating a Document Template to Store Your Styles

To store a bunch of styles so that you can use them over and over, you create a *document template*. Actually, it's a special type of document called a *template*. In the template, you can store all the styles you created, which allows you to use them again for other documents.

You create a document template like you do any new document. Start by creating a new document in WinWord:

1. **Choose the File→New command.**

   The New dialog box opens.

2. **Scan for the New area in the New dialog box.**

   You have two radio buttons: Document and Template.

3. **Choose the Template button.**

4. **Click OK.**

   You see what looks like a new document but is really a document template-thing. (The title bar of the new document indicates that you are working on a template.)

5. **Create the styles for your new document template.**

   Follow the instructions for creating styles in the first part of this chapter, but create a number of styles you want to save or use for particular documents. For example, this book has a document template that has styles for the main text, numbered lists, figure captions, section headings, and a bunch of other stuff I've ignored.

6. **Save the document template to disk.**

   Choose File→Save As, type in a name (1 to 8 characters), and click OK. Then you can close the template document and you're done.

Optional reading on stealing styles

Sometimes you go to the work of creating all these great styles you want to use all the time. But then, how can you stuff them all into a document template so that other documents can use the same styles? The answer, gentle reader, is theft. Pure and simple. Follow these steps to "borrow" a style from another document already on disk:

1. Choose the Format→Style command.

2. Click on the Define button.

3. Click on the Merge button.

   The file list that appears shows you various document templates known to WinWord. You can highlight one to steal its styles (actually, you just borrow them).

   If you want to steal styles from a document, then you need to use the List Files of Type drop-down box and select Word Document (*.doc) to list document files. Locate and highlight the document file whose styles you want to pinch.

4. Click on the From Template button.

   WinWord displays some sort of error box message or some such. Feel free to ignore it.

5. Click OK.

✔ To use a document template when you create a new document, refer to the section "Using a document template" later in this chapter.

✔ Templates are a very special type of document, so special that they even have their own file extension, .DOT. File names and extensions are discussed in Chapter 15.

✔ Be clever with your template names. I send out all my letters using the LETTER template; faxes start with the FAX template. These are accurate file names, brief and legal, that describe the types of templates they represent. Do the same and your WinWord guru will smile upon your face in a delightful manner.

Creating a template complete with text

Templates need not contain only styles. They also can store text, especially text you may use over and over again in certain types of documents. For example, a common type of WinWord template may contain a letterhead, which allows you to use that template for your correspondence. I have a FAX template I use to send out faxes; the first part of the FAX (the To, From, and Re lines) are already typed into the template, which saves me energy I can use to get down to business.

To create a template complete with text, follow these steps:

1. **Do everything outlined in the preceding section, Steps 1 through 5.**

   Gee, a direction like that saves the author a lot of typing.

2. **Before saving your document template to disk, type in some text you want to be part of that template.**

   Anything you type will be saved to disk along with the template's styles. For example, you can create your letterhead and, providing you read various other chapters in this book, make it look like the one shown in Figure 13-3.

3. **Save the template to disk, as outlined in the preceding section.**

   Give it a clever name, something like LETTER or LETRHEAD.

   ✔ You can store lots of text in a document template if you like — anything you normally type into a WinWord document. However, the idea here is to be brief. A specific template isn't as useful as a general one.

   ✔ You also can stuff graphics into a document template. Refer to Chapter 19 for information on using graphics in your documents.

   ✔ Please refer to Chapter 18 for information on Mail Merge — a distant concept from document templates, although the two can be easily confused.

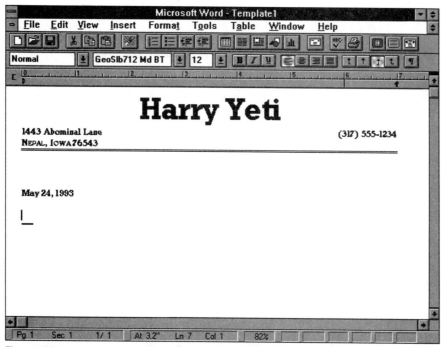

Figure 13-3: A sample letterhead type of document template.

Using a document template

Oh, this is really dumb. To use a document template, follow these steps:

1. Choose File→New.

The New dialog box opens. This is the way you start any new document in WinWord.

2. Under the Use Template list, select the template you want.

Creating a letterhead? Then pick out LETRHEAD from the list. The Normal template is WinWord's own boring normal template (which should be renamed *Yawn*).

3. Click OK!

The template is *attached* to your document, ready for use. You can take advantage of any styles stuffed into the template and view, use, or edit any text saved in the template.

✔ Opening a document with a template does not change the template; your new document is merely "using" the template's styles and any text it already has. To change the template, refer to the following section.

✔ Golly, doesn't this make WinWord kind of easy? Only, of course, if the entire document template and style fiasco hasn't already induced brainlock.

Changing a document template

Changing or editing a document template is identical to changing or editing a normal document. The difference is that a template is opened instead of the document. Yes, WinWord can deal with this just fine. Can you?

1. Open the Template.

Choose File→Open. In the Open dialog box, select Document Templates (*.dot) from the List Files of Type drop-down box. This directs WinWord to list only document templates in the Open dialog box file window. You may have to zoom around your hard drive to find the templates. WinWord is fond of putting them in its own directory, which is probably C:\WINWORD for most of us.

2. Open the template that you want to edit.

Double-click on its filename.

3. Make your changes.

You edit the template just as you would any other document. Bear in mind that it is a template you're editing and not a "real" document. Any style changes or text you edit is made on a template and will be saved to disk as a template again.

4. Save the modified template.

Choose File→Save.

Or choose File→Save As to assign the modified template a new name and maintain the original template.

5. Close the template document.

Choose File→Close.

✔ Any changes you make to a document template will not affect any documents already created with that template. They will, however, affect any new documents you create.

✔ The Normal template is a special beast. Any change that you make to the Normal template will be made in all other templates that you use. The moral to this story is to leave the Normal template alone.

Chapter 14
The Power of Glossaries

The Right Honorable Frederick Alfred Ziconowitz IV, Ph.D., MBA, JD, DD. Just look at that name. How would you like to type it 50 or 60 times a day? Wouldn't it be easier to type, say, **Fred**, and have the rest of that bodacious moniker magically appear thanks to your computer? You bet it would! And, wouldn't it be nice if you could type **fredbye**, for example, and have WinWord automatically zip in the complimentary close to a letter and add The Right Honorable Frederick Alfred Ziconowitz IV, Ph.D., MBA, JD, DD's signature block in a letter? Yup. It's all possible in WinWord, thanks to the miraculous (meaning it's miraculous they included something to make it easier) *glossary* command.

The Tao of Glossaries
(Required reading if you haven't a clue)

Suppose that you are typing a table or a bunch of steps to do something, and you have to type it again, and again, and again. You need a table that is three columns wide, formatted just so, with the company logo in the first cell, and you need it 30 or 40 times a day. Boy, are you are going to be glad that you read this chapter, because with a glossary — it's all a breeze.

A glossary is a shortcut. Forget what you think in your head when you see the word *glossary*. Instead, think of it as an abbreviation. You type in **Fred**, press the special glossary command key, F3, and then `The Right Honorable Frederick Alfred Ziconowitz IV, Ph.D., MBA, JD, DD` appears on-screen. All you type is **Fred;** the computer does the rest. That's what you should think when you see *glossary*.

✔ You must create a glossary entry before you can use the glossary command. The entry is created by selecting text on-screen. That text is then assigned a shortcut by using the Edit➔Glossary command. The details are outlined in the following section.

✔ Glossary entries become a part of the document template. Refer to the preceding chapter for more information on document templates.

✔ Glossaries can contain up to 150 different entries for each template that you create, and each of these entries is almost unlimited in length or complexity. You can store pictures, blocks of text — even scanned images like photographs or signatures — to bring into a document with a flick of the wrist.

✔ Any glossary entries that you attach to the Normal template will be available to every document, regardless of the template that is attached to it. Glossary entries attached to any template other than Normal will only be available to that template.

Creating a glossary entry

To create a glossary entry, follow these steps:

1. **Mark the text you want to use as a glossary entry.**

   Refer to Chapter 6 for the full details on marking a block of text. Keep in mind that all the text you mark will be included in the glossary entry.

2. **Choose Edit➔Glossary.**

   The Glossary dialog box opens, as shown in Figure 14-1. You can see the text you selected (at least some of it) in the bottom part of the dialog box.

3. **Give the glossary entry a name.**

   Type the name, which can be very short, into the Glossary Name box. For example, our friend Fred would have highlighted his full name in the document and then typed only `Fred` into the dialog box.

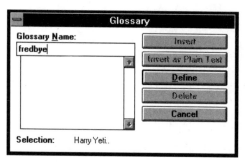

Figure 14-1: The Glossary dialog box.

4. Click on the Define button.

You're done. The glossary entry is now ready to be used, which is covered in the following section.

> ✔ The next time you close your document or exit the program, WinWord asks whether you want to save the document and template changes; answer Yes to keep this glossary entry you just created.

Using glossary entries

To put a glossary entry into a document, follow these steps:

1. Put the toothpick cursor where you want the glossary entry to be placed.

2. Type in the shortcut word.

Fred would type **Fred**. That's all — no space or period after it. Suppose that your glossary entry for your name, address, and city is called *me*. You would type **me** and then . . ..

3. Press the F3 key.

The glossary entry is inserted into the document, replacing the keyword. So Fred becomes his full, obnoxious name and *me* becomes your name and address.

> ✔ You also can choose and insert the glossary by opening the Glossary dialog box (Edit→Glossary).

> ✔ If the toothpick cursor is off by a little bit, WinWord complains that it doesn't recognize the glossary entry. If you're sure you've done everything right, choose Edit→Glossary and look up your glossary entry to verify.

Editing glossary entries

Changing the contents or appearance of a glossary entry isn't difficult. You open the glossary entry, change it, and save the changed entry with the same name. If the bunko squad caught up with Fred and told him that he couldn't tell people that he had a Ph.D. because his alma mater, The Park Bench School of Newspaper Arranging, was not a credited institution, changing his glossary entry would require the following steps:

1. **Put the toothpick cursor where you want the glossary entry to be placed.**

   You need to "go through the motions" here to make the operation run a bit smoother. Yes, this is a shortcut, not sanctioned in the manual. (But, then again, that's why you're reading this book.)

2. **Type the shortcut word.**

   Do this just as if you were inserting the entry.

3. **Press the F3 key.**

   The glossary entry is inserted into the document at the place where the toothpick cursor is, replacing the shortcut word.

4. **Edit.**

   Make any changes you want to the glossary entry just pasted into your document. Once you're done, you'll re-save it using the same name. The net effect here is that the original entry is changed but the name is kept the same (to protect the guilty).

5. **Mark the text you want included as the glossary entry.**

6. **Choose Edit→Glossary.**

7. **Click on the existing glossary name.**

8. **Click on the Define button.**

   A dialog box opens and asks whether you want to redefine the glossary entry.

9. **Click on Yes.**

   You're done. The entry has been edited in an underhanded but perfectly legal manner.

Deleting glossary entries

Nothing stays the same for ever. As a matter of fact, Madam Zuzu was forced to let Fred go when she discovered that he was attempting to sell picture post-cards of his home planet, a little known orb of Betelgeuse, to her customers.

To delete a glossary entry, follow these steps:

1. **Choose Edit→Glossary.**

   The Glossary dialog box opens and lists all glossary entries.

2. **Click on the name of the entry you want to delete.**

   In Madam Zuzu's case, it's Fredbye who's going bye-bye.

3. **Click on the Delete button.**

   The glossary entry's name is removed from the list.

4. **Click on Close.**

   Fred is no longer.

Part III
Working with Documents

"THIS LAVA DISPLAY JERRY DEVELOPED REALLY MAKES OUR DOCUMENTS COME ALIVE."

In this part . . .

Document just sounds so much more important than "that thing I did with my word processor." It implies a crisp, masterful touch. No, this isn't another dreary report; it's a document. This isn't just a letter complaining to the local cable affiliate; it's a document. It isn't a note to Billy's teacher explaining his "rash"; it's a document. It sounds professional, so never mind that you had to tie your fingers in knots and print several hundred copies before you got it right — it's a document!

This part of the book explores the thing you use WinWord for: making documents. This includes printing documents, working with documents and files on disk, and the ugly, sordid story of mail merge, which is right up there next to paying taxes in mental agony and grief.

Chapter 15

More Than a File — a Document

A *document* is what you see on-screen in WinWord. It's the text you create and edit, the formatting you apply, and the end result that's printed. But a document also is a file you store on disk for later retrieval, editing, or printing. This is where things get rough because big bully DOS moves in on the action. To work with your documents on disk, you need to wrestle with DOS filenames. Personally, I'd rather exist on a diet of bird seed and vending machine food, but we're all stuck with DOS, so let's try to make the best of things.

Working on Several Documents Simultaneously

This is handy: WinWord lets you work on up to nine documents at once. Nine! That's as many people as they had in the Brady Bunch, if you count Alice the indentured servant. Depending on the amount of memory you have, you can open up to nine documents without having to close any of them. You don't have to save one to disk and start over, which is nice news for Alice.

In WinWord, each document is stored in its own window on-screen. Normally that "window" uses the whole screen, so that document is all you see in WinWord. To see other documents, you access the Window menu (Alt,W). From there, choose the number, 1 through 9, corresponding to the document you want to see.

WinWord politely shows you the document name, right after its number in the menu. Figure 15-1 shows what the Window menu looks like with a bunch of documents open.

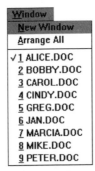

Figure 15-1: Use the Window menu to track open documents.

✔ To switch from one document to another, select its name from the Window menu with the mouse or the keyboard. The names are alphabetized for your convenience.

✔ If you press Ctrl+F6, you'll be taken to the "next" window; Shift+Ctrl+F6 takes you to the "previous" window. If you only have two windows open at a time, then Ctrl+F6 makes for a keen shortcut to skip-to-my-lou between them.

✔ The goings on in one document are independent of any other: Printing, spell checking, and formatting affect only the document you can see on-screen.

✔ You can copy a block from one document to the other. Just mark the block in the first document, copy it (Ctrl+C), open the second document and paste it in (Ctrl+V). Refer to Chapter 6 for detailed block action.

Seeing more than one document

You can arrange all of your documents on-screen by choosing Window→Arrange All. This command puts each document into its own "mini-window" — officially known as the Multi-Document Interface by Windows Well-Wishers.

✔ Although you can see more than one document at a time, you can work on only one at a time: the document with the highlighted title bar. You can work on other documents by clicking on them with the mouse, or by pressing the Ctrl+F6 key.

✔ After the windows have been arranged, you can manipulate their size with the mouse and change their position.

✔ Clicking on a mini-window's Maximize button restores WinWord to its normal, full-screen view.

✔ The Window→Arrange All command works great for two or three documents — when you're comparing text, for example. Arranging more documents than three makes the viewing area so small that it's of little use.

Working on two, or more, parts of the same document

You can look at two or more different parts of the same document — yes, the *same* document — by choosing the Window→New Window command. This creates another window on-screen in which you'll find another copy of your document. Unlike having different documents open in separate windows, each copy of this document is "connected" to the other; changes that you make in one of the copies are immediately included in the other.

✔ This feature is useful for cutting and pasting text or graphics between sections of the same document, especially when you have a very long document.

✔ The title bar tells you which copy of your document you're looking at by displaying a colon and a number after the filename. For example, this document is CHAP15.DOC:1 in one window and CHAP15.DOC:2 in the second window.

✔ You cannot close one window without closing both documents. The second window is merely a new look at the same document.

✔ Another way to view two parts of the same document is by using the old split-screen trick. This feature is discussed . . . why, it's right here.

Using the old split-screen trick

Splitting the screen allows you to view two parts of your document in one window. No need to bother with extra windows here. In fact, I prefer to use WinWord with as little "junk" on-screen as possible. So when I need to view two parts of the same document, I just split the screen — Solomon-like — and then undo the rift when I'm done. You can accomplish the same splitting-screen feat by following these steps:

1. **Place the mouse cursor on the little black area located just above the up-arrow button on the vertical scroll bar (on the upper-right side of your document).**

   When you find the sweet spot, the mouse pointer changes shape and looks like a pair of horizontal lines with arrows pointing down and up.

2. **Hold down the left mouse button, and drag the pointer down.**

   As you drag, a line drags with you and slices the document window in half. That marks the spot where the screen will split.

3. **Release the mouse button.**

   Your screen looks something like Figure 15-2.

   ✔ Each section of the screen can be manipulated separately and scrolled up or down. But the windows still are the same document; changes that you make in one of the copies are immediately included in the others.

   ✔ This feature is useful for cutting and pasting text or graphics between sections of the same document.

   ✔ To undo a screen split, put the cursor on the little black area and drag it back up to the ruler.

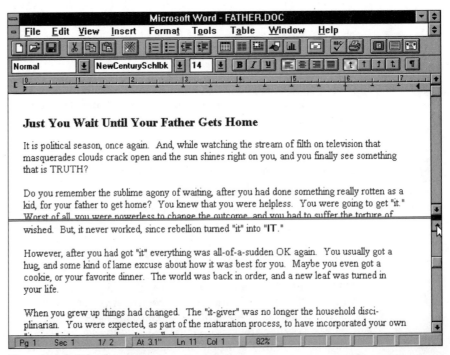

Figure 15-2: Splitting the screen.

Saving a Document to Disk (the First Time)

There's no need to save your document to disk only when you're done with it. In fact, saving should be done almost immediately — as soon as you have a few sentences or paragraphs. Save! Save! Save!

To save a document that hasn't already been saved to disk, follow the steps listed below. If you've already saved the file, skip up to the next section.

1. **Summon the Save command.**

   Choose File→Save, Press Alt,F,S, or press the Shift+F12 shortcut. You see the Save As dialog box shown in Figure 15-3.

2. **Type in a DOS filename for your document.**

   This is the tricky part; DOS filenames can only contain letters and numbers and can be no more than eight characters long. You must be brief and descriptive (which rules out most lawyers from effectively naming files).

3. **If everything goes right, your disk drive churns for a few seconds and eventually your filename appears in the title bar.**

   Your file has been saved.

   If there is a problem, you'll likely see one of two error messages:

```
Do you want to replace the existing filename?
Yes No Cancel Help
```

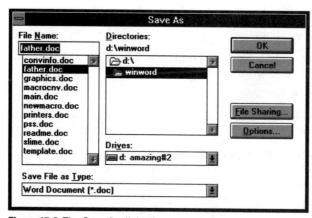

Figure 15-3: The Save As dialog box.

There already is a file on disk with that name. Press N, then skip back up to Step 2 and type in another name. If you press Y, your file will replace the other file on disk, which is probably not what you want.

```
This is not a valid filename OK Help
```

You tried to save a file to disk and there was a problem. Most likely, you used a naughty symbol in the filename or got carried away and made the name too long. Try again at Step 2 above, and use only letters and numbers in the file name.

✔ Additional rules on naming files can be found in Chapter 17 in the section "Naming Files."

✔ You also should organize your files by storing them in special places on your disk called *subdirectories*. This subject is covered in Chapter 17, the section "Finding a Place for Your Work." Technical mumbo jumbo on *subdirectories* is hidden away in Chapter 23, the sections "Organizing Your Files" and "Creating New Directories."

Saving a document to disk (after that)

The instructions in this section assume that you already saved your file to disk once. So why save your file again (and again)? Because it's smart! You should save your file to disk every so often — usually after you write something brilliant or so complex that you don't want to retype it again. (If you haven't yet saved your document to disk, refer to the preceding section.)

Saving your document to disk a second time updates the file on disk. This is painless and quick:

1. **Choose File→Save or press the Shift+F12 shortcut.**

   You'll see the status bar change oh-so quickly as the document is saved.

2. **Continue working.**

   I recommend going back and repeating this step every so often as you continue to toss words down on the page.

   ✔ Save! Save! Save!

   ✔ I recommend saving your document to disk every three minutes or so, or any time after you've written something clever.

   ✔ If you already saved your file to disk, its name will appear in the title bar. If there is no name there, refer to the preceding section for saving instructions.

Here are the shortcut keys for quickly updating your document file on disk:

Press Shift+F12.

Saving a document to disk and quitting

You're done for the day. Your fingers are sore, and your eyes glaze over. Everywhere you look, you see a mouse pointer. You blink and rub your eyes and stretch out your back. Ah, it's Miller time. But before you slap your buddies on the back and walk into the sunset on a beer commercial, you need to save your document and quit for the day:

1. **Exit.**

   Choose File→Exit or press Alt+F4. You see a box that asks

   ```
   Do you want to save changes to Filename? Save document?
   Yes No Cancel Help
   ```

2. **Press Y to save your document.**

   The document is saved and WinWord closes — quit, kaput.

   ✔ If there is a second document in WinWord and changes have been made to it since it was last saved, you'll see the same message again. Press Y to save that document.

   ✔ After you quit WinWord, you find yourself back in Windows. There, you can start another program or exit Windows and turn your PC off for the day.

   ✔ Always quit WinWord and Windows properly. Never turn off your PC or reset when WinWord or Windows is still on-screen. Only turn off your PC when you see the DOS prompt.

Saving and starting over with a clean slate

When you want to save a document, remove it from the screen, and start over with a clean slate, choose the File→Close command. This keeps you in WinWord.

   ✔ You also can start afresh in WinWord and work on a new document by choosing File→New.

   ✔ If you haven't yet saved your document to disk, refer to the section titled "Saving a Document to Disk (the First Time)" earlier in this chapter. Always save your document right after you start writing something.

   ✔ There is no reason to quit WinWord and start it again to begin working with a blank slate.

Here are the shortcut keys for saving your document and starting again with a clean slate. This assumes that you already saved your document to disk:

1. Press Alt,F,C.

2. Press Alt,F,N.

Retrieving a Document from Disk

When you first start WinWord, or after closing one document and starting again with a clean slate, you have the option of retrieving a previously saved document from disk into WinWord for editing.

To grab a file from disk — to retrieve it — follow these steps:

1. Summon the Open command.

Choose File→Open or press Ctrl+F12, the Open shortcut. You see the Open dialog box, as shown in Figure 15-4.

2. Type in the name of the document stored on disk.

You also can use the gizmos in the dialog box to browse through various disks and subdirectories on your PC — providing that you're adept at such things, or have read through Chapter 23, "Contending with Windows (and DOS)."

3. Press Enter.

WinWord will find the document and load it on the screen for editing.

Open		
File Name:	**Directories:**	OK
*.doc	d:\winword	Cancel
convinfo.doc	d:\	
father.doc	winword	
graphics.doc		Find File...
macrocnv.doc		
main.doc		
newmacro.doc		
printers.doc		
pss.doc		
readme.doc		
slime.doc	**Drives:**	
template.doc	d: amazing#2	
List Files of Type:		
Word Documents (*.doc)		☐ Read Only

Figure 15-4: The Open dialog box.

4. Go!

> ✓ If the document isn't found, you'll see an error message and have the chance to try again. Edit the document filename if you want by using the left- and right-arrow keys, Delete and Backspace, or typing a new filename. If you still get an error message, refer to Chapter 25, the section titled "I lost my files!"

> ✓ If you load a file written by another word processor, you may see a dialog box asking whether it's okay to convert it to WinWord speak. Answer Yes. Refer to Chapter 16 for more information on alien word processor documents.

Loading One Document into Another Document

There are times when you want to load one document into another. When you do, follow these steps:

1. **Position the toothpick cursor where you want the other document's text to appear.**

2. **Choose Insert→File.**

3. **At the prompt, type in the name of the file you want to paste into your document.**

4. **Press Enter.**

The document appears right where the toothpick cursor is.

> ✓ If you aren't really sure where you put the file that you want to include, you can select the Find File command to look for it. Refer to Chapter 17 for additional details on Find File.

> ✓ The resulting, combined document still has the same name as the first document.

> ✓ You can retrieve any number of documents into your document. There is no limit, although you should avoid the huge hulking cow document if possible.

> ✓ These steps allow you to retrieve a block saved on disk and stick it into another document. This is often called *boiler plating*, where a commonly used piece of text is slapped into several documents. It's also the way cheap romance novels are written.

Chapter 16

Other Documents — Alien and ASCII

- -

In This Chapter

▶ Loading a DOS text file

▶ Saving a DOS text file

▶ Loading documents created by alien word processors

▶ Saving documents in alien formats

- -

*W*inWord is not the only word processor in the world. (Too bad.) Other folks use other word processors, and occasionally you may tangle yourself with the files they create. You may need to give someone a file in ASCII format. It's these moments when you must deal with non-WinWord documents, what I call *alien* file formats.

Loading a DOS Text File

A DOS text file is a special, non-document file that you can load into WinWord for editing. It's a non-document file because it contains no formatting, no bold or underline, centering, headers, or footers. It's just plain old text.

To open a DOS text file, follow these steps:

1. Do the Open command.

Choose File→Open or press Ctrl+F12, the Open shortcut. The Open Document dialog box appears.

2. Type in the name of the DOS text file you want to load.

Or you can use the controls in the dialog box to hunt down the file you want on your hard drive. (Please see the following tip for information on making this a bit easier.)

3. Choose OK!

Click the OK button or press Enter. Because the file isn't a WinWord document, you see the Convert File dialog box, as shown in Figure 16-1. WinWord guesses the file format, which probably will be Text Only, as highlighted in Figure 16-1. If Text Only isn't highlighted, highlight it in the list (providing that you know for certain — and I mean really truly positively certain — that it's a text file).

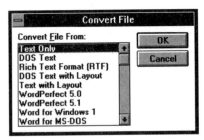

Figure 16-1: The Convert File dialog box.

4. Choose OK!

Click the OK button or press Enter to select Text Only and load your text file. The DOS text file appears on-screen, ready for editing just like any WinWord document, although the formatting will be really cruddy.

✔ Suppose that you don't know the name of the text file. If so, look at the bottom of the Open Document dialog box. There you'll find the List Files of Type drop-down thingy. There you should select All Files(*.*). This allows you to view all the files on your hard drive, not just WinWord documents. Or, if you're totally messed up, you can use the Find File command, which is covered in Chapter 17.

✔ DOS text files are also called *ASCII* files. ASCII is an acronym that basically means "a DOS text file." You pronounce it *ask-EE*.

✔ Information on opening WinWord document files lurks in Chapter 15.

✔ The only difficult thing about dealing with a DOS text file is when you're required to save the file back to disk in the *DOS text format — not as a WinWord document*. These steps are outlined in the following section.

Saving a DOS Text File

If you open a document in one of the alien formats and make even the smallest change, WinWord wants to save the file as a WinWord document. This keeps all the formatting and special stuff intact for the next time you work on the document. However, because some applications need to have files in a DOS text format, saving them as a WinWord document will confuse those applications to no end. Therefore, WinWord is also capable of saving files in the DOS text format, also known as saving a file in ASCII format.

To save a new or existing document in the DOS text or ASCII Format, follow these steps:

1. **Conjure the Save As command.**

   This must be the Save <u>A</u>s command, not the Save command. Choose <u>F</u>ile→Save <u>A</u>s or press the F12 key.

2. **The typical Save As dialog box appears.**

   Normally you enter a filename and WinWord saves it as a document on disk. But you want to save the file as a DOS text file. To do that, you must change the *format*, which appears in the Save File as <u>T</u>ype box.

3. **Click on the down-arrow button beside the Save File as <u>T</u>ype box.**

   This drops down the list of file formats under which WinWord can save your document.

4. **In the list, look for the Text Only (*.txt) format.**

   Use the up- and down-arrow cursor keys to highlight various formats in the list. When you see Text Only (*.txt), highlight it.

5. **Press Enter.**

6. **Select the File <u>N</u>ame box again.**

   Press Alt+N or click with the mouse.

7. **Type in a filename for the DOS text file.**

   Watch that filename! Some DOS text files may need to be saved with a TXT, BAT, SYS, or INI extension. If you get confused about what extension you want to use, type the file name and leave off the period and the extension (the three letters that follow it). There is usually a reason that you edit a text file in WinWord; part of that reason should explain what to name the file when you save it back to disk.

8. **Choose OK.**

   Press Enter or click OK with your mouse to save the file to disk.

If the file already exists, you'll be asked whether you want to replace it; press Y to replace it. This is one of the rare circumstances when it's okay to press Y to replace the file.

- ✔ Saving a DOS text file may be a requirement in some instances — if you're ever asked to edit the special CONFIG.SYS or AUTOEXEC.BAT files, for example. You can load those files as you would any WinWord document. But you *must* save them back to disk as DOS text files.

- ✔ You can save a document as a DOS text file *and* a WinWord document file. First, save the file to disk as a WinWord document with the DOC extension. Then save the file to disk as a DOS text file, again using the extension TXT. The reason behind this is that you'll have a text file, which is what DOS wants, and a WinWord file, which contains secret codes and prints out really purty.

Understanding the ASCII thing

WinWord saves its documents to disk in its own special file format. That format includes your text — the basic characters you type — plus information about formatting, bold, underline, graphics, and anything else you toss into the document. That's all saved to disk so that the next time you use WinWord, you get your formatting back for editing, printing, or whatever.

Every word processor has its own different document file format. So, your WinWord documents are considered "alien" to other word processors, which use their own non-WinWord format. It's been this way since the dawn of the PC. So to keep the confusion low, a common text format was developed. It's called the *plain text* or *ASCII* format.

ASCII is an acronym for something I need not mention because there will be no test on this material and you'd probably forget what the acronym stood for two minutes from now. What's more important than knowing what it represents is knowing how to pronounce it: ASK-EE. It's not "ask-two." It's ASK-EE.

An ASCII file contains only text. There are no formatting codes, no bold, underline, graphics, or anything. Just text. It's also called the *plain text* format or sometimes the *DOS text* format. Whatever you call it, an ASCII file contains only text.

Because ASCII files aren't littered with word processing codes, their text can be read by any word processor. In a way, ASCII files are the Esperanto of document files. Any word processor can read an ASCII file and display its contents. The text will look ugly, but it's better than nothing. Also, to maintain compatibility, WinWord can save your files in ASCII format, as described in the section "Saving a DOS Text File."

Loading Documents Created by Alien Word Processors

Suppose that crazy Earl gives you a disk full of his favorite limericks. Of course, Earl is crazy, so crazy that he actually uses WordPerfect. Without thinking about it, Earl has handed you a disk full of WordPerfect documents and it's making you silly.

First don't panic button: Don't worry about the Windows aspect. Although Earl's WordPerfect is one that doesn't use Windows, it doesn't affect whether or not you do. A PC disk is a PC disk. No problems there.

Second don't panic button: WinWord can safely read Earl's limerick files, although he saved them in that whacko WordPerfect file format. To retrieve the files, just follow the steps outlined in the previous section, "Loading a DOS Text File." Yes, the same steps. The only difference will be in Step 3. WinWord recognizes the WordPerfect documents and automatically highlights `WordPerfect`; it will even recognize the version in the Convert File dialog box. The same holds for any other word processing document; just select its type from the list and you'll be fine.

- ✔ Not only can WinWord read WordPerfect documents, it also recognizes several other popular document formats instantly. Just use the Open command to open the alien word processor document.

- ✔ Nothing's perfect. The alien document you open into WinWord may require some fixing up, adjusting fonts, and whatnot. This is at most a minor bother; at least you don't have to re-type anything.

- ✔ After the file is in WinWord, you can save it to disk in the WinWord format. Just use the Save command as you normally would. WinWord asks whether the old file should be overridden with WinWord formatting. If so, answer Yes.

- ✔ Occasionally, WinWord finds something so utterly bizarre that it won't recognize it. When that happens, you can try to open the document, but it's probably better to ask the person who created the document to save it in ASCII format.

- ✔ Another common document format is RTF, the Rich Text Format. This is better than ASCII because it keeps track of underline, bold, and other formatting. If you'll be sharing files often with other weirdo word processors, try to get everyone to settle on a common format, like RTF. Better still, get everyone to settle on WinWord.

Saving Documents in Alien Formats

Now comes the time for you to give Earl your collection of leprechaun jokes. Alas, those are all saved to disk in WinWord format. You could be lax like Earl and just hand him a diskette full of WinWord documents. But then he'd call you up and complain or ramble on and on about some new word processor conversion program he found. Because you don't have the time for that, just do him a favor and save the file in his own word processor's format.

This is simple: Follow the steps outlined in the previous section "Saving a DOS Text File." In Step 4, however, select the proper alien word processor format from the list. For Earl, that would be `WordPerfect 5.1`. This saves the file in the alien format.

- Users on Venus prefer Ami Pro for Windows.
- Users on Mars prefer WordStar but, hey, they've always been behind the times.

Chapter 17

Managing Files

· ·

· ·

*T*he more you work in WinWord, the more documents you create. And, because you always save those documents to disk, the more files you make. This is how a hard drive gets full of stuff; you create it. In a way, your hard drive is like your closet. It's full of stuff. And unless you have a handy closet orga- nizer — like the one I bought on TV for three low, low payments of $29.95 — things are going to get messy. This chapter tackles the subject of files — using and organizing them.

Naming Files

When you save your precious work to disk, which is always a good idea, you need to give it a specific type of filename. This has nothing to do with WinWord; point your fingers of blame at DOS.

  ✔ DOS is the one that has such restrictive filenames!

  ✔ DOS is the one that limits you to eight measly characters!

  ✔ DOS is the one that lets you use only numbers and letters!

  ✔ DOS is the scourge upon which . . . . Okay. Let's not get carried away.

To save a document to disk you need, to use a DOS filename. Here are the rules:

- ✔ A DOS filename can be no more than 8 characters long. It can be less, sure. A one character filename is okay but not very descriptive.

- ✔ You can use any combination of letters or numbers to name your file. Extra points are awarded for being clever. Upper- and lower-case letters are the same according to DOS.

- ✔ A DOS filename can start with a number. In fact, the name of this file, the document that contains this chapter, is 17.DOC (a one and a seven and then .DOC). That's a perfectly legit DOS filename — and descriptive because it tells me what this file contains. (A filename like CHAP15.DOC would be more descriptive and still legit.)

- ✔ Filenames do not contain spaces!

- ✔ DOS filenames cannot contain symbols. Okay, that's a half truth. But why clutter your brain with the symbols it can and cannot have? It's just better to name files by using only letters and numbers.

- ✔ DOS filenames can have an optional *filename extension*. This follows the filename and can contain one, two, or three characters. A period separates the filename from the extension — and that's the only time you'll see a filename with a period in it. Filenames do not end in periods.

- ✔ WinWord filenames don't absolutely have to have the .DOC extension, but you are asking for major-league headaches if you don't use it.

- ✔ A *pathname* is a super-long filename, describing exactly where a file is on a disk drive. The pathname contains a colon, letters, numbers, and backslash characters. For more information, refer to the following section.

- ✔ Examples of good and bad filenames are provided in Chapter 1, the section "Save Your Stuff!"

Finding a Place for Your Work

A hard drive can be a rugged and unforgiving place — like the parking lot at Nordstroms during a shoe sale. Trouble looms like the last pair of off-white pumps at under $10. Unless there is some semblance of organization, chaos rules.

To work your hard drive effectively, you need organization. It's a big deal: *organization*. There are special places on your hard drive called *directories* or sometimes the nautical *subdirectory* term is used instead. These are like holding bins for files. All files of a certain type can be stored — and retrieved — from their own directories.

The organization and setup of directories is covered in Chapter 23. Your guru or the person responsible for setting up your computer should have built some of these directories and arranged them for your use. (If not, you can create directories as needed; refer to Chapter 23.)

Each of these directories is known by a specific name. That name is called a _pathname_. The pathname includes the disk drive letter, a colon, a backslash, then a directory name. If you have a directory within another directory (a _subdirectory_), then its name also is included in the _pathname_, along with extra backslash characters to make it all look confusing.

Some common pathnames are listed below in Table 17-1. Please write in additional pathnames you use, along with their purposes. Or, if this is all having you shake your head, have your guru fill in the pathnames for you:

Table 17-1	Common Pathnames
Pathname	_Contents/Description:_
C:\	Drive C, main "root" directory
A:\	Drive A, main "root" directory
C:\WINWORD	WinWord's directory
C:\DOS	DOS's directory
C:\WINDOWS	Window's directory
_____	_____
_____	_____
_____	_____
_____	_____
_____	_____
_____	_____

✔ Directing WinWord to use a specific directory is covered in the next section.

✔ You can combine a pathname with a filename for use with the File→Save (Shift+F12) and File→Open (Ctrl+F12) commands. This is a long and complex thing to do with a great potential for typos. Instead of typing in a pathname, I recommend using the mouse to change directories in the dialog boxes. (Only those well versed in DOS talk usually mess with pathnames anyway.)

Using a New Directory

Unless directed otherwise, WinWord always places its files where it got them. This is fine, if you already saved a file to its proper directory. However, when you open a new file, the new file will go to the directory that was open when you created it. In other words, if I open a new file and I am sitting in the c:\winword\dummies directory, the new file will automatically be saved in that directory, unless I tell WinWord otherwise.

To tell WinWord to save a file to a specific directory on your hard drive, follow these steps:

1. **Summon the File→Save As or File→Open command.**

   You can use a new directory when saving a file to disk or opening a new file. If you choose File→Save As or press F12, the Save As shortcut, the Save As dialog box opens, as shown in Figure 17-1. If you choose File→Open, you see the Open dialog box, shown in Figure 17-2.

2. **Make one of the following decisions:**

   ✔ If you're already in the directory that you want to be in, skip to Step 4.

   ✔ If you know the name of the directory where you want to place the file, you can skip to Step 4 and type the file's full name. I don't recommend this because full filenames are a pain (but I had to list it here anyway as an option).

   ✔ Select the disk drive you want from the Drives drop-down list in the Save As dialog box. Click on the down-arrow button or press Alt+V. Select a drive letter from the list. If it's a floppy drive, ensure that you have a disk in the drive *before* you select it.

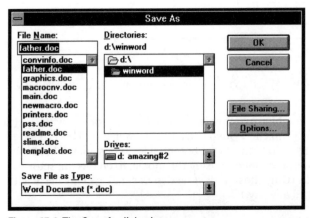

Figure 17-1: The Save As dialog box.

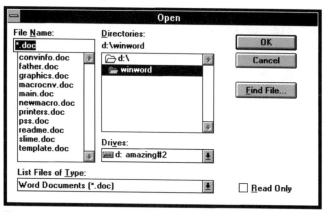

Figure 17-2: The Open dialog box.

> ✔ Select the subdirectory you want from the <u>D</u>irectories drop-down list in the Save As dialog box. Click on the down-arrow button or press Alt+D. Use the up- or down-arrow key to highlight a subdirectory. Move to the directory that you want by double-clicking on it. (More instructions on "working the directories" are offered at the end of this list of steps.)

3. Repeat Step 2 until you find the directory you're looking for.

For example, suppose that WinWord is on drive C and I want to use my \HUMOR\PROMNITE directory on drive D. First, I change to drive D using the Dri<u>v</u>es drop-down list. Then I mosey on over to \HUMOR\PROMNITE using the <u>D</u>irectories drop-down list. When I'm there, I see a list of my WinWord files saved in that directory, and I can save my new files there as well. Cool, yes. Organized — most definitely.

4. Enter the filename in the File <u>N</u>ame box if you're saving a file, or select the file from the list if you're opening.

5. Choose OK.

> ✔ Each directory on your hard drive is like a *folder* — which is how they appear in the <u>D</u>irectories drop-down box. Some folders contain other folders. To see their contents, double-click on the directory's name.

> ✔ The main directory on every disk is the *root directory*. It's the one with a drive letter followed by a backslash. On drive C, it's named C:\. Other directories on the disk have other names, and sometimes the names will give you a clue as to the directory's contents. Sometimes.

> ✔ The files in each directory appear in the list under the File <u>N</u>ame box.

> ✔ Each disk in your system has its own set of directories. If you can't find the directory you want on one disk, try another. For example, scope out drive D if drive C turns out to be a dud.

Finding Files in WinWord

It's really hard to lose a file so thoroughly that WinWord can't find it, even if you have an absolutely horrid memory. I often find it difficult to remember which documents contain the information I want and where the heck I put that file anyway. WinWord's Find File command in the File menu can be a real time saver here.

To locate documents, the Find File feature uses almost any information you can remember — or guess at — about a document. For example, you can find all documents that contain any reference to Fred Ziconowitz or all documents written by a certain person in the month of May.

To search for documents by using the Find File command, follow these mesmerizing steps:

1. Summon the Find File command.

Choose File→Find File. You also can click on any button labeled Find File; these buttons are located in various saving and opening dialog boxes, such as the Open dialog box (refer to Figure 17-2). The Find File dialog box opens, as shown in Figure 17-3.

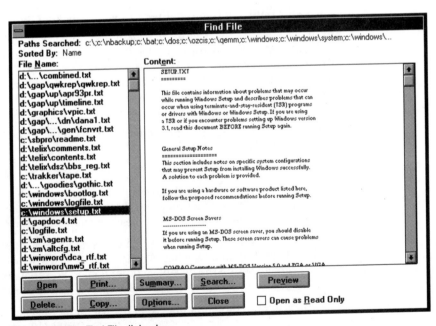

Figure 17-3: The Find File dialog box.

2. Click on the Search button.

The Search dialog box appears, as shown in Figure 17-4.

3. Fill in the blanks!

You don't have to fill in all the blanks — just the ones that deal with what you know about the file(s) you want. For example, the search information entered in Figure 17-4 tells WinWord to "Poke around inside of each file and tell me which ones have the word `father` in them." This works because the word `father` was typed into the Any Text box.

4. Click on the Start Search button.

Word performs the search and lists files meeting your search criteria in the Find File dialog box.

> ✔ You can search for a specific file in the Search dialog box by putting its name in the File Name box. Then look for the Drives drop-down box, open it, and select All Drives from the list. Your file, if it exists, will be located in no time. Highlight it in the Find File box, and click the Open button to begin editing.

> ✔ The Any Text box in the Search dialog box allows you to type in a bit of text and search for all files that contain that text.

> ✔ The Type box in the Search dialog box allows you to control which types of files you search for. For example, you can open the list and select Word Document (*.doc) to look for WinWord documents.

> ✔ If you chose All Files (*.*) from Type in the Search dialog box, you will see some files that consist of cryptic computer instructions and gunk.

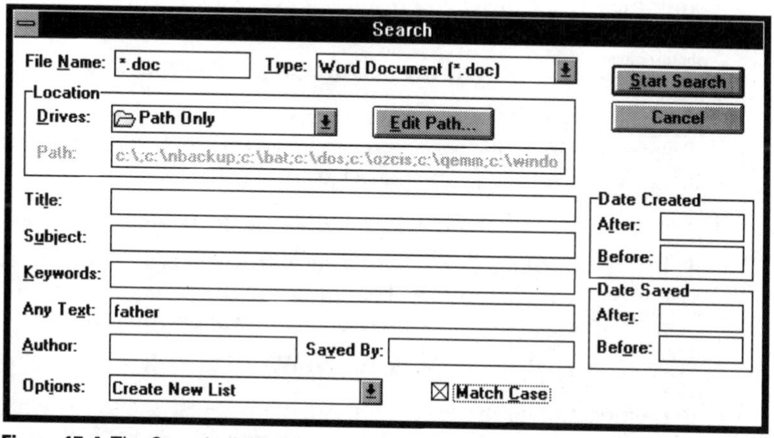

Figure 17-4: The Search dialog box.

✔ Do not try to load any of the weird files into WinWord. Although WinWord won't choke, you won't be able to do much of anything. If you do load a weird file (and I don't know why, seeing how I just warned you), press Alt,F,C to clear it away and start over.

✔ Ignore the Title, Subject, and Keywords boxes in the Search dialog box unless you're typing in *summary info* for each WinWord document you create. (Usually, no one does this.)

✔ Click on the Close button in the Find File dialog box when you're finished.

Locating files elsewhere in the Search dialog box

The Find File dialog's Search button lets you find files all over your hard drive — and maybe even laying on the ground outside your computer if you have a Pentium machine. The key is knowing which buttons to press inside the Search dialog box. This can be tricky, so follow along carefully and just smile and nod through the parts you don't understand.

1. **Open the Find Files dialog box.**

   Choose File➜Find File.

2. **Choose the Search button.**

   There's that horrid Search dialog box!

   The idea here is that you're looking for a file or group of files that could be anywhere. Your hard drive stores files on disks and then in subdirectories (see Chapter 23 for more information on subdirectories). You can look for your files in one of several ways. But first, you must tell WinWord which file you're looking for.

3. **Type the name of your document into the File Name box.**

   If you're looking for a specific file, type in its name exactly: EXACT.DOC or THISONE.DOC. Otherwise, you can leave this box alone. It shows *.DOC, *.*, or some other cryptic message. That's fine.

4. **Optionally specify a file type using the Type drop-down list.**

   The only two types worth bothering with are Word Document and All Files. Other types are listed as well, but most of the time you'll be looking for a WinWord document, so Word Document will be your choice.

5. **Specify a location — a place for WinWord to look for your file(s).**

   In the Location area are several gadgets you can use to tell WinWord where to look for your files. The Drives drop-down list is the best choice. There, you can select one of any of your computer's hard drives, or — and this is a great choice — you can pick the All Drives item. That tells WinWord to look on all your disk drives for the documents you want to find.

Doing it the hard way — taking a
Yellow Line boat tour of the Find File dialog box

All aboard for the boat tour of the Find File dialog box (as shown below); please bring a sack lunch for the first day at sea and don't forget your pills and patches. (Note that the Casino will not be opened until we're at least 12 miles from shore, or when you're seriously bored with shuffleboard.)

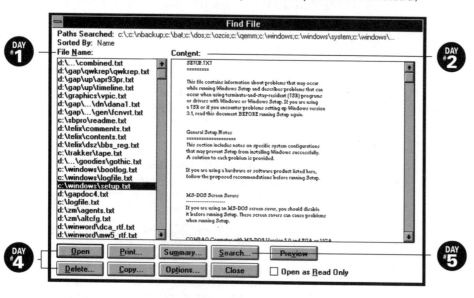

Day #1	**File Name area**	A list of WinWord documents (files), those found by a search command or those "on the path." The files are displayed with their long, cryptic DOS pathnames; the actual name of the file is the last part, after the final backslash (\).
Day #2	**Content area**	This large space shows you a preview of a document. Click on any single file in the File Name area to see its contents. For example, click on LUNCH.DOC to see what's for lunch. Booooon Apetitó!
Day #3	***At sea***	Bingo tonight at 8:00 in the Dramamine lounge!
Day #4	**The Buttons**	You can use the buttons Open, Delete, Copy, and Print to open, delete, copy, or print the highlighted file. Use the Close button to make the Find File dialog box vanish (but don't forget your life preserver).
Day #5	**Search button**	The Search button opens another dialog box that assists you with searching for files. This trip costs more in brain power but makes a fun one-day excursion for those who aren't too sea sick at this point.

6. Specify a pathname if you're using subdirectories.

When you just want to look in a specific subdirectory, dispense with the Drives drop-down list and click on the Edit Path button. You see the Edit Path dialog box, which is where you can tell WinWord to look in certain subdirectories and display only those files. You work the Edit Path dialog box as you would any Open or Save As dialog box; locate the drive and directory you want and click on the Add button. If you don't want to look in a specific directory, highlight it and click on the Delete button (this doesn't delete the directory, it just removes it from the list). When you're done, click on the Close button. Then select Path Only from the Drives drop-down list. Now you're done with this step. (I know — technical stuff, but you were warned.)

7. You're done — almost.

By selecting a filename, file type, and a location (either Drives to look in or a Path), you've told the Search dialog where to look for files. The next step is to start searching . . . .

8. Click on the Start Search button.

WinWord looks for any files located in the places you asked it to look and matches any filename descriptions (or any search text, as covered in the section "Finding text in files" elsewhere in this chapter). The results of the search — the files that matched — appear in the Find File dialog box.

> ✔ Finding files using the Find File dialog really works — honest! But it's not the easiest thing you can do in WinWord.

> ✔ When you're working with a lot of files in the same directory, use the Edit Path button in the Search dialog box to put only that directory on "the path." This makes working with all those files easier (and is another good reason to organize your files into subdirectories; see Chapter 23).

Looking at documents on-disk

Wouldn't it be nice if you could look into a document before you loaded it, like getting a sneak preview? This is entirely possible using the Find Files command and dialog box.

Follow the steps for finding a file:

1. Choose the File→Find File command.

There may or may not be a list of files displayed in the box. If there are, click on a file to highlight it. If it's a WinWord document, you'll see a sneak preview of it in the large Content area on the right of the Find File dialog box. Otherwise, you must continue with Step 2.

2. Follow the steps in the preceding section for locating a group of files.

> ✔ Use the scroll bar on the Content window to peruse the file.
>
> ✔ Click on the Close button in the Find File dialog box when you're finished.

Copying files

You can use the Find Files dialog box to copy files to and fro' in your system. Here's how it works:

1. Select a file to copy from the Find File dialog box.

Highlight that file. Or, if you want to gang-copy, hold down the Ctrl key and click on each filename to mark more than one file. You also can use the instructions in the section "Finding Files in WinWord" to search for other files that aren't immediately visible in the Find File dialog box.

2. Click on the Copy button.

You see the Copy dialog box shown in Figure 17-6.

3. You'll need to type in a destination — a *path* — for the file.

This is trouble. Instead of bothering with the path, you can follow the steps in the section "Using a New Directory" earlier in this chapter for information on winding your way to the correct drive and directory. The same rules apply to the Copy dialog box.

For example, you could enter **A:** to copy the highlighted file to a diskette in drive A. Or you could just select A: from the Drives drop-down list.

Figure 17-6: The Copy dialog box.

4. Choose OK!

Click the OK button or press Enter. The file(s) will be copied.

> ✔ Be sure there is a formatted disk in drive A or drive B before you copy files there. Refer to Chapter 23, the section "Formatting Disks," for more information.

> ✔ If a file by the same name already exists at the destination, WinWord asks whether you want to replace it. My advice is to press N unless you're absolutely certain you're not overwriting something important. Try the Copy command again, but use a different destination or another disk.

> ✔ For help with copying files, destinations and such, refer to *DOS For Dummies, 2nd Edition*. The same information explained in Chapter 3 of that book, "File Fitness," applies to WinWord's Copy command as well.

Deleting files

You can use the Find Files command to flick unworthy files from your hard drive. Before we begin our acts of utter destruction, and lay the files to rest, heed one warning: *Don't delete anything you need!* Instead, delete older copies of files, backups, or just plain old junk (junk files happen).

When you're ready to destroy, follow these steps:

1. Select a file to blow away from the Find File dialog box.

Move the highlight bar to that file. Or, if you're feeling despotic, hold down the Ctrl key and click on file names to mark one or more files.

2. Press the Delete button, the Destroy command!

Okay, it's really the Delete command. A message box asks whether you really want to delete the filename, or if you marked a group of files for slaughter, a dialog box with the appropriate roll call appears.

3. Choose Yes.

The file is no more. Or, if you were needlessly greedy, the files have been vanquished. Gone! Gone! Gone! Purge 'dem files!

> ✔ Oops! If you want to undelete a deleted file, refer to Chapter 25 and look up the section titled "Oops! I deleted my document!"

> ✔ I don't recommend deleting files from WinWord. Use the File Manager for your wanton acts of destruction. Refer to the first section in this chapter.

Finding text in files

You can use the Find Files command to locate text in your WinWord documents. This is great feature for document fishing; those times when you have forgotten a document's name but don't want to wade through the tedium of loading a bunch of documents individually to scan for text. Instead, do this:

1. Open the Find Files dialog box.

Choose File→Find File.

2. Choose the Search button.

Blup! Its dialog box appears.

3. Type the text you're searching for in the Any Text box.

Be specific, be brief. For example, scan for a name, a key phrase, something particular to the document you're hunting down.

5. Press Enter.

WinWord scans all the files looking for your text.

6. When the search is done, WinWord displays any files it found.

Each file contains the text you specified. Highlight one or all and click on the Open button to load them into WinWord.

✔ Refer to the section "Finding Files in WinWord" for more information on the Find File command and Search dialog box.

✔ You can tell WinWord to match the case exactly, to look for Father instead of father, by checking the Match Case box in the Search dialog box.

✔ The Drives drop-down list allows you to limit your search to a path or to specific drives. You can select All Drives if you just don't have a clue about where that critter is. If you are on a network, you may wish to search All Local Drives to keep from spending an entire day watching WinWord search through thousands of files that belong to other people.

Chapter 18
Mail Merge for the Mental

*M*ail merge. Ugh. What it is: a method of producing several customized documents without individually editing each one. We're talking form letters here — but sneaky form letters that you can't really tell are form letters.

Let's face it, mail merge is not fun. However, in an effort to do my civic duty — and in an attempt to hold down the massive medical bills that result from the multitude of slipped disks caused by budding mail mergers picking up and tossing the User's Guide through the handiest window — this chapter contains only the basic, need-to-know steps for mail merging.

Understanding Mail Merge

There are three ways to handle WinWord's (or anybody's) mail merge:

   1. Read this chapter, and then go out and have a drink.

   2. Skip this chapter, and go straight to the booze.

   3. Hire a professional to do it for you while you are in detox.

I'll outline the first part of the first approach here. The second approach you can attempt on your own. The third approach shouldn't be necessary. (If you've been through this before, skip to the section "Preparing the Main Document.")

Mail merge is the process of taking a single form letter, stirring in a list of names and other information, and then merging both to create several documents. Each of the documents is customized by using the list of names and information you provide.

The file that contains the names and other information is called the *data file*. The file that contains the form letter is referred to as the *main document*.

It doesn't make a whole lot of difference which one you create first, because one of the cuter things about mail merge is that WinWord always thinks that you have already created the other one. You can't win; get used to it.

You can start by opening a blank main document in WinWord. You also can start by typing the body of the main document and create it as you would any other document, complete with formatting and other mumbo-jumbo. But leave those spots blank where you would put the address, "Dear Mr. Blather," or anything else that will change form letter to letter. You will put some fill-in-the-blanks special codes here in a bit. These special codes are called *fields*.

The data file contains the names, addresses, and other information you want. But, unlike the main document, this document is created by using a special format. It's almost like filling in names in a database program. (In fact, that's exactly what it is.)

Each of the names, addresses, and other information in the data file composes what's called a *record*. WinWord creates a custom letter by using the main file as a skeleton and filling in the meat with the record in the secondary file. I know — totally gross. But nothing else I can think of now describes it as well.

Because no one commits this routine to memory (and for good reason), the following sections provide outlines to follow so you can create a mail merge document using main and data files. Cross your fingers, count the rosary, and check the kids, we're goin'-a mail-mergin'.

Preparing the Main Document

The main document is the fill-in-the-blanks document. Create it as you would any document: Type away and insert formatting and such as necessary. But leave certain key items "blank," such as names, addresses, and other items that will vary from letter to letter.

You continue creating the main document and leaving nothing where you will want *fields* to appear later. When you're finished, you save the main document to disk but leave it up on-screen. Figure 18-1 shows a sample main document

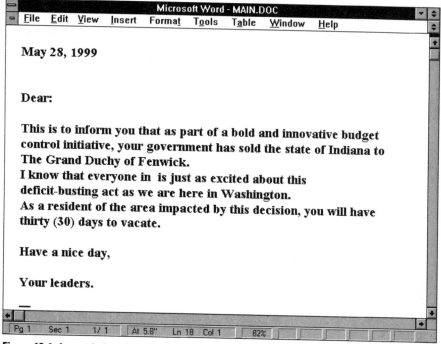

Figure 18-1: A sample form letter.

created in this manner. The parts that don't make any sense or where something appears to be missing (Dear: . . . for example) are where the blanks are to be filled in later.

- ✔ The main document contains all the fill-in-the-blanks stuff.

- ✔ Space has been left in the main document for the mailing address and salutation.

- ✔ The second paragraph has a place to put in the name of the city.

Preparing the Data File

A data file is not a traditional WinWord document. It is a database table of sorts with the list of fields — the blanks that need to be filled in the main document — as its header. The data file then includes several lists or *records* of information that WinWord merges into those fields. The end result is many customized documents. Figure 18-2 shows a typical data file.

Field names   Print Merge toolbar ⌐   Main Document tool

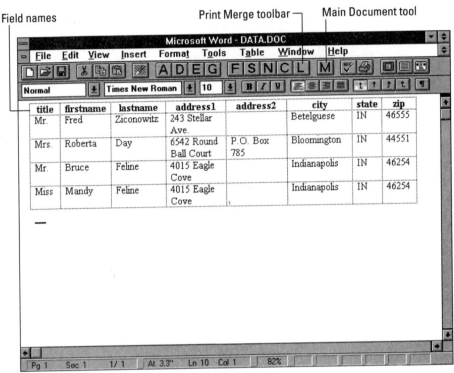

Figure 18-2: A data file with the field names as its header.

To start a data field, follow these steps:

1. **If you already have a main document, open it. If not, open a blank document by choosing File→New.**

2. **Choose File→Print Merge.**

   The Print Merge Setup dialog box opens, as shown in Figure 18-3.

3. **Click on the Attach Data File button.**

   The Attach Data File dialog box, conveniently shown in Figure 18-4 opens. If you already created a data file, you can select it here and skip the rest of this stuff. But, because this is supposed to be instructional, go on to Step 4.

4. **Choose the Create Data File button.**

   And . . . the Create Data File dialog box, shown in Figure 18-5, opens and is ready to accept the names of your fields.

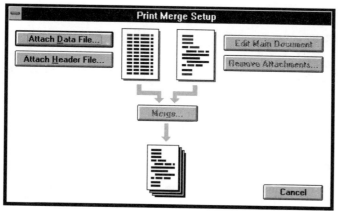

Figure 18-3: The Print Merge Setup dialog box.

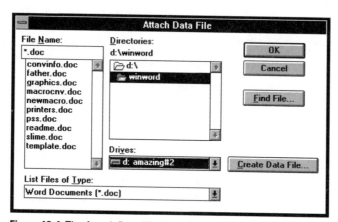

Figure 18-4: The Attach Data File dialog box.

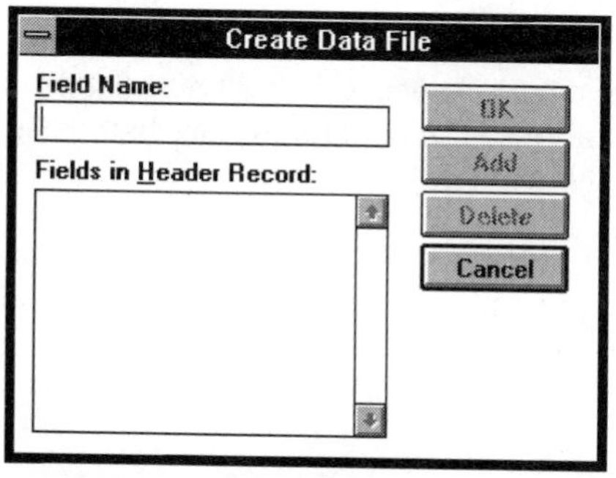

Create Data File

Field Name:

Fields in Header Record:

OK
Add
Delete
Cancel

Figure 18-5: The Create Data File dialog box.

5. Type a field name into the Field Name box.

Here are some suggestions for making this make sense:

- ✔ The field should be named to reflect the kind of information it will contain. For example, a field named *firstname* would contain first names.

- ✔ A field name must begin with a letter.

- ✔ A field name can contain up to 20 letters, numbers, and underscore characters.

- ✔ You cannot use spaces or punctuation marks in field names.

- ✔ When entering addresses, always make separate fields for the city, state, and ZIP codes.

6. Choose the Add button, or press the Enter key.

This inserts the field you created into the list shown in the Fields in Header Record box. This very important-sounding thing, a *header record*, is only a list of titles for the columns that will contain the names, addresses, and other things. (You will see what I mean pretty soon.)

7. Remember that without pain there is little gain.

8. Repeat Steps 5 and 6 for each field that you want to include in your data file.

- ✔ Add fields for all the fill-in-the-blanks items in your documents: name, address, and salutation.

- ✔ You can have up to 31 fields in a data file. That should be enough.

- ✔ No two fields can have the same name.

9. Click the OK button.

The Save As dialog box appears.

10. Give your document a name.

11. Click the OK button.

After the document has a name, a table appears with all of the field names running along the top. This place where all the field names are listed is called the *header record*. You are now ready to insert the information.

Adding data to the data file

Enter your records by plopping the data into the appropriate column in the data file's table. This is where you fill in the blanks, athough you're doing it all at once instead of writing a whole lot of individual letters. WinWord will glue everything together soon enough.

At this point, your screen should look something like Figure 18-2, shown previously in this chapter. If not, you may want to consider Step 2 or Step 3 that was listed under the section "Understanding Mail Merge" at the beginning of this chapter.

> ✔ Move from column to column by pressing the Tab key. The table automatically expands to add space for additional records as you go.

> ✔ When you finish adding records, be sure to save your document. (Choose File→Save or press Shift+F12).

Inserting the fields

Now it is time, finally, to glue the two documents together. It's why they call it a mail merge, after all. To do this, you first need to tell the main document where to put the fields that you so painfully created in the data document. So, return to the main document by clicking on the big M in the data file's toolbar or by choosing File→Print Merge and selecting the Edit Main Document button.

You need to place the fields — the blanks — into your main document. That's done by following these steps:

1. **Position the toothpick cursor where you want the field to be placed.**

   For example, you want a name field after the *Dear* in your letter's greeting, so position the cursor between the Dear and the colon (see Figure 18-6).

   > ✔ The fields created in the data document do not have any punctuation in them. If you want a space or a comma, or anything else, you need to insert it in the main document.

2. **Choose the Insert Merge Field button with the mouse, or press the Alt+Shift+F key combination.**

   The Insert Merge Field dialog box opens, as shown in Figure 18-7.

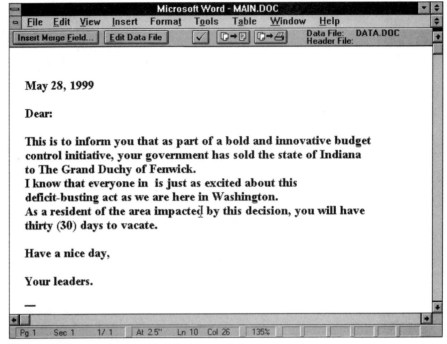

Figure 18-6: The main document in Print Merge window.

3. Highlight the field that you want to place in the document, and select OK.

For example, placing the cursor between Dear and the colon, highlighting the firstname field, and pressing OK enters the cryptic code <<firstname>> into the main document.

✔ You can have more than one field on a line.

✔ If a field is empty, like address2 in most of the sample records, WinWord skips it by default when it merges with the main document. This does not leave unsightly empty lines or anything.

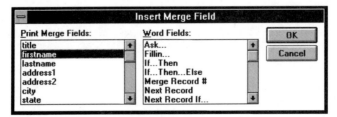

Figure 18-7: The Insert Merge Field dialog box lists all fields in the data file.

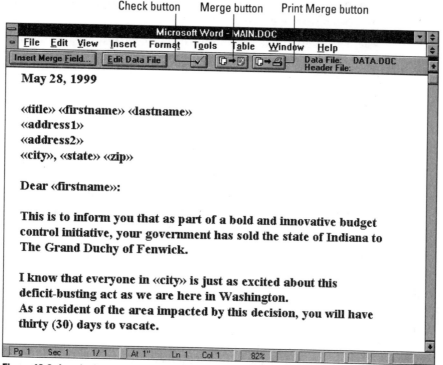

Figure 18-8: A main document all gussied up and ready for merging.

4. Continue adding fields until the document is complete.

When you are finished, your document should look similar to the one illustrated in Figure 18-8.

Merge Mania!

After creating the main and data files, you're ready to merge away! Ensure that both main and data files have been saved to disk. This is very important! When you want to do the merge, follow these steps, which are, you will be glad to learn, a whole bunch simpler than anything else connected with merging:

1. Open the main document.

Choose File→Open or — and this is really handy, if you've been working on the main document recently — select the main document itself from the bottom of the File menu, which shows the last four files used.

2. When the document appears, notice that its toolbar has changed. It now has only five buttons.

✔ The Insert Merge Field button can be used just in case you forgot to put in a field, see "Inserting the fields" previously in this chapter to find out about fields.

✔ Pressing the Edit Data File button whisks you right back to the data file so that you can make additions or changes. See "Preparing the Data File" and "Adding data to the data file" previously in this chapter for information on this fascinating topic.

3. If the whole process of mail merge makes you paranoid, like it does me, click on the button that has the check mark.

This button tells WinWord to look at what you did to see whether you made any really big mistakes, like including a field that isn't in the data record. If you pass the test, WinWord announces:

```
No print merge errors have been found.
```

Be happy.

4. Merge!

Click on the Merge button.

Congratulations, you've just merged.

✔ WinWord merges the names and other information from the data file into the main document and creates lots of little, customized documents. That's what you see on-screen right now. Your options at this point are to review all the documents, save them, or print them. You made it!

✔ Viewing several merges before printing is a good idea. Check for punctuation and spacing.

✔ The main file appears several times on-screen, with information from the data file plugged into each copy. All files are separated by hard page breaks (a row of equal signs).

✔ If your merge isn't humongous, you should save your mail merge in this on-screen format.

✔ You can print right from the screen view of the merged files by selecting File→Print.

✔ To print the merged documents, press the Print Merge button. This opens the Print dialog box whence printing takes place. Click OK, and after a few moments — or longer, depending on how detailed the merge is and how many records you have — you have a complete set of merged documents issuing forth from your printer.

✔ Now you know how to get those custom, uniquely crafted documents out to the foolhardy who actually think you took the time to compose a personal letter. Ha! Isn't mail merge great?

✔ Always examine the results of the merge. Some things may not fit properly, and some editing will no doubt be required.

Part IV
Working with Graphics

The 5th Wave
By Rich Tennant

"HE SAID 'WHY BUY JUST A WORD PROCESSOR WHEN YOU CAN GET ONE WITH A MATH AND GRAPHICS LINK CAPABLE OF DOING SCHEMATICS OF AN F100 AIRCRAFT ENGINE?' AND I THOUGHT, WELL, WE NEVER BUY TOASTEMS WITHOUT BRAN ..."

In this part . . .

Word processing is words, so what's the ugly subject of graphics doing here? After all, you struggle to write; now do they want you to struggle to draw?

Fortunately, graphics in a word processor isn't that painful, especially thanks to Windows, which lives and breathes graphics, and that's the thrust behind this part of the book. It's more than just cutting and pasting pretty pictures and, if you're lucky, there's very little actual drawing involved. (So dash those images of stick figures lining your literary master-pieces.) There are many parts of WinWord that you can use to help create graphics — stuff you'd never otherwise know about. It's all covered here in the cheery manner you expect. Be prepared to make your writing not only literary, but flowery as well.

Chapter 19
Making Purty Pictures

*I*f a picture is worth a thousand words, then isn't that photo of Rocky winning the boxing championship against Apollo Creed worth 500 "Yo, Adrian"s?

Graphics, when well-chosen and relevant to the subject, add another dimension to the understanding of the words you write. You can add illustrations, simple drawings called *line art*, and even photos to enhance your creative work. On multimedia-equipped computers — *multimedia* means "I spent a lot more for this stuff" — you also can add movies with sound or animation with your own voice recorded as a sound track to your WinWord document. Cool, yes! Practical, no!

Adding a Graphic Image

There are three different ways to add a graphic to a WinWord document:

1. You can just paste it in wherever the toothpick cursor happens to be.

2. You can put it in a table.

3. You can put it in a frame.

   Each method has something going for it; each has something going against it, too.

   ✔ Pasting is the latter half of copy-and-paste. You start by finding or creating an image in another program, one suited to graphics. Then you *copy* the image. Windows remembers it. Then you *paste* it into WinWord. This works like copying and pasting text, and the same Ctrl+C (Copy) and Ctrl+V (Paste) keys are used in all Windows programs for this purpose.

✔ Putting an image into a table works just like copying it to the tooth-pick cursor's position. The difference is that the image fits snuggly into a cell in a table. Refer to Chapter 12 for more information on tables; your local hardware store has lots of books on making chairs and lawn furniture.

✔ Putting an image into a frame is nice because you can write text *around* the image. Otherwise, the image kinda sits by itself, all lonely without text to insulate it.

Whence commeth thy graphical image?

Before you write anything, you should have a good idea in your head what you want to write about. (If you don't, and you just stare at the blank screen, then you have what it takes to be a *real* writer!) The same holds true with graphics. You need to have the graphic image you want to use in your text before you paste it in. WinWord can do a lot of things, but you can't exactly draw with it. Not really.

Graphic images — pictures — come from several places. You can create the image in a graphics program, buy a disk full of images or *clip art*, or you can use a device called a *scanner* to electronically convert pictures and other printed images into graphics files you can store in the computer.

✔ WinWord can deal with many popular graphics file formats, which probably are listed in the manual somewhere, and which do appear on the List Files of Type drop-down lists in the various graphics-related dialog boxes. As long as your graphics can be saved in a *compatible* format, WinWord won't balk.

✔ You don't need to have a graphics file on a disk. You also can paste anything you can get onto the Windows Clipboard directly into a WinWord document as a graphic. This means that you can create a graphic with a drawing program, copy it to the Clipboard, and then paste it into your WinWord document. This is the "do it on the fly" school of graphics creation.

✔ The most common graphic file formats are .PCX, .GIF, .WMF, .BMP, and .TIF. These are all file extensions you can find on graphics files on your hard drive. Table 19-1 below explains what the formats mean. If you can save your graphics in any of these formats, you're in business and WinWord is happily-bappily.

Table 19-1	Common Graphic Formats	
Format	*Pronounciation*	*File type*
.PCX	Pee-See-Exchs	PC Paintbrush (also Windows Paint)
.GIF	Jiff (the peanuttier peanut butter)	Graphics Interchange Format, used primarily on CompuServe for "naked lady" images
.WMF	Double-U-Em-Eff	Windows *metafile*, a common graphics file format
.BMP	Bee-Em-Pee	Windows bitmap files, used by Windows Paint and other programs
.TIF	Tiff	Tagged Image Format file, used by some sophisticated drawing programs

Slapping a graphic image into a document

To stick a graphic image already created on disk into your text, follow these whimsical steps:

1. Position the toothpick cursor to the spot where you want your picture.

If there's any text already there, it will be shoved aside to make room for the graphic.

2. Choose the Insert→Picture command.

Use the mouse or press Alt,I,P. You see the Picture dialog box, as shown in Figure 19-1.

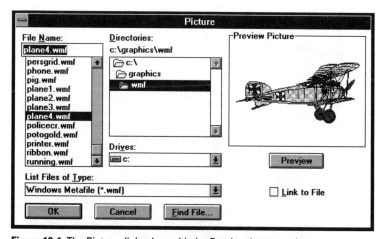

Figure 19-1: The Picture dialog box with the Preview button active.

3. **Navigate through the drives and directories until you find the graphic image you want.**

The graphic image must already be created and saved as a file on disk. Refer to the first two sections in this chapter for additional information. You can find the name of the file that contains the image you want by manipulating the Dri_ves, _Directories, and File _Name lists until you see the file you want.

Clicking on the Pre_view button will let you see a *thumbnail* image of the graphic. This saves a lot of time, especially if you are deciding between several different images.

4. **Select the image.**

Highlight the filename.

5. **Choose OK!**

Splat! The image is pasted into your document, wherever your cursor happened to be.

✔ "Ugh! That wasn't the image I wanted." Hurry and choose the _Edit→_Undo command, or press Ctrl+Z and try again.

✔ You don't have to use the _Insert→_Picture command if you copy and paste an image. To do that, create the image in another Windows application, select it for copying, then return to WinWord and paste. (You can use Paintbrush, which is located in the Accessories program group in the Windows Program Manager.)

✔ The image appears right where the toothpick cursor is. In fact, you can almost treat the image as if it were a "character" in your document.

✔ The following section offers information on adjusting the image by adding a border, for example.

✔ Some images are colorful on-screen. Unless you have a color printer, they'll only print in black, white, and — with a laser printer — shades of gray.

✔ A cool thing to stick at the end of a letter is your signature. Use a painting program like Windows Paint or have it *scanned in* by using a desktop scanner to create your John Hancock. Save it as a file on disk, and then follow the previous steps to insert it at the proper place in your document.

✔ If you have faithfully followed the preceding steps, and that blasted graphic just won't show up on-screen, it's probably because the paragraph formatting got messed up. Put the cursor in the paragraph that has the graphic, open the Format→_Paragraph dialog box, and change the line spacing to something other than `Exactly`.

- This method of inserting a graphic does not allow you to put multiple lines of text next to the image. See "Slapping it in a table" or "Frame the thing" later in this chapter to learn how to do this.

- Although they're not really "graphic images," WinWord has an assortment of oddball characters you can insert into your text, right along with the normal human characters. For example the ☺ or the ♥ are ever-popular with hippie-wanna-bees. Refer to Chapter 9 for more information on WinWord's oddball characters.

- WinWord comes with a small library of clipart located in the \WINWORD\CLIPART directory.

- Nothing slows down WinWord like a few graphical images on-screen. Try pasting them in last.

Slapping it in a table

Tables are wonderful places for a graphic. You can put your image of, say, your favorite politician in a cell and place text in any cell before or after the graphic. This keeps everything neat without interfering much with the text before or after the table.

To insert a graphic in a table, follow these steps.

1. **Make the table.**

   Refer to Chapter 12, "Using Tables and Columns," to learn about tables. Keep in mind that it's okay to make a table with only one "row." You can put the image in one column and text in the other.

2. **Position the toothpick cursor in the cell where you want your picture.**

   Point and click with the mouse.

3. **Choose the Insert→Picture command.**

   Click with the mouse or press Alt,I,P.

4. **Navigate through the drives and directories until you find the graphic you want.**

5. **Select the image and choose OK.**

   Slap! The image is pasted into your table.

- If the image has already been saved in the Windows Clipboard (you copied it from another program), then you just need to press Ctrl+C, the Copy command, in Step 3 and you're done.

- You can "grab" the edges of a cell in a table to change the cell's size or position.

- To change the size of your image, see the section "Adjusting the Graphic Image" later in this chapter.

Frame the thing

The third, and most satisfying, way to put an image into a document is to put it in a frame. Putting a graphic in a frame gives it mobility; you can move the frame all over the document and place it just so. To put a graphic in a frame, you must first make the frame — big surprise.

To make a frame, use these steps:

1. **Switch to Page Layout View.**

   Choose View→Page Layout. You can skip this step, but WinWord will be insistent and finally do it for you. So why not succumb right away?

2. **Choose the Insert→Frame command.**

   The toothpick cursor changes into a little cross-hair doodad.

3. **Put the little cross-hair doodad where you want the upper-left corner of the frame to be.**

4. **Create the frame by holding down the left mouse button and dragging the little cross-hair doodad down and to the right.**

   This creates a rectangle on-screen.

   ✔ Your picture will appear inside that rectangle — okay, "frame."

   ✔ When the frame is constructed, you can move it around by moving the cursor to the edge of the frame until it changes into a four-headed arrow. When this occurs, hold down the mouse button, and drag the frame to its new location.

   ✔ You can combine Steps 1 and 2 above and simply click the Frame tool and respond Yes to the resulting dialog box. The cursor becomes a cross-hair, and you can continue with Step 3.

After the frame has been constructed, you can plop a graphic into it. Use these steps:

1. **Select the frame by moving the cursor to the edge of the frame until it changes into a four-headed arrow.**

2. **Click the left mouse button.**

   The frame becomes selected and is surrounded by a box with "handles" on it.

3. **Summon the all-powerful Insert→Picture command.**

   Click on Picture in the Insert menu or press Alt,I,P.

4. **Navigate through the drives and directories until you find the graphic you want.**

5. Select the image and choose OK.

Plop! The image is pasted into the frame.

> ✔ If something goes wrong, nine times out of ten it is because the frame was not selected before you imported the image.

> ✔ The following section explains how to change the size of your image.

Adjusting the Graphic Image

To get a graphic image into your text, follow the steps in the preceding section. After the image is there, you can adjust its size by clicking once on the image. Keep in mind that this won't let you re-draw the image. But you can certainly tweak its appearance a bit.

Here are the basic "I want to tweak my graphics" steps:

1. Click on the image with the mouse cursor.

The graphic becomes surrounded by a box. The box has *handles* on it, which you can use to manipulate the image (see Figure 19-2).

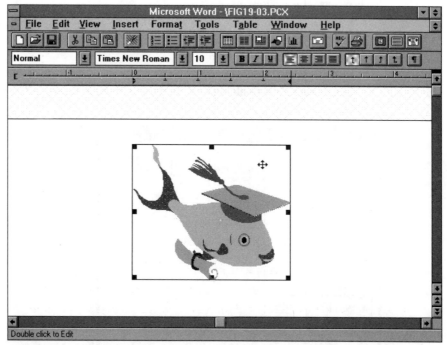

Figure 19-2: An image from the WinWord clip art library shown in Page Layout view and surrounded by handles.

2. Grab any one of the handles and drag it to change the image's size.

- ✔ The graphic can be scaled (made larger or smaller without distortion) by holding down the Ctrl key while dragging one of the corner handles.

- ✔ The graphic can be cropped, or chopped off, by holding down the Shift key while dragging a handle.

- ✔ If adjusting the image's size just isn't enough, you can do some pretty fancy editing of the image by double-clicking on it with the mouse. This opens a link between the image and the program that made it — or a program that can work with the image. Usually, Microsoft Draw opens, although Windows Paint sometimes does instead.

- ✔ Refer to Chapter 20 to learn how to change the graphic by using Microsoft Draw.

Drawing Lines around the Graphic

WinWord treats a graphic, even one in a frame, like a paragraph. Therefore, you can draw various different kinds of boxes around a graphic without the need for a drawing program. Everything can be done right in WinWord.

To box a graphic, follow these steps:

1. Select the graphic by clicking on the image with the mouse cursor.

The graphic becomes surrounded by a box.

2. Choose the Format→Border command.

The Border Picture dialog box opens, as shown in Figure 19-3.

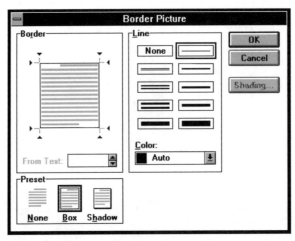

Figure 19-3: The Border Picture dialog box allows you to draw a box, or pieces of a box, around a graphic image.

3. Select a Line style.

In the Line area of the Border Picture dialog box, click on a line style: thin, fat, double, single.

4. Select Box or Shadow from the bottom of the dialog.

The Shadow option gives the frame "depth" by casting a simulated shadow down and to the right.

5. Choose OK.

You got a boxed graphic.

> ✔ This works with all three types of inserted graphics: those pasted in wherever the cursor happens to be; the ones placed in a table; and those placed in a frame.

> ✔ You also can use the Border dialog box to put a box around one or more paragraphs of text in your document. Just highlight the paragraph and choose Format→Border. Select the line style, whether you want a regular box or a shadow box, and then click OK.

Chapter 20

WinWord's Amazing Applets: Equation Editor, Graph, Draw, and WordArt

*W*inWord is not alone. Just as Windows comes with its own "suite" of little programs — mini-applications called *applets* — WinWord comes with its host of li'l programs as well. With Windows, you get: Write word processor; Paintbrush painting program; Terminal communications program; Cardfile data organizer; and a calendar, clock, and calculator. These give the idly interested Windows user something to play with while they save up enough money to buy real programs.

The programs offered with WinWord gear themselves toward word processing, so they aren't as broad as the Windows applets (which implies that they actually appproach being useful). Bothering with these little gems is optional. However, everyone I've shown them seems to enjoy them, so maybe you will too. That would be a nice switch.

The Great WinWord Applet Hunt

Four programs come with WinWord. These may or may not have been installed at the same time you installed WinWord:

✔ The Equation Editor, used to create mathematical-looking equations

✔ Microsoft Graph, a graphical/statistical program

✔ Microsoft Draw, a drawing program (more exact than a painting program)

✔ Word Art, a fancy word/letter display program

To see whether you have these programs installed, follow these steps:

1. Choose the Insert→Object command.

Use the mouse or press Alt,I,O. The Object dialog box appears, similar to the one in Figure 20-1. This box contains a list of objects or things you can stick into a WinWord document. The idea here is that you don't have to go somewhere else, create something, copy it, and paste it back into WinWord. The Object dialog box lets you instantly create something and stick it into WinWord without the excess travel expenses.

2. Scan the list of items.

You're looking for four of them: Equation, Microsoft Drawing, Microsoft Graph, and MS WordArt. These are the four applets mentioned at the start of this section. If you can't find one or more, then you'll need to install the applets as described in the following section. If they're all there, then you're in business.

3. Click Cancel to close the Object dialog box.

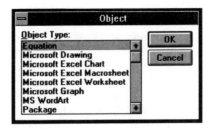

Figure 20-1: The Object dialog box.

✔ Many other items are listed in the Object dialog box. These represent various things you can paste into a WinWord document. For example, if you have Excel, you may see an item representing an Excel Worksheet or Chart.

✔ The WinWord applets are programs unique to WinWord, which you can't access from other programs.

✓ Each applet has a specific function and produces a specific graphical object that you can quite handily insert into your WinWord document.

Installing the Applets

The WinWord applets come with Word for Windows and should have been installed when you first setup WinWord. However, they may not be there for a number of reasons: You don't have enough space on your hard drive; you elected not to include them when you installed WinWord (probably because you didn't know what they were); or someone else set up WinWord and didn't know what to do. In any case, the following steps tell you how to install the applets:

1. **Find your original WinWord distribution diskettes.**

   These are the floppy disks that came with Word for Windows. They might still be in the box or you might have stored them away in a disk caddy or fire safe somewhere. I keep my disks in the original box, which is buried under a mound of stuff in the back corner of my office.

2. **Locate the first diskette, which will be labeled Disk 1 or have the word SETUP on it.**

3. **Place that diskette into your A floppy drive.**

   If it's a 5¼-inch drive, close the drive door latch.

4. **Switch to the Program Manager.**

   Press Ctrl+Esc. The Task List window opens. In the list, locate Program Manager and double-click with your mouse.

5. **Choose the File→Run command in the Program Manager.**

   The Run dialog box appears. The cursor will be flashing inside a text box.

   You also can double-click on the Word Setup icon if you have it in your Program Manager.

6. **Type in the following:**

```
A:SETUP
```

   That's A, a colon, and the word *setup*. There are no spaces and no period at the end.

7. **Press Enter.**

   This runs the Setup program on drive A, the one you originally ran to install WinWord on your PC. (Okay, some one else may have done this for you.)

   It takes some time to run, doesn't it?

   Ho-hum.

8. **Click the Continue button.**

Don't pay any heed to any warning about "overwriting" WinWord.

9. **Click the Continue button again.**

10. **Click the Custom Installation box.**

In the Word Setup Options dialog box, you find a list of items, each with a check box.

11. **De-select each check box, except the one beside Draw, Graph, Equation Editor, WordArt.**

Make sure that only this item has an X in its box. Everything else should be X-less.

12. **Click on the Setup button.**

13. **Continue following instructions on-screen.**

Read everything and answer the questions so that the Applets are installed on your system. If you're faced with a choice, always press Enter. This selects the default item, which is probably the one you want.

14. **Eventually, the Setup program ends.**

Great! The WinWord applets are now installed and you can enjoy using them.

✔ If your disks for WinWord are for your B drive, type b:setup in Step 6.

✔ If you can't find the original WinWord distribution diskettes (or a copy you might have made), then you're out of luck. Sorry.

✔ If there wasn't enough room on your hard drive when you first installed WinWord, there may not be enough room on it now. If so, the Setup program warns you of this. There's nothing you can do, aside from freeing up space on your hard drive. That's a technical subject, so you better grab your DOS or Windows guru and force him or her to help you.

The Gestalt of the WinWord Applets

The WinWord Applets are like little programs that produce what are called *objects*. As far as you or I are concerned, the objects are graphics — things you can paste into your documents. But Windows thinks that the graphics are *objects*, or items of extreme importance around which Windows will hop and jump like a little kid high on Cocoa Puffs.

What if, heaven forbid, you want to toss something like this at your readers (see Figure 20-2):

$$\sigma_X^2 = \frac{1}{n}\left\{\sum_{i=1}^{n} X_i^2 - n\overline{X}^2\right\}$$

Figure 20-2: Sample Equation Editor object.

That's a formula, possibly one for some deadly toxic chemical being dumped by evil scientists right now, just up the street. In WinWord, that item is an *equation object,* created with the WinWord Equation Editor. It's really nothing at all, as is the following graph (see Figure 20-3):

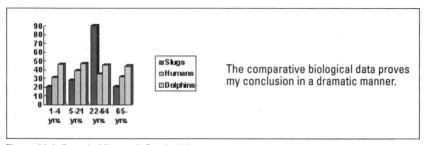

Figure 20-3: Sample Microsoft Graph object.

The above, professional-looking and highly impressive graphic was created with the Microsoft Graph applet by the same unskilled laborers who wrote this book .

The steps to get to these impressive doodads are simple:

1. **Position the toothpick cursor where you want the object to appear.**

   The object is a graphic. In some cases, it can appear right in the middle of a sentence or at the start of a line. Other times, it should go on a line by itself or in the midst of a table where it can be dealt with more easily.

2. **Choose the Insert→Object command.**

   The Object dialog box opens (refer to Figure 20-1).

3. **Select the object you want to insert.**

   Suppose that you want to create a fancy letterhead, such as the one shown in Figure 20-4. You click on the Microsoft Draw object in the Object dialog box and highlight it. (Following sections outline how to use all four of the applets.)

Society to Supply Cats With Unlimited
Numbers of Small Woodland Creatures

123 Outtamy Way
Dead Bird, Montana

Figure 20-4: A fancy letterhead created with a WinWord applet.

4. Choose OK.

This zooms you to the applet where you can create the object or graphic for your document.

5. Toil! Toil! Toil!

Create that object or graphic! This can be really easy, so the toil is misleading (we don't want anyone to assume that you're having fun here, right?). Just last night, I created a simple object for a document by using WordArt. It took maybe 5 minutes, and that was with my left brain soundly asleep.

6. Quit the applet.

The applet asks whether you want to update your document with the new graphical object. Choose the <u>Y</u>es button. This returns you to WinWord and inserts the graphical object into your document.

✔ The advantage of inserting an object into a WinWord document — especially one created by a WinWord applet — is that the object is "hot-linked" back to the program that created it. To fix up your graphical object, all you need to do is double-click on it with the mouse. Zoom! That takes you back to the applet, where you can edit or tweak the object.

✔ The WinWord applets, Draw, Graph, Equation Editor, and WordArt, are available only in WinWord. You cannot use them in any other Windows application. Don't even bother trying. We did for days and could not get it to work.

✔ After the applet places its object into your document, the object functions like a graphic. You can click on the object once and the tell-tale dotted graphical outline box appears. You can use the mouse to change the graphic's size by dragging any of the outline's edges or corners. The image re-sizes itself accordingly.

✔ To maintain the proportion of the art, hold down the Ctrl key while you drag one of the corner handles.

✔ To crop the image (literally, to hack off excess white space around the graphic), hold down the Shift key while dragging the handles as you re-size the graphical object.

✔ To edit the applet's graphical object, click it twice with the mouse. The applet that created the object opens, which allows you to make adjustments and tweaks as necessary.

Employing the Equation Editor

No self-respecting human being would have anything to do with something as totally nerdy as the Equation Editor applet. Yet, we suppose that there may be some users who have a need to express mathematical mysticism in its glorious "how'd they do that?" format. This is much better than trying to use the fractured and fragmented symbols on the keyboard to express your Greek math things. Then, there also may be the curious users. Nothing can be more fun than *pretending* you know advanced hydro-physics and dreaming up some Einstein-level-IQ equation to impress the in-laws in your Christmas letter. Follow these steps:

1. **Move the toothpick cursor where you want your equation to be inserted.**

   It can be anywhere — on a line by itself or in the middle of a sentence.

2. **Choose the Insert→Object command.**

   The Object dialog box opens.

3. **Click on Equation in the list.**

   This activates the Equation Editor applet — a real program. It appears in a window on-screen, right on top of WinWord and your document (see Figure 20-5). Don't panic.

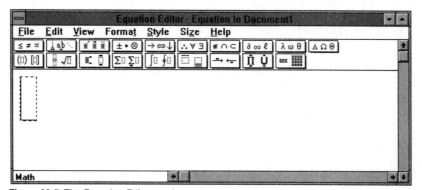

Figure 20-5: The Equation Editor applet.

4. Build your equation.

Below the menu bar is a series of button-menus. Click on one with the mouse, and a palette of equations, doohickeys, and mathematical thingamabobs appears. This is how you select various items to go into your equation — to build the equation graphically.

At this point, you're on your own. The Equation Editor can build just about any equation, but it's up to you to know what you want in the equation. You select items from the button-palettes, fill in the dotted rectangles, and poke and change things with the mouse. Have fun!

5. When you're done editing, choose File→Exit and Return.

WinWord asks whether you want to save the changes in your document. This question is posed because WinWord has, in a way, already updated your document with an Equation Editor object.

6. Choose Yes!

You plop back into WinWord and you can see your glorious equation, there to baffle mankind or whomever you send your memos.

✔ The equation appears in your document like a graphic.

✔ If you click on the equation, it becomes outlined like a graphic window frame. You can use the mouse to re-size the equation by dragging one side of its frame to a new location. The equation changes its shape accordingly.

✔ To edit the equation, click on it twice with the mouse. The Equation Editor opens and allows you to make minor changes.

Grappling with Microsoft Graph

Nothing can spin the dust off numbers better than a real cool graph. You don't even need to mess with a spreadsheet or futz with a "chart program." Everything can be done neatly from within WinWord, thanks to the novel Microsoft Graph applet.

To insert a graph into your document, follow these steps:

1. Move the toothpick cursor to the place you want to insert the upper-left corner of the graph.

Graphs are big square things. WinWord inserts the big square thing into your document, so move your cursor where you want the graph *before* you start.

2. Choose the Insert→Object command.

Or, click the Graph tool.

The Object dialog box appears (refer to Figure 20-1).

3. Choose Microsoft Graph from the list.

The Graph applet opens — a real live program — that appears on top of WinWord and your document on-screen. Figure 20-6 shows what the Graph applet may look like. There are two windows, one for the graph and another for the data. The Datasheet window looks like a spreadsheet or table. The Graph window looks like a graph. Both windows contain bogus data at this point, which you can replace. And you can select another type of graph (pie chart, linechart) if you like.

4. Replace the sample data with the information you want displayed.

You can add and delete columns and rows the same way that you would do this in any table. See Chapter 12 for info about tables. You need to click on the Datasheet window to activate it before you can input new values. To add new rows and columns, use the last two commands in the Edit menu.

5. Change the graphic, if you like.

The Gallery menu contains all the chart options. If you want a pie chart, for example, you can choose Gallery→Pie. You need to follow the instructions on-screen and possibly tweak your data a bit to get the right pie flavor.

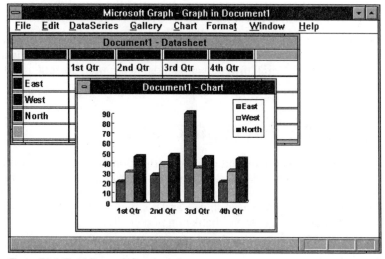

Figure 20-6: The Microsoft Graph applet.

6. Fiddle and play!

The information you enter into the table is immediately updated in the chart. This allows you to see your graph evolve. It can really be fun, but please don't let anyone watching you believe that you're having fun. That isn't fair.

7. You're done!

Choose the File→Exit and Return command. The applet asks whether you want to update the graph in your document.

8. Choose Yes!

Your document now has a beautiful graph, suitable for framing. (See Chapter 19 for information on framing a graphic.)

✔ You also can make a graphical chart from data already in your document. Suppose that you have numbers sitting in a table. To make it into a Microsoft Graph thing, mark the entire table as a block, and then follow all of the preceding steps for creating a new chart. Your data, instead of the "bogus" data, fills in the datasheet for creating the graph.

✔ If you make a chart from a table already in your document, you can use the first cell for the title of the chart. Any words you put in this cell (the upper-leftmost) will be centered above the graph as its title.

✔ There are many different flavors of charts available; poke around in the Gallery menu to find the one that perfectly highlights your data.

✔ After the graph appears in your document, it can be treated like a graphic. If you click on the graph-object, it will be outlined like a graphic window frame. You can use the mouse to re-size the equation by dragging one side of its frame to a new location. The graph changes its shape accordingly.

✔ To edit the graph, for modifying or tweaking the graph or changing the type of graph, click on it twice with your mouse. This re-activates the Microsoft Graph program and loads the graphic-object for editing.

Dealing with Microsoft Draw

Microsoft Draw is a neat little applet with a bunch of uses. It is especially good for making minor additions to clip art or other graphical stuff in your documents. You can get really sophisticated with Microsoft Draw. It has its own toolbar, menus, and everything — and it's free! free! free! with WinWord. Such a deal. Call up Bill Gates and thank him personally.

Obviously, there isn't enough space here to explain the entire Microsoft Draw application. So, instead, I encourage you to explore it on your own — just as you once explored the fun Paintbrush program. Also, refer to the check list at the end of this section for some suggestions on how best to use Draw if your exploration time is hindered by something looming and ominous.

To insert a Microsoft Draw object-graphic thing into your document:

1. Put the toothpick cursor where you want the graphic thing to appear.

2. Choose the Insert→Object command.

Or, click the Draw tool.

The Object dialog box opens (refer to Figure 20-1).

2. Choose Microsoft Drawing from the list.

The Draw applet opens, as shown in Figure 20-7. The applet is another program that appears "on top of" WinWord and your document on-screen. Don't be alarmed by this; it's why you have Windows in the first place.

3. Do something wondrous.

You can create a graphic here, just as you would in any paint program. But with a drawing program, things work differently. Instead of painting pixels on-screen — like drawing with an electronic crayon — you're working with graphical object more like an erector set. When you create a box, for example, you can move the box or change its size *after* creating it. The box is an *object* on-screen, not a set of pixels or electronic crayon gunk. (I'm getting too philosophical here.)

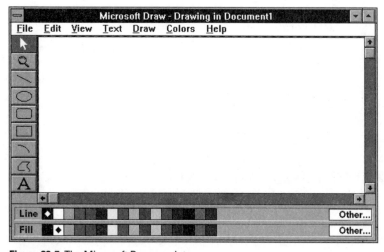

Figure 20-7: The Microsoft Draw applet.

Another fun thing you can do, which was done in Figure 20-4, is to *import* an existing graphical image, one already created in another graphics program. You do this by choosing File→Import Picture in Draw. An Import dialog box opens, where you can pluck a graphic file from anywhere on disk.

4. You're done.

Choose File→Exit and Return. The applet asks whether you want to save the changes to your document.

5. Choose Yes.

You exit the Draw applet and return to WinWord. You see the graphic right there in your document. Stand back and be amazed.

✔ A series of buttons appears along the left side of the Draw applet window. You use these tools to draw straight lines, boxes, and circles. The colors along the bottom of the screen allow you to choose the line colors and a fill pattern (the color for the graphic's "middle").

✔ You can put text into your drawing by using the big A text tool. Unlike a paint program, the text you create appears in its own "box." It can be edited later just like you were editing text in WinWord. The Text menu contains commands for changing the font and text style.

✔ By using the File→Import Picture command in the Draw applet, you can import any graphic into Draw that shows up in the Import Picture dialog's file list. This includes files with extensions of .BMP, .PCX, .WMF, .EPS, .TIF, as well as several others. That's an extensive list, which gives you access to files of strange types that would otherwise baffle WinWord.

✔ I've used the Draw tool to insert some boxes, circles, and triangles into a paper I wrote about trigonometry. It was just easier to draw a triangle in Draw, slap it into WinWord, and write about it than to use the prerequisite 1,000 words to describe what a triangle looks like.

✔ When your Draw drawing is in your document, it behaves like any other graphic. You can click on it it once to "outline" it, and then use the mouse to change its size if you like. The graphic re-sizes itself to fit the outline accordingly.

✔ To edit the graphic in Draw again, click on it twice with the mouse.

Activating MS WordArt

WordArt is very subtle. Most people don't know about it. When they find out, excitement reigns. There are lots of interesting and — dare I use the word — *cool* things WordArt can do to spice up the way your document works.

Like the other applets (Equation Editor, Draw, and Graph), WordArt produces a graphical object in your text. It's not text! For formatting text, you really need to use the character formatting rules and regulations outlined in Chapter 9. WordArt is art.

To put WordArt into your document, follow these steps:

1. Position the toothpick cursor in the spot in your document where you want the WordArt to appear.

It can really be anywhere: at the start of a line, in the middle of a paragraph, or on a line by itself. Whatever the case, move the toothpick cursor to that location first.

2. Choose the Insert→Object command.

The Object dialog box opens.

3. Select MS WordArt from the list.

You may need to scroll through the list to find MS WordArt. I've installed Excel on my PC and there are a few dozen Excel-ish "objects" that appear before MS WordArt. After you select it and click OK, the WordArt applet, shown in Figure 20-8, appears.

4. Type the text you want "artified" into the box.

What you type will replace the `Your Text Here` already highlighted near the top of the window. You can type in more than a single line of text.

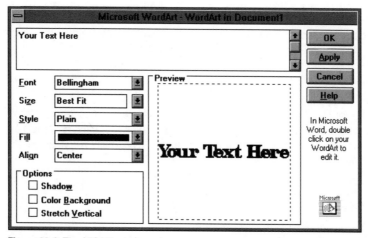

Figure 20-8: The MS WordArt applet.

5. Mess with it!

Along the left side of the dialog box are five items that control your text — that make it arty — Font, Size, Style, Fill, and Align. There are 19 unique fonts in the Font drop-down list. Size makes your text bigger or smaller, and the other three items adjust your text in other ways. Everything is previewed in the box to the right of the drop-down menus. Three check boxes at the bottom of the window also allow you to modify the way your word art looks.

6. When you're done, select OK.

The WordArt object moves into the WinWord document and appears right at the cursor position.

✔ Like any other applet's graphical-object, click on the WordArt graphic twice with your mouse to edit it.

✔ Refer to the section "The Gestalt of the WinWord Applets" earlier in this chapter for more information on tweaking your WordArt.

The initial cap thing ala WordArt

One cute trick you can pull off with WordArt is the interesting "inital cap" token. That's where the first letter of a report, article, chapter, or story appears in a larger and more interesting font than the other characters. Using WordArt, you can make this happen rather easily.

First, position the toothpick cursor at the start of your text — not the title, but the first paragraph of text. It also helps if this paragraph is left-justified and not indented with a Tab or by using any of the tricky formatting discussed in Chapter 10.

Assuming that your story is already written, delete the first character of the first word. For example, delete the O in "Once upon a time." This leaves the word *nce* there, which isn't a word (and WinWord's spell-checker will tell you so over and over). That's okay.

Activate WordArt. Choose Insert→Object, and double-click on MS WordArt to open WordArt's window. Into the sample text area, type an O. Then use the Font and Size drop-down lists to make your O a larger size. You may even want to spruce it up with other options; WordArt is a fun place in which to play.

When you're finished, exit to WinWord and your large, initial cap appears at the start your document. It looks funky at first — which is okay. Click on the graphical object once with the mouse, and then drag the rectangle's various edges to tighten them around the O. It helps if you press the Shift key as you drag.

Chapter 21

Your Basic DTP Stuff

Some graphical things you can do with your document don't involve graphics at all. Instead, these items approach that fuzzy border between word processing and desktop publishing. Indeed, this part of the book would have been considered desktop publishing just a few years ago. So what else is there beside fancy graphics and text? There are boxes. And interesting ways to slap fancy titles and other things into your document. It's not really graphics; it's more along the lines of your basic DTP (desktop publishing) stuff.

Creating Cool Document Titles

Nothing dampens the fire of an exciting paper like a dreary, dull heading. Consider the plight of the hapless garden slug. "Your Garden's Gastropod" can be a creative title (see Figure 21-1). Gastropod comes from the Latin words for stomach and foot. A slug is essentially a crawling stomach, lubricated with a thin coating of slime and built-in fear of salt. But enough biology for now! To make your slug paper stand out you need more than just a title. You need a *creative* title.

Figure 21-1 shows various examples of document titles you can create with WinWord. It's possible to mix and match the styles to create the ideal title you want. The following sections detail how each element is created: formatting text and paragraphs and creating special effects.

Example 1:

```
              The Slug
      Your Garden's Gastropod
```

Example 2:

Slimey, Sticky, Oozy

S L U G S

In Your Garden

Example 3:

Your Glistening Gastropod Gardening Newsletter

SLUG & SNAIL

Vol II, Issue 6   June 11, 1994

Figure 21-1: Sample document titles.

Formatting the text just so

You use three steps for formatting text for your title:

1. Selecting a font.

2. Selecting a type size.

3. Selecting character attributes.

To select a font, follow these steps:

1. Choose the Format→Character command.

The Character formatting dialog box opens.

2. **Click on the drop-down box by the Font option-thingy in the upper-left corner.**

   A drop-down list displays all the fonts known to Windows and WinWord. The best fonts to use for titles are the blocky, no-frills fonts, including Helvetica, Arial, Swiss, Univers, Avant Gard, Optima, and Futura. You're bound to have one of those fonts available in the list. Select it.

3. **Enter a size for the font in the Points box, or use the drop-down button to display a list of available sizes.**

   To make your title big, select a large font size. This means 14pt or more. I like a 24pt title, which is nice and readable from across the hall (with my glasses on).

4. **Select a style from the Style area.**

   Good attributes to give your title are Bold and Small Caps. To select these attributes, click in the little check boxes by each one. When an X appears in the box, that attribute is selected. Notice how the Sample text in the bottom of the dialog box reflects your changes.

5. **Choose OK!**

   Click on the OK button or press Enter after you've made your selections.

6. **Type your title.**

   ✔ Don't worry about centering or shading yet. The character formats come first.

   ✔ More information on formatting characters is offered in Chapter 9.

   ✔ If you have a multi-line title, you can use different type sizes and styles on each line. Avoid the temptation to change the font, however.

   ✔ In Figure 21-1, Example 1 uses the Courier font, 14pt size, bold attribute. This is painfully boring, but it's better than nothing.

   ✔ In Figure 21-1, Example 2 uses the Helvetica font. The first line is 12pt size, bold. The second line is 30pt size, bold, and typed in upper-case. The third line is 18pt size and bold.

   ✔ The third example from Figure 21-1 uses the Helvetica font as well. The first line is 18pt size, bold, and italic. The second line is 24pt size, bold, and small caps. The third line is 12pt size, plain old normal text. (Refer to the Tech box "Fancy — and not required — alignment information" on how the date is shoved to the right side of the box.)

   ✔ To insert the date in your title, use WinWord's Date and Time command. Move the toothpick cursor to where you want the date and choose Insert→Date and Time. Highlight a date format in the list, and then click OK.

   ✔ Don't go nuts.

Fancy — and not required — alignment information

In Figure 21-1, Example 3, at the bottom of the title, you see the volume number on the left side of the page and the date on the right. Both these items of text are on the same line. The trick is to use WinWord's justification to slam one against the left margin and the other against the right. Blithely follow these forbidden steps.

1. **Press Enter to start writing text on a new line.**

   It's best to start with a blank line, so if you're already on a blank line, there's no need to press Enter. I'm just being safe, that's all. You know, careful instructions are my trademark.

2. **Type the text you want aligned along the left side of the page.**

   Type away, la, la, la.

3. **Don't press Enter when you're done!**

4. **Instead, click on the right-align tab button on the ribbon.**

   The button has an up-arrow, but its tail points to the left. Click on that button with the mouse.

5. **Click the mouse on the ruler, just to the left of the right-margin triangle.**

   The right-margin triangle is on the right side of the ruler, and it points to the left. (If you can't see it, click on the left-pointing arrow on the bottom-horizontal scroll bar.) Click the mouse about a quarter inch or so to the left of that triangle. This places the right-align tab-thingy right there and erases all the other tab stops on that line.

6. **Press the Tab key.**

   The cursor hops over to the right side of the page.

7. **Type the text you want aligned along the right side of the page.**

   Type away, la, la, la. Or insert the date, as discussed in the previous section.

8. **Press Enter. You're done.**

Centering your title perfectly

After writing the text, it's time to align things on-screen. You do this by formatting the paragraphs, which means centering or *justifying* the titles.

The typical title is centered. To center text you already typed on-screen (assuming you've been through the preceding section), follow these steps:

1. **Mark the text you want to center as a block.**

   Refer to Chapter 6 for all the block-marking instructions you'll ever need to know.

2. Choose the Center command.

Click on the Center button on the ribbon.

You also can choose Format→Paragraph, Alignment, Centered, and choose OK.

This centers the block on-screen.

✔ To center the page from top to bottom, refer to the section "Centering a page, top to bottom" in Chapter 11.

✔ Additional information on formatting a block of text is found in Chapter 10, "Formatting Sentences and Paragraphs."

Using the Format→Border command

You also can make titles more interesting by putting a box around them — or maybe just some lines along the top and bottom or some fancy shading, as seen in Figure 21-1. You can do this to any text in WinWord. If you want to set aside a paragraph of text from the rest of the page, for example, you can box it or shade it. Just choose the Format→Border command.

Drawing a box around your text

If you're creating a title, you can draw a nice square box around it. Or, you can draw a box around any paragraph or group of paragraphs in any document. To do so, follow these steps:

1. Mark the paragraph you want to box as a block.

Use the handy block-marking instructions in Chapter 6 to carry out this deed. You can mark any text, such as a title you want to snazz up.

2. Choose the Format→Border command.

The Border Paragraphs dialog box opens, as shown in Figure 21-2.

3. Look for the area at the bottom labeled Preset.

4. Double-click on the Box icon.

Your title now has a box around it, similar to the one shown in Figure 21-1, Example 3, but without the shading inside the box. To get shading, refer to the following section.

✔ To put a border with a shadow around your text, double-click on the Shadow icon.

✔ To remove any border from your highlighted text, double-click on the None icon.

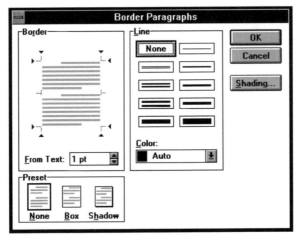

Figure 21-2: The Border Paragraphs dialog box.

Putting less than a box around your text

In Figure 21-1, Example 2, the boxed title has lines only on the top and bottom. To make that happen with your title or any other text, follow Steps 1 and 2 as outlined in the preceding section. And then do the following:

1. **Select a line style from the Line area in the Border Paragraphs dialog box by clicking on it.**

   You can choose from several thicknesses, double, or single line patterns. Notice that the text in the Border preview box changes to match the line style you select.

2. **To eliminate one or more lines around your text, click the mouse on that line in the Border preview box.**

   To eliminate the line on the left side of your text, for example, click on it in the Border preview area with your mouse. That click *selects* that border, and only the two triangles pointing at that side of the box are highlighted.

3. **Click on the None line pattern.**

   This option removes the pattern for the highlighted side of the box, the left side if you followed the example in the preceding step. WinWord actually replaces that side of the border with a new style — *none* in this case.

4. **Repeat Steps 2 and 3 to eliminate another side of your box.**

5. **Click OK when you finish making your newfangled box.**

You can select one of several line styles from the Border dialog box. If you want thicker lines on the top and bottom, for example, select those two sides of the box and click on their new line styles.

Shading your text

The neatest Border dialog box effect of them all is shading your text — or a title, such as the sample shown in Figure 21-1, Example 3. You can shade a title with or without a border around it. Use these steps:

1. **Mark your text or entire title as a block.**

   Refer to Chapter 6 for efficient block-marking instructions. If you want the shaded area to cover more than the title line, highlight the lines before and after the title.

2. **Choose Format→Border.**

   The Border Paragraphs dialog box appears (refer to Figure 21-2).

3. **Choose the Shading button.**

   The Shading dialog box appears, as shown in Figure 21-3. Lots of interesting things can happen here, but your concentration should focus on the Pattern drop-down box where it says Clear.

4. **Choose the Pattern drop-down box.**

   You see a list of shading patterns. The first few shades of gray, or percentages of black in the pattern, vary from 5% to 95% (including clear and solid). A value of 50% is equal parts black and white — solid gray. The 95% value is almost solid black. Other patterns appear at the end of the list, but you don't care about them.

   The best values to select for shading your text are 10%, 20%, or 30%. I prefer 20%, because it prints on my laser printer not too dark to overpower the title text but still dark enough to see that it's the all-important shading that's so hard to do in other word processors.

Figure 21-3: The Shading dialog box.

5. **Select your shading from the list.**

   For example, highlight the 20% Shaded Fill item from the list.

6. **Click OK to exit the Shading dialog box.**

7. **Click OK to exit the Border dialog box.**

   Your text appears shaded on-screen! This is definitely the coolest way to head off your in-depth slug report.

   ✔ Nope, just because you visited the Border dialog box doesn't mean you have to put a border around your text.

   ✔ If the shading stinks (and we're all allowed a little latitude for screwing up here), then you can remove it. Just follow the steps outlined previously, but select the Clear pattern from the list in Step 5.

   ✔ Shaded titles look best when they're at the top of your first page — not on a page by themselves.

Printing white on black

After shading, the next most fun thing to do is print white text on a black background. This is a very bold move and stands out prominently in your text — like being hit in the face with a cinder block. So don't use this technique casually.

Oh, La-di-da

To produce white-on-black text, you must do two things. First, you must create a black background; and second, you must create white-colored text. Here is how you create a black background:

1. **Mark your text as a block.**

   Chapter 6 has all the details. It's best to start with text already on-screen. At some point here, you will have black text on a black background, which you cannot see. If you already have the text written, it will be easier to see when you're done.

2. **Choose Format→Border.**

   The Border Paragraphs dialog box appears (refer to Figure 21-2).

3. **Choose the Shading button.**

   The Shading dialog box appears (refer to Figure 21-3).

4. **Click on the Background drop-down box.**

   You see a bunch of colors displayed in the drop-down list. The current color will probably be Auto. Select Black as the next background color.

5. Click OK to exit the Shading dialog box.

6. Click OK to exit the Border dialog box.

Now you don't see anything on-screen, since you have black text on a black background. (Actually, with the block highlighted, you will see what looks like a large white block floating over a black block. Don't freak!)

With the block of text still highlighted, you need to change the text color to White. This is done by using the Character dialog box, as follows:

1. Choose Format→Character.

The Character dialog box opens. Look for the <u>C</u>olor drop-down list in the dialog box, just above dead-center.

2. Activate the <u>C</u>olor drop-down list.

You'll see a bunch of colors displayed.

3. Select White **from the list.**

This is the "color" you want; white text over the black background you already created.

4. Click OK in the Character dialog box.

You can now un-highlight your block. The text appears on-screen and printed in *inverse* white letters on a black background.

✔ Yes, although we said you can't print in color in Chapter 8, you can print with white text on a black background.

✔ I don't recommend reversing vast stretches of text. White text on a black background prints poorly on most computer printers. This stuff is best used for titles or to highlight smaller blocks of text.

✔ You cannot highlight a word or part of a paragraph with white text on a black background. The black background can be applied only to an entire paragraph.

✔ When you highlight a block of white text on a black background, it appears on-screen "normally." That is, the reversed text will appear inverted — or black-on-white — when you mark it as a block. This can really goof you up, so just try not to go mental when you highlight reversed text.

✔ You should use the preceding steps to create a reverse text, white-on-black *style* in WinWord. Refer to Chapter 13 for more information; you can use the <u>B</u>order button in the Style dialog to help you create this style.
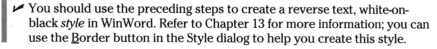

Part V
Help Me, Mr. Wizard!

The 5th Wave   By Rich Tennant

"Hurry, Stuart!! Hurry!! The screen's starting to flicker out!!"

In this part . . .

WinWord is not the sole cause of your woes. When you use a computer, you have several things to contend with: the computer, DOS, Windows, your printer, phases of the moon . . . . It's like starring in a bad French farce with too many villains. Fortunately, some humans — yes, humans — really like computers. When you're in dire straits, you can call on their expertise. Call them wizards, call them gurus, call them when you need help. And when you can't call on them, refer to the chapters in this part of the book to help you through your troubles.

Chapter 22

Face to Face with the Interface

*B*y now, you probably have noticed that approaching WinWord, and the strange and unusual ways it shows stuff on your screen, is about as calming as having the pilot assure you personally that the plane is okay and that sputtering noise is no cause for concern — but he's wearing a parachute. Don't you agree that there are too many buttons, icons, gizmos, and whatzits? Don't answer too quickly because there are even more than that — including some wild things you've never seen and probably don't want to see. This chapter mulls over the lot, explains just what's what on-screen, and tells you whether it's important and why.

"My Toolbar (Ribbon, Ruler) Vanished!"

Missing something? Notice that the sample screens in this book or in the manual don't look a darn thing like your screen? Frustrated? That's because everything on-screen is adjustable. You can change the looks of just about anything and make various parts of the display appear or disappear quite easily and most often accidentally. The culprit is the View menu, shown in Figure 22-1.

Figure 22-1: The View
menu with the
Toolbar, Ribbon, and
Ruler all selected.

The View menu shown contains all sorts of options for controlling the display.
The three main "long things" on the screen are listed in the middle section:
Toolbar, Ribbon, and Ruler. If any of those items has a check mark by it, then
you can see it on-screen. If you don't want to see the Toolbar, Ribbon, or Ruler,
select that menu item from the View menu. Likewise, if you want to see it, select
the proper item.

✔ The first three items in the View menu control how you "see" your document. Normally, you see your document in Normal mode. (They must have
   been in a good mood that day in the Microsoft Menu Naming Dept.) If the
   screen ever looks funky or you see a "background" behind your document,
   Choose View→Normal.

✔ The ribbon may change into something else entirely. Refer to the section
   "The Ruler Changed into a Line of Arrows!" later in this chapter.

✔ Oh, other funky things can happen to the display; just keep reading.

✔ WinWord also has the capability to view multiple documents at a time.
   Refer to Chapter 15 for additional information.

"All My Words Have Spots Between Them!"

```
This·can·be·very·annoying.¶
```

What you see on your screen when your text looks like that above are *non-printing characters*. These symbols represent spaces (produced by the space bar), end-of-paragraph marks (the Enter key), and Tabs. They show up on-screen, but — fortunately — not when printed. There are two ways to feel about this:

1. The marks let me see things that would otherwise be invisible, such as rogue tabs and spaces and other stuff that may foul up my document but which I would otherwise be unable to see.

2. The marks look gross on-screen; who wants to edit a document that looks like it has the chicken pox?

 You turn off the specks in two ways. From the ribbon, you can click on the last button on the right, which is the *paragraph* symbol. That shuts off the effect.

You also can make the change by choosing T<u>o</u>ols→<u>O</u>ptions. The Options dialog box opens. In the Nonprinting Characters area, make sure nothing — not one check box — has an X in it. Then click the OK button.

"There's a Line Down the Left Side of My Screen!"

Ah, that annoying line down the left side of the screen doesn't mean your monitor is out of whack. Instead, you have discovered the *style area*. That thing shows you what style is applied to what paragraph, and it was discussed in Chapter 13 briefly.

To turn off the style area, follow these steps:

1. **Choose T<u>o</u>ols→<u>O</u>ptions.**

   The Options dialog box appears.

2. **At the top of the window, in the** Window **area, you see a text box titled Style Area <u>W</u>idth.**

3. Type in the number 0 (zero).

This sets the width of the style area thing to zero inches, which effectively makes it nonexistent. Yeah!

4. Click OK.

The style area is forever gone.

Although the style area is annoying, having it visible can really help you edit strange documents. If you're having trouble applying styles to your document, I recommend switching the style area back on. Just follow the preceding steps again and enter a value of .5 or 1 for a half-inch or inch-wide style area.

"What's Wrong with the Margins?"

Fresh out of the box, the settings of WinWord are only barely okay. If you look on the ruler, the left margin — represented by two little triangles sitting on top of each other — probably is set to zero. This is good. You also see the right margin — represented by a big triangle — set somewhere around six inches. This isn't so good. That right margin setting probably means that you have a lot of wasted screen space.

The margins can be set by following these steps:

1. Choose the Format→Page Setup command.

The Page Setup dialog box opens, as shown in Figure 22-2. The settings for the left and right margins you see in the two appropriately titled text boxes will probably be 1.25". Wasteful and ecologically unsound. If you change them to .75" or less, you use more of the paper when you print your work. A monkey or a bird will thank you.

2. Select the Left text box and type in .75 (period, 7, 5).

3. Select the Right text box and type in .75 (same thing).

4. Click on the Use as Default button.

This automatically applies the new margins to all documents you open that use the Normal template. (Styles and templates are covered in Chapter 13, "Formatting with Style.")

✔ Chapter 10 contains additional information on formatting with the ruler.

✔ If something is wrong with your margarine, I recommend switching back to butter.

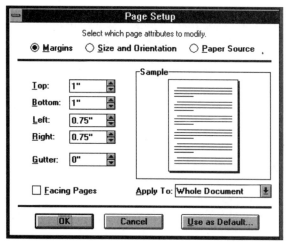

Figure 22-2: Changing the margins in the Page Setup dialog box.

Don't read this info on screen resolutions and text size

The amount of a document you can see on-screen depends on your video card resolution, the size of your monitor, and the settings you select when you install Windows. At standard VGA resolution (what we're all probably using), you can see 7 ¼" of the ruler. When you change to SuperVGA resolution (which means you paid more for your monitor), you can see a little more than 7 ½" of the ruler. If you change to a higher resolution (way too much money), you can see just about 8 inches, and at higher resolutions, the ruler extends for a little more than 10 inches. This makes a humongous difference to the eye.

I usually use a 17-inch monitor, and I like the 1,024 x 768 resolution for WinWord. On a smaller monitor, the best compromise is an 800 x 600 resolution, if I work with normal-sized paper. This is on my system. Unfortunately, each different combination of monitor and video card is different. You need to experiment with your own setup to see what is most comfortable for you.

In the Windows Program Manager, click on the Windows Setup icon in the Main Program Group or use the File→Run command and type setup to run the SETUP program. From there, you can adjust your monitor's resolution. This is technical stuff — but stuff you should expect from a darkly shaded sidebar, such as this.

- ✔ Another way to adjust the margins is to use the mouse to manually "grab" the little triangles and slide them to where you want on the ruler. However, this method doesn't change the margins for all your documents, as the above steps do.

- ✔ After you change the margin size, you can view the whole length of the line on the monitor by pressing the Zoom Page Width tool, which is the last button on the right in the toolbar.

"The Ruler Changed into a Line of Arrows!"

When this happens, you've simply discovered Outline view. This is a real neat gizmo designed especially by Microsoft for people who really, really love to outline stuff.

WinWord's outlining function isn't covered in this book, because it's kind of an "advanced" subject. But if you stumble onto the Outline view and see those weird arrows instead of a ruler, you can choose View→Normal to return to Normal view.

"The Text Doesn't Look Right — It's All the Same Size, and I Don't Like It!"

Patience, Grasshopper. You must have found Draft view. This is useful for viewing complex documents on a slow computer. Aside from that, stumbling over Draft view induces instant panic because you're led to believe that WinWord suddenly purloined all your text formatting. Believe me, it isn't so! Turn off Draft view by choosing View→Draft.

Okay, I confess. If WinWord is acting a bit slow, or you keep getting those Not enough memory warnings, you can switch to Draft mode on purpose by choosing View→Draft.

"What Are the Last Three Faces on the Toolbar?"

The last three buttons on the toolbar have a dramatic effect on the display. If you've put up with teeny-tiny text for too long, or if you want to see how your text looks in relation to the entire page, then those three buttons will really help out. They could almost be called "secrets" (especially by those who write those *SECRETS* books).

 Clicking the Zoom Whole Page tool displays one whole page of your document all at once. Your text will be teensy tiny, but you can still edit. This is the same as choosing View→Page Layout.

 The Zoom 100 Percent tool expands the view of your document to Normal view, where you see your document at what WinWord assumes is 100 percent of the size it will print. Most of your writing will be done in this view, because the screen is in its most comfortable viewing mode.

 When you click the Zoom Page Width tool, you display the entire width of the page of your margin area, from left margin to right margin. If you notice that your text is a bit small on the screen — or maybe it's too wide — selecting this button forces WinWord to show you everything at once. (This is the "secret" button they write about in those *SECRETS* books.)

Chapter 23

Contending with Windows
(and DOS)

· ·

In This Chapter

▶ Using the Windows File Manager

▶ Organizing your files

▶ Creating new directories

▶ Putting Windows on the path

▶ Formatting disks

▶ Backup your files!

· ·

*I*f WinWord is setup just so, you'll never have to mess with DOS, your computer's disk operating system. You will skip it entirely, and just have to mess with Windows, your computer's other operating system. Uh-huh. And the check is in the mail, your kid really doesn't know who broke the lamp, and "I'm from the government, I'm here to help you." You would think that with Windows it's possible to avoid DOS most of the time. Sadly, even this isn't true. When you use WinWord, DOS rears its ugly head all too often. When that happens, you can turn to this chapter for the help you need.

This is seriously optional reading for the typical WinWord user! Only peer into these pages if you're stuck and have nowhere else to turn.

Using the Windows File Manager

Nobody gets everything right all of the time. And, just to prove this fact, the programmers at Microsoft invented File Manager. Actually, I have heard that the invention of File Manager was the result of an assignment given to the candidates for Minor Demon status at good old Malevolent U. I am led to believe that as a result of this project, all candidates were promoted on the spot. Given all that, you can do all kinds of spiffy stuff with the File Manager: move files from hither to yon, make directories, and direct, organize, and choreograph the awesome file dance.

Now here's the news: File Manager is not a part of WinWord. No, it's part of Windows itself — another program, one that you use to manage files. You must use it, because WinWord doesn't do squat about managing files (at least, not the kind of squat I can write about here in a happy, friendly manner).

To run the File Manager, do the following:

1. **Look for the Program Manager.**

   The Program Manager is the Windows main program, the place whence you started WinWord (way back in Chapter 1 if I remember). A quick way to find the Program Manager is to press Ctrl+Esc and look for Program Manager in the Task List. Double-click on it with your mouse.

2. **Look for the File Manager.**

   The File Manager has a wee li'l icon that looks like a file cabinet. Figure 23-1 illustrates this rather well. Find that little icon and you're almost home.

3. **Double-click on the File Manager icon.**

   Lo, the File Manager appears.

Figure 23-1: The File Manager icon.

If the File Manager is already running, which happens often in Windows, you need to "switch to it" from within Windows. The safest way to do that is to follow these two steps:

1. **Press Ctrl+Esc.**

   This opens the Task List of programs Windows is currently juggling simultaneously. No need to concern yourself with the juggling, nor should you be prepared to duck when Windows whips out the flaming bowling pins.

2. **Search in the list for the File Manager.**

   Hey! There it is!

3. **Double-click on it.**

   You're now using the File Manager. Aren't you lucky?

✔ Because you have the Windows File Manager, you might want to learn how to use it. If so, there is an absolutely wonderful book available that has a whole chapter devoted just to this one subject. It is called *Windows For Dummies* — ta da!

✔ The author acknowledges that he hates the File Manager and shall, therefore, avoids discussing it as much as possible.

Organizing your files

DOS's main job is to put files on disk — even if you're using Microsoft Windows. DOS gobbles up your WinWord documents in memory and spits them out on your hard drive for later retrieval, editing, and printing. This is immensely handy, and I recommend that everyone save all their documents to disk; refer to Chapter 1 for the details.

The drawback to your hard drive is that it can get cluttered quickly. To avoid the clutter, DOS lets you organize files on the hard drive into separate storage places called *directories*. Each directory contains its own, separate set of files, yet all the files are stored on the hard drive. The directories keep you organized.

I recommend that everyone use directories to organize their various projects. You can even have directories within directories for two and three levels of organization. It can be fun — but it's not without its cryptic aspect.

✔ The subject of naming files and storing them on disks is covered in Chapter 17.

✔ If your guru has organized your hard drive, refer to Chapter 17, in the section "Finding a Place for Your Work." Use the table there to locate various subdirectories your guru may have set up for you.

Creating new directories

Creating a new directory is like making a new garage or closet. Suddenly, you have all the storage space you dreamed of. Think of your power tools neatly organized and no more boxes piled waist high. And for you men out there, think of all the shoes you could put into that closet! Too bad real life isn't as handy as a computer.

To create a new directory, you must use the File Manager. Follow these steps:

1. Activate the File Manager.

In case you don't know how this is done, the steps for this process are outlined at the start of this chapter. You actually have to escape the confines of WinWord to create a new directory.

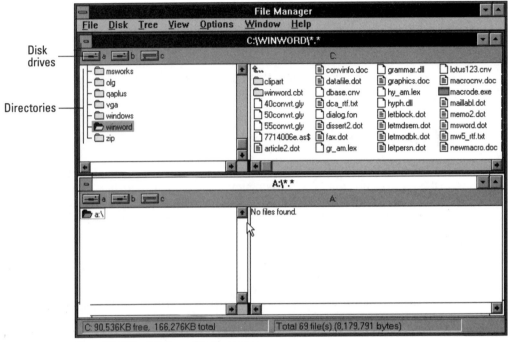

Figure 23-2: The Windows File Manager.

2. **In the File Manager, click on the disk drive icon for the disk on which you want your new directory (see Figure 23-2).**

   The drive icons are on a toolbar right below the menu bar and a little to the right of the oyster bar. When you click on the disk drive icon, a sub-window opens and displays directories already "on" that hard drive.

3. **Locate a directory.**

   Start by finding the directory you want to contain your new project directory. If this baffles you, highlight the main directory, the first one in the list. Otherwise, hunt down the directory you want to contain your new project directory. (Yes, this is confusing, which is why it's more DOS here than Windows.)

4. **Highlight that directory.**

   Click on it with your mouse.

5. **Choose File→Create Directory from File Manager menu bar.**

   This opens up a dialog that lets you give your newborn directory a name (see Figure 23-3).

Create Directory	
Current Directory: C:\WINWORD	OK
Name: [ ]	Cancel
	Help

Figure 23-3: The Create Directory dialog box.

6. **Give the directory a name.**

Fred would be OK, but something like *letters* would be better. The object here is to be descriptive but not use more than 8 characters. You can use numbers and letters to name your directory — *but no spaces!*

7. **Press Enter.**

You've just made your new directory. Congratulations. Have a cigar.

8. **Press Alt+Tab.**

This returns you to WinWord. If you go to another application, press Alt+Esc a few times until WinWord is the *only* thing you see on your screen again.

✔ New directories must be created in the File Manager (it's one of the few things WinWord can't do by itself).

✔ You name a new directory just like you name a WinWord document — but without the DOC extension. Directory names can be from 1 to 8 characters long and include both letters and numbers. They cannot contain spaces or the "assorted nuts" of other symbols.

✔ Two other sources of information include the *DOS for Dummies, 2nd Edition,* and *Windows for Dummies.* The DOS book contains all the filename and subdirectory basics. The Windows book tells you more about the File Manager.

✔ Boy! This is sure complex. If you agree, have your guru do it all for you.

Formatting Disks

Formatting diskettes is something we all have to do. Disks begin life "naked." All the disks in a new box are blank, like blank audio cassettes and videotapes. But unlike recording music or a TV program, you must *format* a computer disk before you can use it. You can't do that in WinWord.

To format a disk follow these steps:

1. **Summon the File Manager.**

   Refer to the start of this chapter for information on summoning the File Manager.

2. **In the File Manager, choose Disk→Format Disk.**

   The Format Disk dialog box opens, as shown in Figure 23-4.

3. **Use the Disk In drop-down box to select the disk drive containing the disk you want formatted.**

   It's already set to Drive A, so if you want to format a disk in drive A you're already half there.

4. **Double check that a disk is in the drive ready to be formatted.**

   If it's a 5¼-inch drive, make sure the drive's door latch is closed.

5. **Press Enter.**

   You see a message box that asks you whether you are sure that this is what you want to do. Say Yes again. The machine whirs and groans for what seems forever.

6. **When the disk is formatted, the File Manager asks whether you want to format another.**

   Say No, and you return to the File Manager.

7. **Press Alt+Tab to return to WinWord.**

   If this doesn't work, press the Alt+Esc key combination until WinWord is the *only* thing you see on your screen.

Figure 23-4: The Format Disk dialog box.

- ✔ Breathe in and out slowly; the rapid pulse caused by so much excitement will pass.

- ✔ DOS uses two disk sizes: the small and compact 3½-inch disks, and the larger and floppier 5¼-inch disks. Buy the right size for your computer. Compare sizes by measuring your floppy disk drive's gaping maw.

✔ There also are two disk *capacities*. Always buy the largest capacity your system can handle. For most of us, that's *high-capacity* or *high-density*. As long as you use these diskettes, formatting won't be a problem.

✔ Sometimes, you can buy formatted diskettes. They're a tad more expensive than the other diskettes, but they save you time and the hassle of repeating the above steps every time you want to use a floppy disk.

✔ Chapter 12 in *DOS for Dummies* goes into great detail on buying, formatting, and using diskettes.

Backup Your Files!

Backing up your stuff is as important as saving a document to disk. But when you backup, you create duplicate documents on a second disk, usually a floppy disk. That way, should anything ever happen to your computer or its hard drive, you can recover quickly by using the backup copy. If Earl comes over and sits by your computer and — since Earl has a big butt — accidentally knocks your computer off the table and breaks it, you won't feel so bad knowing that you have a safety copy of your files well-distanced from Earl.

Backing up is usually done by running a special Backup program, such as DOS's BACKUP command. If you're using DOS 6 or later, you also can run the BACKUP command within Windows. This is definitely something your guru needs to setup for you. Also, the guru needs to give you a list of instructions on how and when to backup.

The second way you can backup is to use the WinWord Save <u>A</u>s command in the <u>F</u>ile menu. When you need to save your files to a different place, a floppy is best. This is a royal pain, but one well worthwhile, until your guru teaches you about BACKUP.

✔ Backing up your files should be done every day. If you're using some sort of Windows Copy command to copy files (either in the File Manager or elsewhere), check the file dates and copy everything that has today's date on it. That means you will have "backed up" all the files you worked on today. When asked whether you want to *replace* files already on the backup disk, press Y; you always want the newer backup files to replace the older ones.

✔ To prepare a floppy disk for use, it must be formatted. Refer to the section titled "Formatting Disks" in this chapter for additional information.

✔ The <u>F</u>ile→<u>F</u>ind File command also can copy files to a floppy disk. Just wrestle with the controls in the Find File dialog box, highlight a gaggle of files, then click on the Copy button to put duplicates on a floppy disk. Refer to Chapter 17 for more info on the Find File dialog.

✔ If you accidentally delete a file, you may be able to undelete it without having to resort to a backup copy. Refer to Chapter 25, the section titled "Oops! I deleted my document!"

Chapter 24

The Printer Is Your Friend

*I*s the printer your friend? Perhaps. Unfortunately, friend or foe, the printer is just as stupid as the computer. This means that you must beat it with a stick a few times to get it to behave, or else you wind up hitting yourself in the head with the same stick. But give yourself a second to repose, and consider leafing through this chapter before causing yourself or your printer any physical harm.

Feeding It Paper

The way the paper feeds into your printer depends on which printer you have. Some printers eat paper one page at a time. Other printers may suck up continuous sheets of *fan-fold* paper directly from the box (the "spaghetti approach"). And laser printers delicately lift one sheet of paper at a time from their paper tray and then weld the image to the page by using dusty toner and inferno-like temperatures. Printing can be quite dramatic.

Whichever way your printer eats paper, make sure that you have a lot of it on hand. The end result of a word processor's labors is the printed document. So buy a box or two of paper at a time. I'm serious: You'll save money and trips to the store in the long run. And as a suggestion, look for a huge paper store or supplier and buy your printer paper from them instead of an office supply or computer store. The prices will be better.

✔ Try to get 20 lb. paper. The 18 lb. paper is too thin. I like 25 lb. paper, which is thicker and holds up very well, but it's more expensive. Paper that's too thick, such as "card stock" may not go through your printer.

✔ Colored papers and fancy stuff are okay.

✔ Do not print on erasable bond paper! This paper is awful. After all, the point behind erasable bond is that you can erase it, which doesn't happen much with a computer printer.

✔ Avoid fancy, "dusted" paper in a laser printer. Some expensive papers are coated with a powder. This powder comes off in a laser printer and gums up the works.

✔ Only buy the "two-part" or "three-part" fan-fold papers if you need them. These contain carbon paper and are commonly used for printing invoices and orders. Also, the old "green bar" paper makes for lousy correspondence. It has "nerd" written all over it.

✔ If you need to print labels in your laser printer, get special laser printer labels. I recommend the Avery labels.

✔ Laser printers can print on clear transparencies — but only those specially designed for use in a laser printer. Anything less than that will melt inside your printer and you'll have to clean out the gunk. If you are going to print transparencies, it's cheaper to print on a piece of paper and then have that photocopied onto transparency film, anyway.

Un-Jamming the Printer

Next time you're in San Francisco, there's a little psychic you can visit on The Haight. She'll do a chart for your printer, which will explain why it jams on some days and not on others. This is the best solution I can offer to the question: "Why can't the paper always go through the printer like it's supposed to?"

If you have a dot-matrix printer and the paper jams, cancel printing in WinWord. (Refer to Chapter 8, the section "Canceling a Print Job.") Then turn the printer off. Rewind the knob to reverse-feed the paper back out of the printer. Don't pull on the paper or it will tear and you'll have to take apart the printer to get the paper out. (If that happens, call someone else for help.)

For laser printers, you need to pop open the lid, find the errant piece of paper, remove it, and then slam the lid down shut. Watch out for various hot things inside your printer; be careful of what you touch. There's no need to cancel printing here, because laser printers have more brain cells than their dot-matrix cousins. However, you may need to re-print the page that got jammed in the printer. Refer to Chapter 8, the section "Printing a Specific Page."

If the jam was caused by using thick paper, re-trying the operation probably won't work. Use thinner paper.

Stopping Incessant Double-Spacing!

Nothing is quite as disenchanting as a printer that constantly produces double-spaced documents, whether you want them or not. This is a terribly annoying problem, but it has a handy, one-time solution — if you kept your printer manual when you bought your printer.

Somewhere on your printer is a tiny switch. That switch controls whether your printer double-spaces all the time or only single spaces. Right now, the switch is set to double-space no matter what. You need to find that switch and turn it off.

✔ Sometimes, the little switches are on the back or side of your printer; sometimes they're actually inside your printer.

✔ Turn your printer off and unplug it before you flip the switch. This is especially important if the switch is inside the printer. It also prevents people from trying to print while your fingers are in the way of the printer's buzz-saw-like gears.

✔ The switch may be referred to as "LF after CR" or "Line feed after carriage return" or "Add LF" or "Stop double spacing!" or something along those lines.

Changing Ribbons and Toner

Always have a good ribbon or toner cartridge in your printer. Always! Most printers use ribbons; laser printers use toner cartridges. This is something you should never skimp on, lest the Printer Pixies come to you in your dreams and smear ink on your fingers.

✔ Keep a supply of two or three extra ribbons or toner cartridges. This will hold you in case you need a new one over a working weekend.

✔ When the ribbon gets old and faded, replace it. Some places may offer re-inking services for your ribbon. This works, if the ribbon fabric can hold the new ink. If your ribbon is threadbare, you need to buy a new one.

✔ You can revitalize an old ribbon by carefully opening its cartridge and spraying some WD-40 on it. Re-assemble the cartridge and put the ribbon on some paper towels. Let it sit for a day before re-using it. This should give the ribbon some extra life, but it can only be done once (and only works with ribbons — not toner cartridges!).

✔ Ink printers use ink cartridges. Replace these when they run low on ink, just as you should replace a ribbon or toner cartridge.

- ✔ When a laser printer's toner cartridge gets low, you see a flashing "toner" light or the message Toner low displayed on the printer's control panel. You can take the toner out and "rock" it a bit. This makes it last about a week longer. When you see the message again, you should replace the toner immediately.

- ✔ There are services that offer "toner recharging." For a nominal fee, they take your old toner cartridges and refill them with new toner. Then, you can use the toner cartridge again and squeeze some more money out of it. Nothing is wrong with this, and I recommend it as a good cost-saving measure. But never recharge a toner cartridge more than once, nor should you do business with anyone who says it's okay.

"Where Did the Weird Characters Come From?"

If strange characters appear on your output — almost like the printer burped — it's a sign that WinWord may not be set up to use your printer properly. Those stray @ and # characters that appear on paper but not on-screen indicate that your *printer driver* may be improperly installed.

Refer to the section titled "Changing Printers" later in this chapter. Check the current printer (the one that is highlighted) and make sure it has the same name as the printer hooked up to your PC. If not, select the proper printer from the list. And if your printer isn't on the list, refer to the following section, "Setting Up a New Printer," for information on setting up your printer to *properly* work with WinWord.

Setting Up a New Printer

Setting up your printer has physical and mental parts. The physical part involves a cable connecting your PC and the printer. The part that makes you mental is the software part, where you gracefully grab WinWord by the throat and scream, "Look, bud, this is my printer! And I paid lots of money for it! Use those special fonts I paid for!"

Hopefully, someone else will set up your printer for you. This is done when you first install Windows. One of the many questions it asks is "Which printer do you have?" Windows knows all about most of the popular printers, and the printer makers have included all the necessary information for those that Windows doesn't. Chances are, you'll get to use all the printer power you paid for.

One of the nicest things about Windows is the fact that once you install a printer, you can use it in any program that runs under Windows. It will be available to WinWord, Draw, Paint, or anything else that uses the Windows operating system.

If WinWord isn't set up to use your printer, or you've changed printers and need to reset everything for your new printer, you need to install it from the Windows Control Panel. Follow these steps:

1. **Summon the Program Manager.**

   Press Ctrl+Esc. The Task Manager window opens. In that window, you see a list of programs. Look for the Program Manager. Highlight the Program Manager by clicking on it once, and then click on the Switch To button. This zooms you over to the Program Manager program thing.

2. **Look for the Control Panel icon and start the Control Panel program (see Figure 24-1).**

   The Control Panel is a program in Windows that controls such devices as your printer. You can find the Control Panel icon just as you find the WinWord icon used to start Windows. When you find the icon, double-click on it with your mouse.

   If you can't find the control panel, type Alt,F,R, type **CONTROL** and press Enter.

3. **Look for the Printers icon in the Control Panel main screen (see Figure 24-2).**

4. **Double-click on the Printers icon.**

   This opens the Printers dialog box. Yes, you're almost done. Remember that Windows makes things easier but there is no Abracadabra button. Not yet.

5. **Click on the Add button**

   This produces the drop-down list, shown in Figure 24-3.

Figure 24-1:
The Control Panel icon.

Figure 24-2:
The Printers icon.

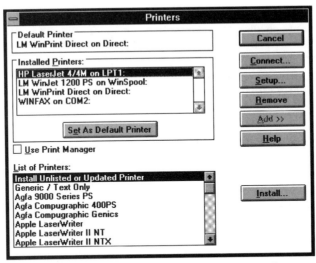

Figure 24-3: The Printers dialog box with the List of Printers list open.

6. Scroll through the list and select the printer that you want to install.

For example, click on Apple LaserWriter II NT if that's your new printer. If you're installing a printer that is not on the list, choose the very first item, `Install Unlisted or Updated Printer`. If you're installing an updated printer driver, choose the very first item, `Install Unlisted or Updated Printer`.

7. Click on the Install button.

The computer churns and whirls, perhaps even groans and complains, and will most likely ask you to insert one of the disks that came with the Windows program. Continue following the instructions on-screen. (This is why setting up a printer is really a Guru's job.)

8. After the printer is installed, quit the Control Panel program.

Press Alt+F4 or choose Settings→Exit menu.

9. Return to WinWord.

Press Alt+Tab. If that doesn't work, press Alt+Esc a few times until WinWord is the only program you see on your screen.

✔ When setting up printers for WinWord, install every possible printer you think you'll ever use. For example, I set up WinWord for every printer in the office, although my PC has always used the same printer. I even added a few printers I'd like to buy but can't afford. That way, if I ever switch printers in the future, I won't need to go through the above steps.

✔ If you don't have the disks that came with the Windows program, or a disk with the new or updated printer driver on it, you are stuck. I recommend you go looking for the guy that has the disks that you need and beat him up.

✔ If you can't find a disk for your printer, call up the printer's manufacturer. The number can usually be found in your printer manual. Either that, or call up the store where you bought the printer and harass the second person you talk to.

✔ These steps will add the printer to a list of possible selections. To learn how to select the printer after it has been installed, read the next section.

Changing Printers

The multiple choice printer game is necessary because a single PC may be connected to or have the potential of using several different printers. For example, you may change printers in the future or one day walk into your office and find out someone else has changed the printer for you. (How nice.) When you do, you'll need to tell WinWord that you're using another printer.

To select another printer for WinWord, follow these steps:

1. **Choose File→Print Setup.**

   The Print Setup dialog box opens, which is actually a function of Windows and not WinWord itself. Inside the dialog, you see a list of all installed printers, those printers you or your guru was wise enough to install on your PC.

2. **Highlight (click on) the printer that you want.**

   The printer currently selected will be highlighted. For example, my current printer may be my Panasonic, which I use for quick drafts. If I want to use the LaserJet 4, I would click on it.

3. **Choose OK.**

   This closes the dialog box, and you're now ready to use the new printer.

✔ You can access the Print Setup dialog box by clicking on the Setup button when you see the main Print dialog box. Refer to Chapter 8 for additional information on printing.

✔ Selecting the proper printer in WinWord is very necessary. It means that WinWord will talk to your printer in a language they both understand and, if the entrails are favorable that day, things will print as beautifully as you intended.

✔ There's little point in changing printers unless you have the new printer hooked up and ready to use with your computer. If not, don't mess with things!

✔ Hey, and no point in printing unless the printer is on and ready to print.

✔ If you don't see your printer listed, refer to the section "Setting Up Your Printer," earlier in this chapter.

✔ Selecting a new printer with the Print Setup dialog box also is the way you send faxes in WinWord. Instead of selecting a printer, you select a fax "card" installed in your computer. For example, the `WINFAX ON COM2` "printer" is really a fax card (refer to Figure 24-3). This is how you send a fax in Windows; you "print" to a fax card.

Selecting a Network Printer

If your computer is shackled to a network, the odds are pretty good that you use a network printer. This is the type of occasion worth wearing black for. When you use a network printer, it usually means that the printer isn't there, tied directly to your computer via the printer umbilical cord. Instead, the printer is elsewhere, somewhere out there, in the network ether.

Printing to a network printer works just like printing without one. You'll still use the Print Setup dialog box under the File menu to select it, and all WinWord's printer commands and whatnot work the same. The difference is that the printer may not be in the room with you. You have to walk over to the "printer room" or to the boss's office to pick up your stuff from the printer.

✔ Follow the instructions in the section "Changing Printers" for information on selecting a specific network printer. You may also need to contact your network human to see which printer is in which office (although it may say so right on-screen, you never know).

✔ Why is it that only the boss (or the biggest PC crybaby — often both one and the same) always gets The Printer in her offices? Why can't we people who really use the printer have it in our offices? Revolt! Revolt!

Chapter 25
Help Me! I'm Stuck!

In This Chapter

▶ "I can't find Windows!"

▶ "I can't find WinWord!"

▶ "I lost my files!"

▶ "Where did my document go?"

▶ "Where am I now?"

▶ "It's not printing!"

▶ "Oops! I deleted my document!"

▶ "Oops! I just reformatted my disk!"

▶ "What's a non-hyphenating hyphen?"

"There I was, minding my own business, when all of a sudden — for no apparent reason — WinWord *fill-in-the-blank*. Where is my baseball bat?"

It happens all too often. And it happens to everyone. "It worked just great when I did this yesterday. Why doesn't it work today?" Who knows? Retrace your steps. Check the grounds for signs of gypsies. But in the end, turn to this chapter for some quick solutions.

"I can't find Windows!"

Nothing induces that sensation that you just stepped through a door marked "Twilight Zone" better than typing **WIN** at the DOS prompt and seeing Bad command or file name. Uh-oh. Looks like Windows found the car keys and is gone, gone, gone. But where did it go?

Type in the following at the DOS prompt:

```
C:
```

This "logs" you to drive C, your main hard drive. You may have tried to run Windows from an alien hard drive. If so try typing **WIN** at the DOS prompt now.

If the **C:** trick doesn't work, try typing in this command:

```
CD \
```

That's **CD**, followed by a space, then the backslash character (not the forward slash you find under the question mark). Press Enter, then try typing **WIN** to start Windows again.

If this *still* doesn't help, reset your computer. Press and hold the Ctrl and Alt keys, then press the Delete key. Release all three keys. Your computer resets. When it's done, start over.

  ✔ You also might try finding the file WIN.EXE. Refer to the section, "I lost my files" later in this chapter for the details.

"I can't find WinWord!"

Sometimes WinWord takes a vacation. Where did it go? It all depends on how you "lost" it.

If you just started your computer, started Windows, and can't find WinWord, you have a few options. The first is to locate the Program Manager and look for the WinWord icon. There may be several mini-windows in the Program Manager, one of which has the WinWord icon in it. Some of these windows may overlap; use the Program Manager's Windows menu to find them all.

If you were just using WinWord and now . . . it's gone! . . . several things may have happened. Most commonly, you probably "switched away" from WinWord by pressing Alt+Esc, Ctrl+Esc, or Alt+Tab. To get back into WinWord, take these steps:

  1. **Press Ctrl+Esc.**

     The Windows Task List opens, which is a list of programs Windows is running.

  2. **Locate WinWord or Word for Windows or Microsoft Word in the list.**

     If the list is long, you may have to scroll through it to find WinWord.

  3. **Highlight WinWord in the list.**

  4. **Click on the Switch To button.**

     You're back in WinWord.

✔ If none of these steps work, then you've probably quit WinWord accidentally, which has been known to happen in the "easy-to-use" (and goof-up) Windows environment. Just re-start Windows as discussed back in Chapter 1.

✔ WinWord does not self-destruct. If you used your computer and WinWord yesterday, it's still there today. It just may be hidden or out of reach. Under no circumstances should you re-install WinWord unless your guru directs you to do so.

✔ If you can't find the WinWord icon, it may be hidden or deleted. To un-hide it, you must look through all the Program Manager's windows to find it (they can move, you know). If the icon was deleted, then WinWord is still there; only its picture is gone. To restore the picture, you need to add the "WinWord item" back to the Program Manager. Have your guru do this, or consult with IDG Books' *Windows For Dummies*.

"I lost my files!"

Sometimes DOS has a hard time bolting files down on a disk. Because the disk is constantly spinning, I assume that centrifugal force flings the files outward, plastering them to the inside walls of your disk drive like gum under a school desk. That's the mental picture I get. Whatever the case, you can find a lost file quite easily. It just takes time, putty knife optional.

If you're in WinWord, finding files can be done with the handy Find File command. This is covered in detail in Chapter 17, in the section "Finding Files in WinWord."

If the Find File command doesn't help you locate your file, you need to use Windows File Manager program. Follow these steps:

1. **Switch to the File Manager program, or start the File Manager if it hasn't been started already.**

   These steps are outlined at the start of Chapter 23. You need to use the File Manager because WinWord is too inept by itself to find files (unless you think the Find File command is worthy of the name).

2. **In the File Manager, choose File→Search.**

   The Search dialog box opens, as shown in Figure 25-1. There are two text boxes worth noting: Search For and Start From.

3. **Type the name of the file you're looking for into the Search For box.**

   For example, type **WHERZITS.DOC** into the box.

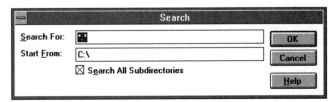

Figure 25-1: The Search dialog box, used for finding lost files.

4. Press the Tab key.

5. Type the drive letter of the disk you want to search into the Start From box.

For example, if you want to search the hard drive C, type in the following:

```
C:
```

That's C and a colon.

6. Click the OK button or press the Enter key.

Churn, churn. Thucka-thucka.

7. You see the Search Results dialog box.

The Search Results dialog box holds a list of files found by the File Manager. If one of them is the file you want, double-click on it. Otherwise, you can repeat the above steps and search some more.

If the file isn't found, then a dialog appears proclaiming No matching files were found. Click the OK button in despair, but re-work the above steps to search another disk drive.

✔ If more than one matching filename appears, you may need to check them all to see which one is the one you want.

✔ Consider that you may have saved the file under a different name.

✔ If the search is a bust, press Ctrl+Esc and select WinWord from the list to return to WinWord: Press Ctrl+Esc, highlight Word in the list, and click on the Switch To button.

"Where did my document go?"

Ever get the sensation that the computer is making faces at you when you turn away? Sometimes, when you look back, the computer won't even have your document on-screen. In the rush to hide its sneering grin, the computer may have put up DOS on-screen. Or you may not see your document at all.

The first thing you should try is pressing a key, any key. Little gremlins like to install things like screen savers on unsuspecting computers. These will turn your file into flying toasters, starfields, alien landscapes, or — worst of all — nothing. Pressing a key, or moving the mouse, will bring all back to where it should be.

✔ If you see the DOS prompt, you should try typing the **EXIT** command. For example, suppose that your screen looks something like this:

```
C:\WINWORD>
```

Type **EXIT** and press Enter. This takes you back into Windows instantly with your document intact. (This trick also deserves a major *Whew!*)

✔ Try moving the cursor up and down a few pages: Press PgUp or the PgDn keys. What may have happened is that the next page in your document is blank and you're only seeing the blank part on your screen. Fiddling with the cursor keys should get you re-oriented.

✔ Look in the Window menu to see whether you accidentally switched windows.

✔ Press Ctrl+Z as a last resort, just in case you deleted everything.

"Where am I now?"

If the keys appear to be too close together, or your fingers suddenly swell, you may find yourself accidentally pressing the wrong cursor keys and, lo, you're somewhere else in your document. But where?

Rather than use your brain to figure things out, press Shift+F5. Shift F5 is the Go Back command, and pressing it moves you to the previous cursor position and resets your document as you remember it. (Also refer to Chapter 2.)

"It's not printing!"

Golly, the printer can be a dopey device. You tell WinWord to print and the printer just sits there — deaf as a post! "Doe, dee, doe," it says. "Aren't you glad you paid twice as much money for a laser printer? Yuck! Yuck! Yuck!"

Believe it or not, the printer is not being stupid. In fact, you should check to make sure that the printer is on and working. Then, you need to check for paper to print on. Then, confirm that the printer cable is still connected. Only then should you slap it.

But wait! Before slapping it, try the following:

Press Ctrl+Esc to open the Task Manager. Look in the list to see whether Print Manager appears. If so, highlight that item and click the Switch To button. In the Print Manager, read the message on-screen. That will tell you whether WinWord knows what's wrong. Then resume or cancel the print job. Press Alt+Tab to return to WinWord when you're done.

- ✔ If a large picture or drawing has been inserted into your document, this will make the computer and printer think harder before it starts to print. Have patience.

- ✔ Do not try printing again; don't try pressing harder on the keys. When the printer doesn't work, it doesn't work. This requires more attention then telepathy.

- ✔ Refer to Chapter 8 for additional information about printing.

- ✔ Make sure that the computer and printer are off — and unplugged — before you plug in a printer cable.

"Oops! I deleted my document!"

Deleting files is necessary, just like stepping on cockroaches. But what if you found out a cockroach was really a reincarnation of your Aunt Shirley? Wouldn't you want her back? The same thing holds true with files. Sometimes you may accidentally delete a file. If you do, follow these steps to reincarnate your file in WinWord:

1. **Panic. Hate yourself. Say a dirty word.**

2. **Press Ctrl+Esc to open the Task Manager.**

   The Task Manager window appears. Look in the list for the Program Manager.

3. **Highlight the Program Manager and click on the Switch To button.**

4. **In the Program Manager, choose File→Run.**

5. **Type UNDELETE. Press Enter.**

   You see a bunch of interesting stuff on-screen. Eventually, at the bottom, you see a line that starts with a question mark and ends with the prompt `Undelete (Y/N)?` (The question mark is displayed instead of the deleted filename's first character.)

6. **Is the filename that starts with the question mark the file you want to undelete? If so, press Y. If not, press N and repeat this step until your filename is displayed.**

7. **After pressing Y, you are asked to type in the first letter in the filename. Do so. (You know what the first letter was better than I.)**

8. **You'll see the message** `File successfully undeleted`. **It lives! It lives!**

9. **Press Enter to return to Windows.**

10. **Press Alt+Tab to return to WinWord.**

✔ Don't save anything to disk after deleting a file!

✔ If the file cannot be recovered — and this happens — you see the message `No entries found` or `File cannot be recovered`. Oh well. Be more careful when you delete next time.

✔ You cannot use the Undelete command on a network drive. Contact your network guru and explain the problem. Try not to refer to anything as "dumb" or "asinine."

"Oops! I just reformatted my disk!"

This is why we label disks, so we don't accidentally format something that contains important files and other information. If you do pull this boo-boo, follow these steps immediately to recover:

1. **Hurry up and get to the Program Manager.**

Refer to the first four steps from the previous section.

2. **Choose File→Run.**

3. **In the command box, type UNFORMAT A:**

That's the UNFORMAT command, followed by a space, then A, and a colon.

4. **Press Enter.**

5. **Follow the directions on-screen. Insert the diskette you just re-formatted when you're told to. This operation will take some time to complete, so sit back and be patient.**

✔ Unformatting a disk works best if you use the UNFORMAT command before putting any new files on the disk.

✔ After your disk is recovered, your documents may not have their original names. The UNFORMAT command may give them mechanical-sounding filenames. That's okay; the file's contents are unchanged. You can use the Find File command in WinWord to help view the files and rename them. Refer to Chapter 17.

"What's a non-hyphenating hyphen?"

The hyphen key, which also is the minus key, works to hyphenate a long word at the end of a line. But sometimes you may not want the hyphen to split a word. For example, you may not want a phone number split between two lines. Yet, when you press the hyphen key, that's exactly what happens.

To create a non-hyphenating hyphen, press the Ctrl and Shift keys while you press the hyphen. This inserts a "hard" hyphen into your document, one that won't split a phone number, part number, figure number, or mathematical problem between two lines.

Part VI
The Part of Tens

The 5th Wave   By Rich Tennant

MOUSE PADS THAT NEVER MADE IT

The Road-Kill Pad

The Chia-Pad

The Plastic Vomit Pad

The Pad-Thai

In this part . . .

Don't you just love trivia? And what's the best type of trivia? Lists! For example, "Ten ways to cheat at Hearts," or "Ten things to do that pester your sister's bird," or "Ten best elderly female relatives who like to smoke a good cigar and tell bawdy jokes after dinner." This book deals with WinWord, so this part of the book is devoted to interesting lists about WinWord.

Most of the chapters in this section contain ten items. Some chapters will contain more, others will contain less. After all, if I was as thorough as I could be in Chapter 29, "Ten Features You Don't Use But Paid For Anyway" it would be as fat as those other books on WinWord.

Chapter 26

The Ten Commandments of WinWord

- -

In This Chapter

▶ Thou shalt not use spaces

▶ Thou shalt not press Enter at the end of each line

▶ Thou shalt not neglect thy keyboard

▶ Thou shalt not reset or turn off thine PC until thee quittest WinWord

▶ Thou shalt not manually number thy pages

▶ Thou shalt not use the Enter key to start a new page

▶ Thou shalt not quit without saving first

▶ Thou shalt not press OK too quickly

▶ Thou shalt not forget to turn on thy printer

▶ Thou shalt not forget to backup thy work

- -

*J*ust imagine Bill Gates as Moses. He looks like a 16-year-old wearing a blinding-white pocket protector and a ridiculous pair of taped white glasses. But, he also has the glow of E Pluribus on his face as he walks down the mountain with the Ten Commandments of WinWord emblazoned upon a sequined laptop.

And, lo, it came to pass that the tablet was transcribed. And over the course of time, found its way to this book. Ahem! It's very hard for me to write stiffly, like the characters in a Cecil B. deMille movie. Rather than drag this thing out, this chapter contains a bunch of do's and don'ts for working in WinWord. Most of these items are covered previously in this book, particularly in Part I.

I: Thou shalt not use spaces

Generally speaking, you should never find more than two spaces in a row in any WinWord document. If so, then you should be using the Tab key instead. Use the space to separate words and to end a sentence. If you align lists of information or create tables, use the Tab key.

II: Thou shalt not press Enter at the end of each line

WinWord automatically wraps your text down to the next line as you approach the right margin. There is no need to press Enter, except when you need to start a new paragraph. (Of course, if your paragraph is only a line long, that's okay as well.)

III: Thou shalt not neglect thy keyboard

WinWord is Windows and Windows is mousy. You can get a lot done with the mouse, but some things are faster with the keyboard. For example, I routinely switch documents with Ctrl+F6. And stabbing the Shift+F12 key to quickly save a document works better than fumbling for the mouse. You don't have to learn all the keyboard commands, but knowing those few outlined in this book (and on the keyboard template) will help a lot.

IV: Thou shalt not reset or turn off thine PC until thee quittest WinWord and Windows

Always exit properly from WinWord and especially from Windows. Only shut off or reset your computer when you see the DOS prompt on-screen — never when you're running WinWord or have Windows active. Believeth me, if ye do, ye are asking for mucho trouble, yea, verily.

V: Thou shalt not manually number thy pages

WinWord has an automatic page numbering command. Refer to Chapter 11 in the section, "Where to Stick the Page Number."

VI: Thou shalt not use the Enter key to start a new page

Sure, it works: Press the Enter key a couple of dozen times and you'll be on a new page. But that's not the proper way, and you'll mess up your new page if you go back and re-edit text. Instead, to create a new page instantly, press Ctrl+Enter. This inserts a *hard page break* into your document. Refer to Chapter 11, in the section "Starting a New Page — a Hard Page Break" for the details.

VII: Thou shalt not quit without saving first

Save your document to disk before you quit. Shift+F12 is the key combo to remember.

VIII: Thou shalt not press OK too quickly

WinWord has many Yes/No/OK-type questions. If you press OK without thinking about it (or press Enter accidentally), you could be deleting text, deleting files, or performing a bad Replace operation without knowing it. Always read your screen before you press OK.

IX: Thou shalt not forget to turn on thy printer

The biggest printing problem anyone has is telling WinWord to print something and the printer isn't on. Verify that your printer is on, healthy, and ready to print before you tell WinWord to print something.

X: Thou shalt not forget to backup thy work

Keeping emergency copies of your important documents is vital. Computers are shaky houses of cards, which can collapse at any sneeze or hiccup. Always make a safety copy of your files at the end of the day or as you work. Refer to Chapter 23, in the section titled "Backup Your Files."

Chapter 27
Ten Cool Tricks

*W*inWord is, in some ways, smarter than Spot. Sure, Spot can sit up and beg, roll over, get the newspaper and, unfortunately, use the newspaper, too. WinWord, on the other hand, knows a whole bunch more tricks. And WinWord will never lick your face, interrupt you when you are doing people things, or demand to go for a walk in the park. (By the way, Spot is a dog here.)

This chapter explains some of the neater WinWord tricks. Some are simple and straightforward; some take a little longer for the human brain to grasp.

Select All

There are times when you want to block the whole shooting match — highlight everything from top to bottom, beginning to end — your whole document. When you want to do this, hold down the Ctrl key and press the 5 key on the number keypad. Zap, Zowie! There you go.

Zoom

People seldom approach their computer in the same mood every day. Sometimes we feel removed and want to keep our distance. Sometimes we want to get up close and personal. WinWord understands and can get as close or as far removed as its human's mood dictates.

 Picking Zoom from the View menu (Alt,V,Z) allows you to choose how big or small WinWord displays your document. This isn't how big it prints — nor the text size. The Zoom command only controls how big the document *looks* on-screen.

 When you choose Zoom, you're presented with a Zoom dialog box. Of particular use in that dialog are the two buttons, Page Width and Whole Page. Page Width expands your document so that it just fits on your monitor from left to right margin. This is about as big as it is convenient to use. The second button, Whole Page, fits the document in the window top to bottom. This is pretty small.

There are two keen advantages to using Zoom. The first is that, if your eyesight is poor, you can select a high Zoom percentage, say 200% (or higher if you type in your own Custom value). The second advantage comes when you have a big monitor. When the monitor gets bigger, WinWord (and all of Windows) looks "smaller" on-screen. Zooming out a bit will make your documents more visible, and it's a lot easier to use with text-intensive applications.

If you prefer the toolbar, you can use the Zoom 100 Percent, Zoom Page Width, and Zoom Whole Page With tools. Just click on one for an instant change of view. (See Chapter 22 for details.)

Bullets and Numbering

Often, you need to drive home several points and nothing brings that home like putting bullets in your text. No, these aren't the lead-propelled things used to kill tourists and innocent bystanders. Bullets are typographical dingbats, like this:

● Bang!

● Bang!

● Bang!

To apply bullets to your text, highlight the paragraphs you want to shoot and choose Tools→Bullets and Numbering. There's no need to dawdle in the dialog box, just click OK and your highlighted text will be all shot up, nice and neat. (You also can click on the Bulleted list tool.)

 You can also apply numbers to your paragraphs. When you see the Bullets and Numbering dialog box, click on the Numbered List radio button at the top of the dialog, then click OK. (Or click on the Numbered List tool.)

Draft View

WinWord demands a lot of its owner. If you have a file that has a lot of graphics or a lot of different fonts, a slower computer can take simply forever to display a page of text. You can avoid this by selecting Draft from the View menu. Everything will be changed into one, easy-on-the-computer, font.

There is a problem here, however. Because no graphics are displayed, and because you can't see the different fonts, you might as well be using WordPerfect 5.1. Yech! Buy more memory; buy a better machine; sell your dog; anything but that!

Revealing the Style Area

If you use a lot of styles, you'd probably like to see them in a place that's more accessible than the Style box in the ribbon. You can.

Choose Tools→Options, and choose the View Category. In the Window section, choose Style Area Width. Click on the up-arrow button until the box reads 0.5". Then click OK.

When you return to your document, the style area appears along the left side of your document.

Constructing a Master Document

This is a real neat trick, but it is advanced stuff so don't let anyone else catch you reading it here. When you are writing a real long thing — this book is a good example — you don't normally start at the preface and type through all of the chapters to the end. You skip around. "Gawd, I don't want to tackle Mail Merge yet — think I'll write about . . . ." So, you wind up with a bunch of individual files, the sum of which makes up the book.

Actually, the individual file approach is preferred by most writers. In this and nearly all computer books, each chapter represents a file on disk. We didn't stick the whole thing into one long file for two reasons: speed and memory. There isn't enough of either to go around. Also, very long documents increase the risk of something, well, *strange* happening to everything at once.

There is a way to manage multiple files, like you'd have in this book and other novels you're bound to write. It's complex, but there is a way. Open up a new document, call it MASTER. Choose View➔Field Codes. Choose Insert➔Field. Select Include from the list displayed in the Field dialog box, and then enter the name of the file that you want, CHAPT01.DOC for example. Repeat this over and over until the whole book or whatever has been "included" in your MASTER document. This stitches the files together without actually loading each and every one of them.

A neat extra added benefit to this is that your headers and footers become connected too, so page numbers will continue from file to file uninterrupted. You also can print the master document and have all the chapters and other pieces print sequentially — without having to bother with the painful Find File command as outlined elsewhere in this book. (This is an "advanced" tip because it's primarily used by those who work with long documents but want to keep the chapters or other elements separate on disk.)

Sorting

Sorting is one of WinWord's funner tricks. When you learn it, you go looking for places to use it. You can use the Sorting command to arrange text alphabetically or numerically. You can sort paragraphs, table rows, and columns in cell tables and tables created using tabs.

Always save your document before sorting.

Sorting is not that difficult; all you have to do is save your document before sorting, highlight the stuff that you want to sort — after you save your document first — and then choose Tools➔Sorting. Oh, did I mention that you should save your file first? Then, mess around in the dialog box and decide how you want the information in that file you saved to be sorted.

Why all of this safety? Well, sorting takes a bunch of memory, and the machine could hang, or crash. Or, you could just decide that you didn't like the way it looked after you hit the spacebar or typed a letter — no more Undo command — and have to go back to square one.

Organizing Windows

This is a kinda cute trick. If you have a bunch of files open, you can choose Window→Arrange All to line them all up. This lets you see each document in its own proper window on-screen.

Show All

 Back in the fifth grade, there was this lass who gave an entirely new meaning to show and tell. Well, WinWord, not to be outdone by a 10-year-old, can be an exhibitionist, too. Pressing the Paragraph button on the ribbon instructs WinWord to show you all of its stuff. You can see the spaces between the words as dots, tab marks as tiny arrows, paragraph marks as backward P-like things, and all manner of wonderful jots and titles. Nothing prints out that way — it's just for look-see only.

WordPerfect Help

I suppose that I could go on and on about how the title of this section wastes a perfectly good word; anyone who uses WordPerfect needs help as a matter of definition. Anyway, the folks at Microsoft seem to think that WordPerfect users can be saved from the multi-colored loony bin.

If you are a born-again WinWord convert from WordPerfect, there is a special section of WinWord designed just to unconfuse you and put you back on the path of productive and sane word processing. Choose Help→WordPerfect Help to learn how the big boys do it. This lets you grow accustomed to WinWord's commands as your contorted WordPerfect function key fingers learn to grow straight again.

Chapter 28

Ten Weird Things You Probably Don't Know About

I'm an old WinWord warrior. I go all of the way back to Version 1.0, and that is simply eons in the software universe. I was alone and lonely. Fortunately, so many long years of writing with the same software offers me some insight I'd be more than happy to share. After all, I wouldn't want anyone else to have to use this product for so long without knowing about these ten weird things.

Automatic Save

When the Auto Save feature is active, your document will be periodically saved to disk. This isn't the same as pressing Shift+F12 to save your document. Instead, WinWord makes a secret backup copy every so often. In the event of a crash, you can recover your work from the backup copy — even if you've never saved the document to disk.

To turn on Auto Save, choose Tools➔Options. From the scrolling Category list, select Save. This opens the Save Options dialog box. Click on the `Automatic Save Every` box to insert a check mark. Into the corresponding text box, you can enter the backup interval in minutes. For example, I type **10** to have WinWord backup my documents every ten minutes. If the power is unstable at your home or office, type 5, 3, 2, or even 1 minute as the backup interval. Press Enter to return to your document.

With the Automatic Save, you won't recover all your document in case of a mishap, but you will get most of it back.

Fast Saves

Fast Saves is one of those ideas that sounds real good . . . until you use it. The idea is to avoid having to save everything every time. "Why not just save the changes? This will make things go oh so much faster," the folks at Microsoft said. "Because," retorted this WinWord Dummy, "you can't give a Fast-Saved file to anybody else and expect them to be able to read it on their computer."

The idea is, if WinWord only saves your changes to disk, what's someone else going to make of such a file? What if Tolstoy only changed a character's name in Chapter 43? He would have turned in a disk to his publisher with a Chapter 43 file that contained only the single word *Ludmilla*. That just doesn't work.

My advice is to disable Fast Saves. Choose Tools➔Options. Then select Save from the scrolling list. This opens the Save Options dialog box. If the Allow Fast Saves box is checked, click on it with the mouse. Make it empty. Press Enter to return your document.

NEWMACRO.DOC

A *macro* is a little program that someone has written to do some neat thing in WinWord. There is a whole special programming language devoted to macros; therefore, writing macros is a job for the truly advanced or insane. However, you can be neither advanced nor insane to use macros. WinWord even comes with a bunch of them, all ready to use.

Lurking about in your WINWORD directory is a file called *NEWMACRO.DOC*. Open this file as you would any other document. In it you see a list of all of the macros that come with WinWord — stuff you paid for but never knew about! You can test out each macro by pressing the Demo button. Go ahead. Be bold!

If you like what you see, click the Install button. You are given the option of installing the macro on a *template* (choose the Normal template if you want the macro to apply to all of the templates; choose any other template to have the macro apply to only that one). From then on, you can use the macro in your documents as a handy shortcut.

TEMPLATE.DOC

Resting in your WINWORD directory, right near the NEWMACRO.DOC file (see the previous section), is a file called TEMPLATE.DOC. This document describes two of the templates that came with WinWord, TERM2 and DISSERT2. If you are a student, or have to turn in a paper or dissertation, this template will be of great use. The TEMPLATE.DOC file explains the proper layout of these documents and provides macros for tracking all manner of scholastic stuff.

SmartQuotes

One of the things that makes books and reports look so professional is that the quotation marks are different at the beginning and the end of a quoted passage. On your screen, they're always the same. In fact, those things aren't really quotation marks at all — they're called tick marks. Just like the blood-sucking insects! But don't despair. WinWord can do the "real" quote marks too, it can even keep track of which flavor of mark goes where (the start or ending double quotes). This feature is called SmartQuotes, and it is one of the macros that came with WinWord — stuff you didn't know about. Doesn't this book have *value*?

To install this macro, open the NEWMACRO.DOC document file. It's a WinWord document, located in the WINWORD directory. Select the List Macros button in that document. When the drop-down list of macros appears, select SmartQuotes, then click on the Install button. When it asks you where to install the macro, select the Normal template in the Edit menu. (Assigning shortcut keys to these macros is still a little buggy — it doesn't work too well — so, skip that part.) Select OK.

The options Enable SmartQuotes and Disable SmartQuotes will now appear on your Edit menu. To turn on SmartQuotes, select Enable SmartQuotes. To turn them off, select Disable SmartQuotes. Now you're set. Just don't misquote anyone.

DropCap

Drop caps are those fancy characters that lead off sentences in books. They're larger than other characters, but drop down below the baseline to add extra whiz-bang. WinWord gives you a way, through one of the macros, to come up with something that looks almost, but not quite, good enough to use. Here's the low-down on drop-downs:

Follow the steps in the previous section and install the DropCap macro from the NEWMACRO.DOC file. That sets you up for drop-capping. To make your drop cap, position the toothpick cursor in the paragraph that you want the initial letter dropped. Choose Tools→Record Macro. In the drop-down list, select DropCap. The computer will whir and stutter, the screen will assume amazing looks, and eventually, perhaps, the dropped cap will appear.

Cool? Probably not. Remember, Ctrl+Z is the Undo key.

Cool Characters

The Symbol command in the Insert menu is used to stick odd and wonderful characters into your document. Quite a few of Windows fonts may have a few weird and wonderful characters in them. The "normal" font, usually Times Roman, has several cool characters in it; the Symbol font is fun; and the Wingdings font has all sorts of fun doodads in their typecase. You can insert any of these into your document at your whim. Simply put the toothpick cursor where you want the symbol to appear, choose Insert→Symbol (Alt,I,S), point at the cool character you want inserted and click your mouse.

Refer to Chapter 9 in the section "Inserting Oddball Characters" for more information.

Insert Date

WinWord's date command is named Date and Time and is hanging under the Insert menu. Selecting this option displays a dialog box full of date and time formats, one of which you're bound to favor — but there's a shortcut involved here. Move the toothpick cursor to a spot you want to insert the date in your document and press Alt+Shift+D. That inserts the current date into your document just as if you typed it yourself (or had bothered going through the Insert menu).

Undo Character Formatting

Sometimes, you'll get carried away with your character formatting. Or maybe there's this paragraph that contains a lot of bold and underline and, quite frankly, you don't have the patience to seletively mark and un-bold, un-italic or un-underline the thing. Here's your shortuct: Mark everything as a block, and then press Ctrl+spacebar. That un-does all character formatting in a snap.

Unbreakable Space

There are times, I suppose, that you would want to be sure that a space was not interrupted by something as mundane as the end of a line. For example, suppose that you work for Mr. John Jacob Jingleheimer Smith and, by golly, he doesn't want his long name to be split between two lines. To insert a nonbreaking space, use the Ctrl+Shift+spacebar key combination. That will ensure that when you insert a nonbreaking space between words, they will always be stuck together, just as gum always keeps pages of a book together.

Chapter 29

Ten Features You Don't Use But Paid For Anyway

*W*inWord comes with many more features than you'll ever use. There are definitely more than ten, and probably several dozen I've never heard of. Some people writing those massive "complete" WinWord tomes have been known to disappear into a room and not emerge for months — or years! Indeed, I seriously doubt if anyone who knows everything about WinWord has kept their sanity.

This chapter lists ten of the more interesting features you bought when you paid for WinWord. (I'm not even bothering to mention some of the things Windows lets you do with WinWord, such as embed sounds and other cute but useless things.) You probably didn't know these goodies existed. That's okay — they're a bit technical to work with. This chapter covers each one briefly, but don't expect to learn how to use any of the paid-for-but-forgotten features.

Annotations

If you're reading someone else's work, and you want to make a comment about it, but don't want to make any changes, you can include an annotation. You can insert a comment like: "Charles, it cannot both be the 'best of times' and 'worst of times.' Try to add more clarity to your writing." in such a way that it won't print in the document. The Annotation command is found in the Insert menu. You won't be able to see the Annotations unless you choose View→Annotations.

Table of Contents

It used to be that figuring out a table of contents could make a grown human of the masculine persuasion cry. Who, in their right mind, would want to go to the front of a document, type in all of those names, then all of those dots, and then figure out what page what should be on?

WinWord, Man, that's who! If you have been careful with your styles (see Chapter 13 to learn about styles) inserting a table of contents is a sure bet. Well, almost. The Table of Contents command, found in the Insert menu, will look through your entire document and take everything that has been tagged with a style of Heading (followed by some number), determine what page it is on, and build the Table of Contents for you.

Sounds like fun? Yeah, but it's complex to set up. If you didn't do this when you created your document, then you might as well do it the old fashioned way, weeping bitterly and all that.

Hyphenation

Hyphenation is an automatic feature that splits long words at the end of a line to make the text fit better on the page. Most people leave it off, because hyphenation tends to slow down the pace at which people read. However, if you want to hyphenate a document, choose Tools→Hyphenation. Continuously jab the F1 key when you need Help.

Index

This is an interesting feature but complicated to use. The Index Entry command in the Insert menu marks a spot in a document to include in an index. For example, you can select that command to mark a word and tag it for inclusion as an index entry. Then, using other commands too complicated to mention here, you can have WinWord generate an automatic index at the end of the document. This is a handy thing to have, but it takes time to learn, and you often don't need a full index for a five page letter to Mom.

Language

This feature is for those of you ('cause it's definitely not me) who like to spice up their writing with tidbits from another language. Nothing makes you so — *je ne sais quoi* — as being able to spike your text with utterances in Latin, Italian, French, or Japanese. Never mind whether your reader has a Harvard education. If he doesn't, well then, he wouldn't understand your English text, either!

The Language command in the Format menu allows you to mark a block and tag it as being written in another language, say Norwegian Bokmal. The only reason to do this is for a spell-check. When that happens, WinWord uses that language's dictionary to proof the text instead of attempting to decipher those words as English.

Macros

Macros are an entirely different can of worms. A macro is basically a shortcut. You can create a macro that automatically records something in your document, a set of commands, or anything that you normally have to repeat over and over. Macros automate the process. In WinWord, macros do more and comprise an actual programming language you can use to extend WinWord's abilities. This is heady, technical stuff and is only touched upon in this book in Chapter 28. Venture there if you dare.

Math

Did it ever dawn upon the WinWord people that Math and English are two separate subjects for a reason? The Math and English parts of the SAT scores are separate. Math and English are always taught as separate courses. So who needs a math function in a word processor? I don't know. Even if you did, it's still easier to calculate the numbers by using your desk calculator and type them in manually.

Complaining aside, the Math command in WinWord is Alt,O,C. But before pressing those keys, you have to highlight the stuff that you want mathisized. WinWord can add (+), subtract (-), multiply (*), divide (/), do percentages (%), and powers (^). Doesn't it make you proud? Highlight the equation and select the Calculate function from the Tools menu; the result of the calculation appears in the status bar and is placed on the Windows Clipboard, so you can paste it in wherever you want. Yech!

There is one interesting application to this feature. If you have a column of numbers in a table and wish to quickly add them up, mark that column as a block. Then choose Tools→Calculate. Use Ctrl+V to paste in the total.

Outlining

Outlining in WinWord isn't as bad as outlining in other word processors, but it's still like a completely new program you have to learn before you can try it. To switch on WinWord's outline feature — and really begin a long process of head pains — choose View→Outline. This activates Outline mode, where you get a whole new replacement for the ruler, re-arrange the way your text looks on the screen, and single handedly run up the value of the stock of every aspirin manufacturer there is. (My advice: Don't do this unless you have some serious time to kill.)

Random Statistics

This feature is something you never use, because it is a very unpopular thing. Besides that, it is a royal pain in the digit. WinWord tracks all sorts of statistics about your document. To see them, choose File→Summary Info. Then, click the Statistics button. Then you click on the Update button. WinWord tells you all sorts of things about your document, such as how many words it contains. Writers who are paid by the word use this feature to make sure they get their full load in. It can also give you a good idea of how "big" your document is, although this is really all silly stuff.

Repagination Nonsense

In the beginning, Microsoft Word was a mere DOS application (and a slow one at that.) To make the program faster, Microsoft left out a bunch of "features" that were standard in most word processors. One of those was *repagination*, or the capability of the word processor to automatically insert "page breaks" on the screen (those dotted lines of death). In WinWord, this is done automatically. However (to be compatible I suppose), there is still a Repaginate Now command in the Tools menu. In the old days, that would force WinWord to show you where the page breaks were. Today, it's like a cigarette lighter in a Canadian car; a useless holdover from the past.

Chapter 30

Ten Shortcut Keys Worth Remembering

*T*his is sacrilege! You are forbidden — *forbidden* — to use the keyboard in Windows! Shame on you! Seriously, there are lots of interesting things you can do with the keyboard, things that can be done quite rapidly and without breaking off any nails. Although WinWord has a whole armada of key combinations — well over the 53 mentioned in the first part of this book — there are only a handful worth knowing. This chapter contains the best, a shade more than ten but those I feel you'll grow fond of as time passes.

General-Purpose Shortcut Keys

Thank goodness this isn't WordPerfect. Those folks have lots of function keys, all of them required just to work the program. In WinWord, using the function keys is optional . . . so why bother? Actually, there are five function keys you might want to become friendly with. There is no handy mnemonic here. You'll just have to get used to them, but fortunately there are only five of them:

F1, the Help! key

In any Windows program, pressing F1 displays helpful information. In WinWord, the F1 key is geared to whatever you're doing. If you're in the Save dialog box, press F1 to get help on it. If you see an error message, press F1 for more information (hopefully).

Shift+F3, the Switch Case keys

To change the case of your text between all caps, lower-case, and mixed case, mark the text as a block and then press Shift+F3 until it looks the way you like.

F4, the Repeat key

If you're applying formatting to a number of paragraphs or various text or just doing the same command over and over, press the F4 key. That directs WinWord to pull a "do-over" and work the same command again. (To repeat the Find command, use Shift+F4). A common use for this may be when pasting in symbols. If you're using the Symbol command in the Insert menu to poof-up your document a bit, just press F4 to repeat the insert.

Shift+F5, the "Take me back to where I was" keys

It's easy to get lost in WinWord. If you just pressed Ctrl+End for no apparent reason and suddenly find yourself at the end of your document, press Shift+F5 to get back to where you once were. This key is a big time saver.

Shift+F12, the Save keys

Save! Save! Save! Always save your document. Get in the habit of reaching up and pressing Shift+F12 often as you work.

Block and Editing Shortcut Keys

Any time you're editing your document, even if you're not marking text as a block, the block and editing shortcut keys can come in handy. The three basics are Cut, Copy, and Paste. But don't neglect the all-important Undo key. It has saved many a butt.

The Kindergarten Keys: Cut, Copy, Paste

When you're working with blocks, three shortcut keys will come in most handy:

Ctrl+X, Cut
Ctrl+C, Copy
Ctrl+V, Paste

To use these keys, first highlight a block. Then press Ctrl+X to cut the block or Ctrl+C to copy. Move the toothpick cursor to where you want the block pasted, then press Ctrl+V. Refer to Chapter 6 for more information on playing with blocks.

Ctrl+Z, the Undo keys

The Ctrl+Z key is WinWord's Undo key. It will undo just about anything WinWord can do. The only limitation is that you must Undo immediately; it has a short memory.

Text-Formatting Shortcut Keys

You can use these three shortcut keys — either as you type or on a marked block of text — to affect that text's character formatting:

Ctrl+B, Bold
Ctrl+I, Italics
Ctrl+spacebar, Normal

Type Ctrl+B when you want unbolded text made bold. Or, if the text is already bold and you mark it as a block, Ctrl+B will un-bold the block. The same holds true with Ctrl+I and italics.

The Ctrl+spacebar key returns text to normal. So if you mark a block of text that has all sorts of crazy, mixed-up formatting, press Ctrl+spacebar to see a sea of sanity. Pressing Ctrl+spacebar as you're entering text can be used to instantly switch off whatever formatting you're currently using.

Chapter 31
Ten Unpopular Error Messages And How To Fix Them

*W*inWord doesn't really have that many unpopular error messages. They're really only unfriendly, not unpopular. Most of them have simple explanations and are very easy to correct. In fact, the only one that really bugs me is the out of memory error, which Microsoft claims you can easily fix by adding more memory to your computer. And if I could do the same thing to my head, I would be on Jeopardy! next week. ("I'll take Subatomic Particle Physics for $50,000, Alex.")

All of these error messages appear in dialog boxes. Some of them are produced by Windows; others are WinWord's own property. In most cases, you're resigned to pressing the OK (or "Oh, well") button. The following sections will help you track down the problem and, if you're lucky, make amends.

This document does not exist

Meaning: You used the Open command or Insert File command and the file you named just isn't there.

Solution: Check your typing; you may have misspelled the filename. The file may also be in another directory or on another disk. Refer to Chapter 25 for more information on finding lost files.

This is not a valid filename

Meaning: You tried to save a file to disk and used a forbidden filename or an offending character in the filename.

Solution: Filenames can be from 1 to 8 characters long. They can contain letters (A to Z) and numbers (1 to 9). Anything else and you run the risk of getting the above error message.

Cannot read from drive A

Meaning: You tried to open or save a file to a disk in drive A and there is no disk there or the disk there is unformatted.

Solution: Make sure there is a disk in drive A. Make sure the disk is all the way in the drive and that it's right side up and all that. If you still get the message, then the disk is either unformatted or damaged in some way. Try another disk.

The disk drive is not valid

Meaning: You specified some whacko drive letter.

Solution: WinWord can save files only to disk drives you have. If you specify another drive letter, say Q, then you'll get the above message. If you're on a network, ensure that the network is "up" before trying the command again. You may also want to have your guru look over your machine in case "it worked yesterday."

The path is not valid

Meaning: You tried to save the file to a subdirectory that doesn't exist.

Solution: Odds are that this error was caused by you specifying a backslash in a filename. Or, if you know what a path is and swear you were doing everything just fine, check your typing and try again.

Do you want to save changes to document?

Meaning: You've closed a document or quit from WinWord and the document(s) you were working on haven't yet been saved to disk. Shame on you.

Solution: Click the Yes button to save the document to disk. You may have to give it a filename if it hasn't been saved at all.

Not enough memory

Meaning: WinWord can't find any more memory in your PC. No, it doesn't matter how much memory you had to begin with; WinWord runs out as a matter of course.

Solution: Click the OK button. Then Save your document(s) to disk and quit WinWord. Restart it. If, in the rare circumstance, WinWord won't let you quit (it happens to me about once a month), then switch to Draft mode and try again (Select Draft from the View menu). If that doesn't work, delete any graphics from your document and try again. If that doesn't work, try Save As and save your document to disk as a text file. You'll lose your formatting, but at least you won't have to retype anything. And if that doesn't work, try printing your document. Then get on the blower to Microsoft and scream and yell as I once did.

Word reached the end of the document

Meaning: Your Find, Replace, or Spell command has done its job and reached the end of the document.

Solution: Click OK, or select the option that lets you start over again from the top of the document.

Do you want to replace the existing file?

Meaning: You've tried to save a file to disk using the name of a file already on disk.

Solution: Click No. In the Save As dialog box, type in a new name for a file.

This file is read-only

Meaning: You tried to save a file to disk, and a file with the same name is already on disk. Further, that file has been tagged as "read-only" by DOS. You cannot overwrite the file or change it in any way.

Solution: Save the file to disk using a new name.

Chapter 32
Ten Things Worth Remembering

There's nothing like finishing a book with a few, heartening words of good advice. As a WinWord novice, you need this kind of encouragement and motivation. WinWord can be unforgiving but not necessarily an evil place to work. This book shows you that it's also possible to have a lot of fun with WinWord and still get your work done. To help send you on your way, here are a few things worth remembering.

Don't Be Afraid of Your Keyboard

Try to avoid pressing Enter repeatedly to start a new page, using the spacebar when the Tab key will do better, or manually numbering your pages. There's a handy WinWord command to do just about anything. You'll never know that if you're afraid to try the commands.

Have a Supply of Diskettes Ready

You need diskettes to use your computer, even if you have a hard drive! You need diskettes for backup purposes and for exchanging files with other PCs running WinWord, such as between home and the office.

Keep one or two boxes of diskettes available. Always buy the proper size diskette for your PC, either 5 ¼- or 3 ½-inch disks. And make sure you buy the proper capacity as well. This is usually the high-capacity or high-density diskettes. And format those diskettes!

Keep Printer Paper, Toner, and Supplies Handy

When you buy paper, buy a box. When you buy a toner cartridge or printer ribbon, buy two or three. Also keep a good stock of pens, paper, staples, paper clips, and all the other office supplies (including diskettes) handy.

Keep References Handy

WinWord is a writing tool. As such, you need to be familiar with and obey the grammatical rules of your language. If that language just happens to be English, then you have a big job ahead of you. Even though they're an electronic part of WinWord, I recommend that you keep a dictionary and a thesaurus handy. Strunk and White's *The Elements of Style* is also a great book for finding out where the apostrophes and commas go. If you lack these books, visit the reference section of your local bookstore and plan on paying about $50 to stock up on quality references.

Keep Your Files Organized

Use subdirectories on your hard drive for storing your document files. Keep related documents together in the same subdirectory. You may need someone else's help to set this up. Refer to Chapters 15 and 17 for additional information.

Remember the Ctrl+Z Key!

The Ctrl+Z key is your "undo" key. If you're typing away in WinWord, press it to undelete any text you may have mistakenly deleted. This works for individual letters, sentences, paragraphs, pages, and large chunks of missing text. But be quick, since the Undo command only remembers the last chunk of text you deleted.

Save Your Document Before a Find and Replace

About the only nasty thing that's not un-doable in WinWord is the find and replace command. I once had an assistant who carefully replaced all the spaces in a document with . . . nothing! The end result was a document with three long words instead of three paragraphs of many words. The only way to undo that mistake is to retrieve an original version of the document. And the only way you can do that is if you saved the document before you started the find and replace.

Save Your Document Often!

Save your document to disk as soon as you get a few meaningful words down on the screen. Then save every so often after that. Even if you're using the auto-save feature (discussed in Chapter 27), continue to manually save your document to disk: Shift+F12.

Use a Glossary for Often Typed Stuff

To quickly insert things that you type over and over, like your name and address, use a glossary entry. Type it in once, then define it as a glossary entry under the Edit menu. Then use the shortcut key to zap it in whenever you need it. See Chapter 14 for more about glossaries.

Use Clever, Memorable Filenames

A file named LETTER is certainly descriptive, but what does it tell you? A file named LTR2MOM is even more descriptive, but still lacking some information. A file MOM0023 may indicate the 23rd letter you've written to Mom. Even better is LTR2MOM.23. You get the idea here: Use creative and informative filenames.

DOS gives you only 8 characters to name a file. You can use letters and numbers in the filename, and you can add a period and up to three characters as an "extension." This doesn't leave much room for being descriptive, but it opens wide the door to being creative.

Sadly, the short filenames also make room for the extremely cryptic. To help you hunt down a file, use the handy Find File command. Refer to Chapter 17 for additional information.

The 5th Wave — By Rich Tennant

Installing Word for Windows

• •

This book assumes that you already have WinWord installed on your computer up and ready to run. Further, you also should have DOS and Windows installed, plus some games because life isn't supposed to be the cradle-to-grave torture the computer industry is pushing on us.

If you have yet to install WinWord on your system, or you're going through the upgrade process, then this is the appendix for you. But first, a warning we're required to give:

This book is not a replacement for your WinWord manual.

It is assumed that you own a copy of WinWord and that you have the manual. If you are "borrowing" a copy of WinWord, or if you purchased only the diskettes from some seedy character, then you are stealing and it's not appreciated no matter how good a nature you claim to have.

System Requirements

Before you can run WinWord, you need to have the following:

A computer that runs Windows

If you can run Windows, specifically Version 3.1 or later, then you can run WinWord. No sense in bogging everyone down in the details here.

Installing Microsoft Word for Windows

To install WinWord, follow these steps:

1. **Start everything.**

   Turn on your computer. Start Windows. If you don't see Windows when your computer starts, then type **WIN** (as in the opposite of lose) at the ugly DOS prompt. That runs Windows. (If not, refer to Chapter 25 on how to find Windows.)

2. **Fumble around for the WinWord installation diskettes.**

   There definitely will be more than one. The diskettes are numbered and the first one is — and this may come as a shock — Disk 1. It will also have the word Setup written on it somewhere.

3. **Stick the Word Setup disk (Disk 1) in your floppy drive.**

   Insert it into your A floppy drive, your first or only floppy drive. If you have two floppy drives, Drive A is on the top. If you have a 5 ¼-inch disk drive, then be sure to close the drive door latch after you insert the diskette; 3 ½-inch drives chomp down on the diskettes automatically once they're pushed in far enough.

4. **Locate the Program Manager.**

   This is Windows' main program. If you can't find the Program Manager, then press the Ctrl+Esc key combination. This opens a window called the Task List. In the list, locate Program Manager. (You may have to scroll the list to see it.) Highlight the Program Manager by clicking on it once with the mouse. Then, click on the Switch To button. You're there.

5. **Choose Run from the Program Manager's File menu.**

   This opens the Run dialog box, where you can type in the name of a DOS command to run. In this case, the command is the SETUP program on the disk in drive A, the program that installs WinWord on your computer.

6. **In the Command Line box, type the following:**

   ```
   A:SETUP
   ```

   That's A, a colon, then the word SETUP. There are no spaces between anything and the command does not end in a period. Double-check what you type. Use the Backspace key to backup and erase.

7. **Press the Enter key.**

The SETUP program runs, beginning WinWord's installation. The floppy drive churns and grinds. Eventually, you see a dialog box then maybe a full screen display. Here are some suggestions for getting you through the rest of the installation process:

- ✔ Type in your name and business affiliation if you want. Your name will be used by WinWord as the author of documents. Your initials will be used by WinWord for comments you may leave in documents. You don't have to put in a business name, unless you want to make up a really cool one. Dan's copy says `Dan Gookin` and lists `The KGB` as the company name. Ray's copy says `Ray Werner` and lists `The Electronic Editor` as his company name.

- ✔ Before the SETUP program can install WinWord, it asks for a _path_. It will suggest the following cryptogram: C:\WINWORD. If this doesn't create any trauma for you, click the Continue button. If you know what you're doing, and would prefer the program to install on a different drive or in a different directory, type in that information.

- ✔ When faced with the type of installation question, select Complete. This installs all of WinWord's files, including the applets Draw, Graph, Equation Editor, and Word Art (see Chapter 20). This takes about 14MB of hard disk space. If that's too much space for your hard drive, select the Minimum installation.

- ✔ Read everything. Follow the directions that appear on the screen.

- ✔ When faced with an option, select the one WinWord has preselected for you — the one you can do by pressing the Enter key (what the nerds call the "default" option). As long as you read the screen and maybe understand what's going on, this should be the proper choice. (Try a Vulcan mind meld with the monitor and see if that helps.)

- ✔ Swap disks as they are called for. As the files are copied, and as SETUP installs WinWord, you'll see a graphical "thermometer" track your progress. At certain intervals, you'll be asked to insert a new diskette. Remove the old one and place it in the "already done" stack. Then take a new diskette and insert it properly into your A floppy drive. Click the Continue or OK buttons to proceed.

- ✔ When Setup is complete, click the OK button and you will be returned to Windows. You can then start using WinWord as described in Chapter 1 of this book.

- ✔ Isn't Windows fun and easy to use?

Index

—E—

—N—

—O—

—T—

IDG Books · ...For Dummies Quick Reference Series

COMPUTER BOOK SERIES FROM IDG

...For Dummies Quick Reference books are the smart way to keep the vital computer information you need always close at hand.

They're fun, they're fast and they're cheap! Here, in a concise, useful format, are quick reference books no computer user can afford to be without. All are written in clear, non-technical language, by bestselling authors and experts on the subject at hand. And each is cross-referenced to its main ...For Dummies counterpart. They're great memory refreshers to have close by your PC.

Every book in the series guides you through complex commands keystroke by keystroke, to give users of all skill levels easy access to solutions. They're loaded with helpful icons throughout, to highlight tips and point out special features. Humorous icons are interspersed to indicate suitability and the general safety of the task being described.

DOS For Dummies™ Quick Reference
by Greg Harvey

Explains every DOS command. Special section lists and explains batch commands and configuration commands. Covers all versions, including DOS 6. 44 illustrations, 132 pages.

ISBN: 1-56884-007-1   **$8.95 USA/$11.95 Canada**

Windows For Dummies™ Quick Reference
by Greg Harvey

Includes all major Windows functions. Covers File Manager and Print Manager basics; Windows modes and Windows Help. Covers Windows 3.1. 48 illustrations, 175 pages.

ISBN: 1-56884-008-X   **$8.95 USA/$11.95 Canada**

WordPerfect for DOS For Dummies™ Quick Reference
by Greg Harvey

Explains WordPerfect's menus and tools, manipulating documents, text blocks; formatting and printing. Covers all versions of WordPerfect through 6. 49 illustrations.

ISBN: 1-56884-009-8   **$8.95 USA/$11.95**

For More Information Or To Order By Mail, Call 1-800-762-2974. Call For A Free Catalog!
For volume discounts and special orders, please call Tony Real, Special Sales, at 415-312-0644.

Order Form

Order Center: (800) 762-2974 (8 a.m.-5 p.m., PST, weekdays) or (415) 312-0650

For Fastest Service: Photocopy This Order Form and FAX it to : (415) 358-1260

Quantity	ISBN	Title	Price	Total

Shipping & Handling Charges

Subtotal	U.S.	Canada & International	International Air Mail
Up to $20.00	Add $3.00	Add $4.00	Add $10.00
$20.01-40.00	$4.00	$5.00	$20.00
$40.01-60.00	$5.00	$6.00	$25.00
$60.01-80.00	$6.00	$8.00	$35.00
Over $80.00	$7.00	$10.00	$50.00

In U.S. and Canada, shipping is UPS ground or equivalent.
For Rush shipping call (800) 762-2974.

Subtotal _____

CA residents add
applicable sales tax _____

IN residents add
5% sales tax _____

Canadian residents
add 7% GST tax _____

Shipping _____

TOTAL _____

Ship to:

Name _____

Company_____

Address_____

City/State/Zip _____

Daytime Phone _____

Payment: ❑ Check to IDG Books (US Funds Only)   ❑ Visa   ❑ MasterCard   ❑ American Express

Card # _____ Exp. _____ Signature _____

Please send this order form to: IDG Books, 155 Bovet Road, Suite 310, San Mateo, CA 94402.
Allow up to 3 weeks for delivery. Thank you!

BOBFD

IDG BOOKS WORLDWIDE REGISTRATION CARD

RETURN THIS REGISTRATION CARD FOR FREE CATALOG

Title of this book: Word For Windows For Dummies

My overall rating of this book: ❏ Very good [1] ❏ Good [2] ❏ Satisfactory [3] ❏ Fair [4] ❏ Poor [5]

How I first heard about this book:

❏ Found in bookstore; name: [6]

❏ Advertisement: [8]

❏ Word of mouth; heard about book from friend, co-worker, etc.: [10]

❏ Book review: [7]

❏ Catalog: [9]

❏ Other: [11]

What I liked most about this book:

What I would change, add, delete, etc., in future editions of this book:

Other comments:

Number of computer books I purchase in a year: ❏ 1 [12] ❏ 2-5 [13] ❏ 6-10 [14] ❏ More than 10 [15]

I would characterize my computer skills as: ❏ Beginner [16] ❏ Intermediate [17] ❏ Advanced [18] ❏ Professional [19]

I use ❏ DOS [20] ❏ Windows [21] ❏ OS/2 [22] ❏ Unix [23] ❏ Macintosh [24] ❏ Other: [25]_____
(please specify)

I would be interested in new books on the following subjects:
(please check all that apply, and use the spaces provided to identify specific software)

❏ Word processing: [26]

❏ Data bases: [28]

❏ File Utilities: [30]

❏ Networking: [32]

❏ Other: [34]

❏ Spreadsheets: [27]

❏ Desktop publishing: [29]

❏ Money management: [31]

❏ Programming languages: [33]

I use a PC at (please check all that apply): ❏ home [35] ❏ work [36] ❏ school [37] ❏ other: [38] _____

The disks I prefer to use are ❏ 5.25 [39] ❏ 3.5 [40] ❏ other: [41]_____

I have a CD ROM: ❏ yes [42] ❏ no [43]

I plan to buy or upgrade computer hardware this year: ❏ yes [44] ❏ no [45]

I plan to buy or upgrade computer software this year: ❏ yes [46] ❏ no [47]

Name: _____ Business title: [48] _____ Type of Business: [49]

Address (❏ home [50] ❏ work [51]/Company name: _____)

Street/Suite#

City [52]/State [53]/Zipcode [54]: _____ Country [55] _____

❏ **I liked this book!** You may quote me by name in future
IDG Books Worldwide promotional materials.

My daytime phone number is _____

IDG BOOKS

THE WORLD OF
COMPUTER
KNOWLEDGE

❏ YES!

Please keep me informed about IDG's World of Computer Knowledge.
Send me the latest IDG Books catalog.